Microsoft

Excel 2000
Visual Basic for Applications

Fundamentals

Reed Jacobson

PUBLISHED BY
Microsoft Press
A Division of Microsoft Corporation
One Microsoft Way
Redmond, Washington 98052-6399

Copyright © 1999 by Reed Jacobson

Library of Congress Cataloging-in-Publication Data
Jacobson, Reed.
    Microsoft Excel 2000 Visual Basic Fundamentals / Reed Jacobson.
       p. cm.
    ISBN 0-7356-0593-9
    1. Microsoft Excel (Computer file)   2. Microsoft Visual BASIC.
    I. Title.
    HF5548.4.M523J337   1999
    005.369--dc21   99-13030
                                             CIP

Printed and bound in the United States of America.

5 6 7 8 9 QWE 6 5 4 3 2

Distributed in Canada by H.B. Fenn and Company Ltd.

A CIP catalogue record for this book is available from the British Library.

Microsoft Press books are available through booksellers and distributors worldwide. For further information about international editions, contact your local Microsoft Corporation office or contact Microsoft Press
International directly at fax (425) 936-7329. Visit our Web site at www.microsoft.com/mspress. Send
comments to *mspinput@microsoft.co*m.

For Helios Productions
Project Editor: Sybil Ihrig
Technical Editor: Douglas Giles

For Microsoft Press
Acquisitions Editor: Eric Stroo
Project Editor: Sally Stickney
Editorial Assistant: Denise Bankaitis

PartNo. 097-0008195

To Brian, who was there
in the beginning

Contents

Part 4

Making Macros Easy to Use   207

Part 5

Appendixes   325

Introduction

Microsoft Excel is a powerful tool for analyzing and presenting information. One of the strengths of Excel has always been its macro language. Since Excel first appeared, it has always had the most extensive and flexible macro language of any spreadsheet program. Visual Basic for Applications (VBA) first appeared as part of Excel in version 5. In fact, Excel was the first major application to include this exciting new architecture. Starting with Excel 97, VBA became a complete development environment, consistent with the stand-alone version of Visual Basic, and shared by all Microsoft Office applications.

When you start writing macros in Excel, you really need to learn two different skills. First, you need to learn how to work with VBA. Everything you learn about VBA will be true not only for Excel, but also for other applications that incorporate it. Second, you need to learn how to control Excel. The more you know about Excel as a spreadsheet, the more effective you can be at developing macros that control Excel. While this book focuses on VBA as Excel's development environment, much of what you learn will help you to be more effective using spreadsheets as well.

Microsoft Excel 2000 Visual Basic for Applications Fundamentals walks you through tasks one at a time, keeping you on track with clear instructions and frequent pictures of what you should see on the screen. In each lesson, you'll become familiar with another important aspect of Excel or VBA.

Important This book is designed for use with Excel 2000 (version 9.0) or any edition of Microsoft Office 2000 for Microsoft Windows 95 or later, and Microsoft Windows NT 4.0 operating systems. To find out what software you're running, you can check the product package, or you can start the software, click the Help menu, and click About Microsoft Excel. If your software isn't compatible with this book, a Step by Step or Fundamentals book for your software is probably available. Visit the Microsoft Press World Wide Web site at http://www.microsoft.com/mspress/ or call 1-800-MSPRESS for more information.

Finding Your Best Starting Point in This Book

This book is designed for Excel users who are starting to write macros and for programmers familiar with another programming system (such as Visual Basic or COBOL) who want to use Excel as a platform for developing applications. You'll get the most from this book if you're already familiar with the basic capabilities of Excel, such as entering values and formulas into worksheets.

Learning about VBA and about how Excel works with VBA can seem overwhelming. That's why you need this book. It starts with simple, practical tasks and then takes you on to advanced concepts and powerful applications.

The book is divided into four parts:

- **Part 1: Automating Everyday Tasks** starts you off with practical, straightforward ways to use macros in Excel. It also introduces the macro recorder and the VBA development environment.

- **Part 2: Exploring Objects** helps you understand how VBA talks to Excel. In this part, you'll learn what objects are, how they relate to one another, and how you can find the objects you need when you're writing macros. You'll get practical experience using some of the most important types of objects in Excel: ranges, charts, and PivotTables.

- **Part 3: Exploring Visual Basic** teaches you how to get VBA to move beyond the limitations of a recorded macro. You'll learn how to write macros that make decisions and repeat actions in a loop. You'll also learn how you can write your own functions that you can use from a worksheet as well as from other macros.

- **Part 4: Making Macros Easy to Use** moves you into the world of a complete application. You'll learn how to make applications easy for others to use by adding ActiveX controls to the worksheet and to custom forms. You'll learn how to make applications that respond to actions that a user takes, such as clicking on a worksheet. You'll also build a complete application that retrieves information from an external database and presents it to the user.

Use the following table to find your best starting point in this book.

If you are	Follow these steps
New...	
To Microsoft Excel	**1.** Install the practice files as described in "Installing the Practice Files," later in this Introduction.
To VBA programming	**2.** Become acquainted with the basic features of Excel, referring to the online Help system and other documentation as necessary.
	3. Learn how to create practical macros by working sequentially through Chapters 1 and 2 and the "Review and Practice" section for Part 1. Then, as you want to understand more about advanced macros, work through Chapters 3 through 8 and the "Review and Practice" sections for Parts 2 and 3. If you need to create macros that others can use, continue to Chapters 9 through 12 and the "Review and Practice" section for Part 4.

If you are	Follow these steps

Switching...

| From Microsoft Visual Basic | **1.** Install the practice files as described in "Installing the Practice Files," later in this Introduction. |
| From another Microsoft product that uses VBA | **2.** Work through Chapters 1 and 2 and the "Review and Practice" section for Part 1 to become familiar with Excel's powerful macro recorder. Work through Chapters 3 through 6 and the "Review and Practice" section for Part 2 to become familiar with important Excel objects. Skim Chapters 7, 8, and 10, because the features and functions discussed in those chapters are very similar in all versions of Visual Basic. Then, work through Chapters 9, 11, and 12 and the "Review and Practice" section of Part 4 to learn aspects of creating applications that are unique to Excel. |

If you are	Follow these steps

Upgrading...

| From Excel for Windows 95 | **1.** Install the practice files as described in "Installing the Practice Files," later in this Introduction. |
| From a previous version of Excel | **2.** Complete the chapters that cover the topics you need to learn more about. Use the Contents to locate information about general topics. You can use the index to find information about a specific topic or a feature from a previous version of Excel. |

If you are	Follow these steps

Referencing...

This book after working through the chapters	**1.** Use the index to locate information about specific topics, and use the Contents to locate information about general topics.
	2. Read the Chapter Summary at the end of each chapter for a brief review of the major tasks that have been covered. The Chapter Summary topics are listed in the same order in which they are presented in the chapter.
	3. Find examples in the "Review and Practice" for each part of this book, and look for cross references to the chapters, by section, in the tables at the end of each "Review and Practice."

Installing the Practice Files

The CD inside the back cover of this book contains practice files that you'll use as you perform the exercises in the book. By using the practice files, you won't waste time creating the samples used in the chapters—instead, you can concentrate on learning how to write macros in Microsoft Excel. With the files and the step-by-step instructions in the chapters, you'll also learn by doing, which is an easy and effective way to acquire and remember new skills.

Important Before you break the seal on the practice disc package, be sure that this book matches your version of the software. This book is designed for use with Excel 2000 (version 9.0) or any edition of Microsoft Office 2000 for the Windows 95 or later and Windows NT version 4.0 operating system. To find out what software you're running, you can check the product package, or you can start the software and then on the Help menu click About Microsoft Excel.

Install the practice files on your computer

Follow these steps to install the practice files on your computer's hard disk so that you can use them with the exercises in this book.

1. Remove the CD from the package inside the back cover of this book, and insert it in your CD-ROM drive.

2. On the taskbar at the bottom of your screen, click the Start button, and then click Run. The Run dialog box appears.

3. In the Open box, type **d:setup** (or, if your CD-ROM drive uses a drive letter other than "d," substitute the correct drive letter).

4. Click OK, and then follow the directions on the screen. The Setup program window appears with recommended options preselected for you. For best results in using the practice files with this book, accept these preselected settings. However, you can choose to install the practice files in a drive or folder other than the default drive and folder suggested by the Setup program.

5. When the files have been installed, remove the CD from your drive and replace it in the package inside the back cover of the book.

If you accepted the default settings offered by the Setup program, a folder called ExcelVBA has been created on your hard disk and the practice files have been copied to that folder. A shortcut named Excel 2000 VBA Sample Programs has also been placed on your desktop to make it easy to acccess the practice files.

Be prepared to install additional components

In addition to the components installed during a default installation of Excel 2000, you'll also need the Visual Basic Help files (referenced throughout this book) and Microsoft Query (for Chapter 12). Excel 2000 will automatically install those components when you need them, but you should keep the installation CD or network location available.

Using the Practice Files

Each chapter in this book explains when and how to use any practice files for that lesson. When it's time to use a practice file, the book lists instructions for how to open the file. You should always save the practice file with a new name (as directed in the chapter) so that the original practice file will be available if you want to go back and redo any of the lessons.

The folder into which you installed the practice files contains a subfolder named Finished. This contains a copy of each workbook as it will appear at the end of a given chapter, with all macros that you create in the chapter already completed. If you have problems with an item in any chapter, you can see how the macro works in the Finished folder to help you understand how to correct the problem.

Here's a list of the files included on the companion CD, along with information about where each file is used in the book. Depending on how your Windows system is configured, you might not see the extensions for the files.

Chapter	Filename	Description
1, 11	Budget.xls	A workbook containing the annual budget for the fictional Miller Textiles company.
2, 6, 7, 12	Orders.dbf	The Miller Textiles order history database. This file contains the monthly orders for different shirt designs. This file is stored in a format that can be accessed either by Excel or by the database drivers that come with Excel.
2	Nov2000.txt	A text file containing the most recent month's order information.
Part 1 Review and Practice	Expenses.xls	A workbook containing a list of expenses.
3	Objects.xls	Simple macros that demonstrate what objects are and how to use them.
4	Ranges.xls	Macros along with sample data that demonstrate how VBA controls Excel ranges.
5	Graphics.xls	Simple graphical objects that you will create macros to manipulate.
Part 2 Review and Practice	Tables.xls	A workbook containing three worksheets that you will use macros to manipulate.
7	Flow.xls	Simple macros that you'll enhance using VBA.
8	Function.xls	Simple macros that you will enhance using VBA.
Part 3 Review and Practice	List.xls	A workbook containing a list of monthly orders that you'll filter and print using macros.

Chapter	Filename	Description
9	Events.xls	An otherwise empty workbook that contains some simple prerecorded macros to help you learn how to link macros to events.
10	Loan.xls	Sample values on a worksheet that you'll use to create an easy-to-use loan payment calculator.
12	Map.wmf	A picture file containing a map that will be used as the basis of the user interface.
12	Code12a.txt Code12b.txt Code12c.txt Code12d.txt Code12e.txt Code12f.txt Code12g.txt Code12h.txt	Code that you'll enter to create the custom application. Long sections of code are included as importable files so you won't need to type in the code.
Part 4 Review and Practice	Savings.xls	A workbook that contains financial formulas you'll adjust using a form and worksheet controls.

Uninstall the practice files

Use the following steps to delete the practice files added to your hard drive by the Setup program on the companion CD.

1. Click the Start button, point to Settings, and then click Control Panel.

2. Double-click the Add/Remove Programs icon.

3. Select Excel 2000 VBA Sample Programs from the list, and then click Add/Remove. A confirmation message appears.

4. Click Yes. The practice files are uninstalled, and the Excel 2000 VBA Sample Programs folder is removed from your desktop.

5. Click OK to close the Add/Remove Programs Properties dialog box.

6. Close the Control Panel window.

Every effort has been made to ensure the accuracy of this book and the contents of the CD-ROM. If you do run into a problem, Microsoft Press provides corrections for its books through the Web at

http://mspress.microsoft.com/support/

Using Shortcuts

Excel can accomplish almost any action in several different ways. For most actions, you can select a command from a menu, press a shortcut key, click a toolbar button, and so forth. Different people prefer different techniques. To minimize confusion, the body of the text describes only a single method for most actions. Appendix A lists all the alternative ways that you can carry out the actions described. You might find that you prefer a different method from the one described in the text.

Resolving Possible Configuration Differences

This book assumes that Excel is configured as it would be using a default installation. You might, however, have customized Excel to your preferences. In most cases, customizing Excel won't affect the way you can use this book. In some cases, however, you could customize Excel in such a way that what you see on the screen doesn't match the illustrations in the text or in such a way that the steps in this book don't work exactly as described. Appendix B describes all the possible configuration settings that could affect the way that you use this book. If something in the book isn't working the way it should, and if you've customized Excel in any way, compare your settings with those in the appendix.

Conventions and Features Used in This Book

When you use this book, you can save time by understanding, before you start the chapters, how the instructions, keys to press, and so on, are shown in the book. Please take a moment to read the following sections, which also point out other helpful features of the book.

Procedural Conventions

- Hands-on exercises for you to follow are given in numbered lists of steps (1, 2, and so on).

Typographic Conventions

- Text that you are to type appears in **boldface**.

- New terms, special program code words within body text, and the titles of books appear in *italic*.

- Names of keyboard keys for you to press appear in normal body text font. A hyphen (-) between two key names means that you must press those keys at the same time. For example, "Press Alt-Tab" means that you hold press and hold the Alt key while you press Tab.

- Program code (on a separate line or lines) appears in monospace type:

```
Me.AllowEdits = False
```

Supplementary Features

The following types of special paragraphs identify the various kinds of supplementary information:

Notes labeled	Alert you to
Note	Additional information for a step.
Tip	Suggested additional methods for a step or helpful hints.
Important	Essential information that you should check before continuing with the chapter.

Other Features of This Book

Run Macro button

- You can perform many operations in Excel by clicking a button on the toolbar or a tool in the toolbox. When the instructions in this book tell you to click a toolbar button, a picture of the button appears in the margin next to the instructions. The Run Macro button in the margin to the left of this paragraph is an example.

- Screen capture illustrations show sample user interfaces and the results of your completed steps and frequently include text that indicates the part of the illustration you should notice.

- Sidebars—short sections printed on a shaded background—introduce special programming techniques, background information, or features related to the information being discussed in the main body of text.

- You can get a quick reminder of how to perform the tasks you learned by reading the Chapter Summary at the end of each chapter.

- You can quickly determine what online Help topics are available for additional information by referring to the Help topics listed at the end of each chapter.

- The four "Review and Practice" sections, one at the end of each part, provide additional exercises that help you gain further experience in the skills introduced in the preceding chapters.

Corrections, Comments, and Help

If you have comments, questions, or ideas regarding this book or the practice files on the companion CD, please send them to Microsoft Press. Send e-mail to

mspinput@microsoft.com

Or send postal mail to

Microsoft Press
Attn: Fundamentals Series Editor
One Microsoft Way
Redmond, WA 98052-6399

Please note that support for the Excel software product itself is not offered through the above addresses. For help using Excel, you can call Microsoft Technical Support at (800) 936-5700, or visit Microsoft Online Support on the Web at

http://support.microsoft.com/support/

Visit the Microsoft Press Web Site

You can visit the Microsoft Press Web site at the following location:

http://www.microsoft.com/mspress/

You'll find descriptions for all Microsoft Press books, information about ordering titles, notice of special features and events, additional content for Microsoft Press books, and much more.

You can also find out the latest in software developments and news from Microsoft Corporation by visiting the following Web site:

http://www.microsoft.com/

Automating Everyday Tasks

Chapter 1

Make a Macro Do Simple Tasks

Estimated time: 40 minutes

In this chapter, you'll learn how to:

- Record and run a macro.

- Understand and edit simple recorded macros.

- Run a macro by using a shortcut key.

Last month we lost the remote control to our VCR. It was awful. I wanted to set the machine to record "Mystery Science Theater 3000" at 1:00 A.M. one night, but I couldn't do it because all the scheduling features were built into the remote control. Fortunately, after about two weeks, my wife detected a bulge in the cloth backing of the recliner and retrieved the precious controller. I'm so happy that I can now record old movies. Someday I might even watch some of them.

If you haven't yet installed the practice files that come with this book, refer to "Installing the Practice Files and Additional Microsoft Excel Tools" in the Introduction to this book.

Microsoft Visual Basic for Applications (VBA) is Microsoft Excel 2000's remote control. Sure, you can use Excel without ever using VBA, but not only can the VBA "remote control" make your life more convenient, it also allows you to take advantage of features that you can't get to with the standard "front-panel" controls. And once you become acquainted with Excel's remote control, you'll wonder how you ever got along without it.

How Visual Basic for Applications Talks to Excel

The first spreadsheet macro languages mimicked the user interface. For example, if you typed **R** (for "Range"), **N** (for "Name"), and **C** (for "Create") in the user interface, you would enter **RNC** into the macro to automate the process. This approach had inherent weaknesses. Not only were keystroke macros difficult to read, but they didn't adapt well to the graphical user interface. What do you use to represent dragging a rectangle with the mouse?

To solve these problems, the early versions of Excel contained a new type of macro language that made the macro commands independent of the user interface. For example, in Excel version 4 you could copy a range in at least three different ways: press Ctrl-C, click the Copy toolbar button, and click Copy on the Edit menu. All those user interface sequences translated to a single macro function, =COPY(). These function-based macros had two major drawbacks: First, Excel macros were very specific to Excel; the language couldn't be adapted to other applications. Second, the number of functions kept increasing with each new version, and there was no good way to organize or group the thousands of possibilities.

Automation

Excel with VBA incorporates *Automation* (once known as OLE Automation), a powerful way of automating applications. Excel was the first major application to take advantage of this concept. In this approach, VBA acts as a general-purpose language that's independent of the application. Suddenly, anyone who knows how to work with any version of Visual Basic has a big head start in automating Excel, and anyone who learns how to write Excel macros in VBA can transfer that knowledge to other types of Visual Basic programming.

Note   VBA is a version of Visual Basic that's hosted by an application, such as Microsoft Excel. A VBA macro can't run independently of its host application. VBA and the stand-alone version of Visual Basic both use the same language engine, editor, and most supporting tools. In this book, we'll use "VBA" to refer specifically to the macro language in Excel, and "Visual Basic" to refer to anything that's shared by all versions of Visual Basic.

Even though Excel hosts VBA, VBA doesn't have any special "hooks" into Excel's internals. Rather, Excel *exposes* its capabilities to VBA by means of a special set of commands called an *object library*. VBA talks to Excel's object library.

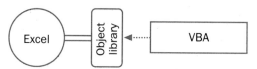

VBA can control not only Excel, but also any application that provides an object library. All Microsoft Office applications provide object libraries, and several other Microsoft and non-Microsoft applications do, too.

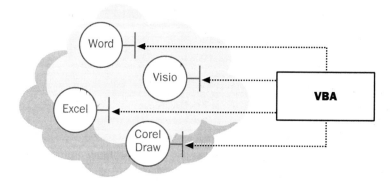

The VBA that comes with Excel isn't the only language that can communicate with the object library. Any language that supports Automation can control Excel. You can control Excel not only with the VBA hosted by Excel, but also with a VBA project hosted by Microsoft Word, with the stand-alone version of Visual Basic, or even with C++ or Inprise Corporation's Delphi program.

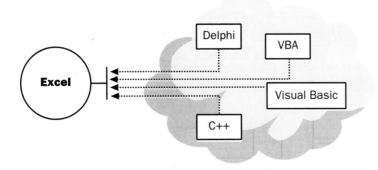

Excel Objects and You

Not only does the object library expose Excel's capabilities to VBA, but even more important, the object library exposes Excel's capabilities to you. Once you know how to read and interpret an object library, you can discover new features and figure out quickly how to put them to work. The best way to start finding out about how VBA communicates with Excel's objects is to record some simple macros. Eventually, however, you'll want to move beyond the limitations of the macro recorder.

In Part 1 of this book, you'll learn how to record and modify simple macros. In Part 2, you'll learn how Excel objects work. In Part 3, you'll learn some secret powers of Visual Basic for Applications. And in Part 4, you'll learn how to make a macro easy to use.

Start the lesson

1. Start Excel.

2. On the Standard toolbar, click the Open button, and then in the Open dialog box, click the Favorites button.

3. Double-click the folder that contains the practice files installed from the companion CD, and then double-click the Budget workbook.

4. Save the Budget file as **Chapter1**.

Creating a Simple Macro

Excel has a large collection of convenience tools readily available as shortcut keys and as buttons on toolbars. Sometimes a built-in convenience tool doesn't work quite the way you want. Enhancing a built-in tool is a good first macro to create.

Open button

See the readme.txt file on the companion CD for instructions on how to install the practice files for this book.

Show the Visual Basic toolbar

Before you start creating the macros, take one small step that will make your work with macros much easier.

1. Point to any toolbar, and click the right mouse button. (This is called "right-clicking.") The toolbar shortcut menu appears, showing most of the available toolbars.

2. Select Visual Basic from the toolbar list. The Visual Basic toolbar appears. You can change the location and shape of this toolbar just as you can any other Excel toolbar.

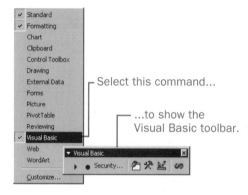

Now, when you're ready to record a macro, just click the circle on the toolbar. When you're ready to run a macro, click the triangle.

Format currency with a built-in tool

On the Formatting toolbar, Excel has a button that formats the current selection as currency: the Currency Style button.

1. In the Chapter1 workbook, select cells D3:F4 on the Budget2000 worksheet.

Currency Style button

2. Click the Currency Style button on the Formatting toolbar. Excel reformats the selected cells as currency.

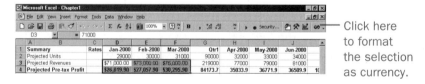

The currency format that Excel applies when you click the Currency Style button has two decimal places. Sometimes you want to display currency with two decimal places—perhaps in your checkbook. But other times you don't want two decimal places—perhaps your budget doesn't warrant that kind of precision. You might want to create a macro to format a cell as currency with no decimal places instead.

Record a macro to format currency

1. On the Budget2000 worksheet, select cells D7:F8.

2. On the Visual Basic toolbar, click the Record Macro button.

3. Replace the default macro name with **FormatCurrency**, and then click OK.

*Record Macro
button*

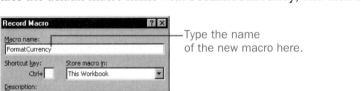

Type the name
of the new macro here.

*A macro name
can contain
uppercase and
lowercase letters,
underscores,
and periods, but
no spaces.*

The word *Recording* appears in the status bar, and a Stop Recording
toolbar appears. You're recording.

4. On the Format menu, click the Cells command, and then, if necessary,
click the Number tab.

5. Select Currency from the Category list.

6. Replace the value in the Decimal Places box with a zero, and then click OK.

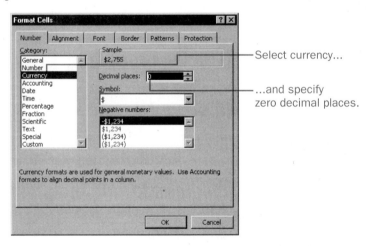

Select currency...

...and specify
zero decimal places.

Excel formats the selected cells as currency without decimal places.

7. Click the Stop Recording button.

8. Save the Chapter1 workbook.

*Stop Recording
button*

That's it. You recorded a macro to format a selection with the currency format you want. Now you probably want to try out the macro to see how it works.

Run the macro

1. On the Budget2000 worksheet, select cells D9:F10.

Run Macro button

2. On the Visual Basic toolbar, click the Run Macro button.

3. Select the FormatCurrency macro in the list, and click Run.

Your macro gives the selected cells your customized currency format. Running the macro from the Macro dialog box isn't much of a shortcut, though.

Assign a shortcut key to the macro

1. On the Visual Basic toolbar, click the Run Macro button.

Run Macro button

2. Select the FormatCurrency macro in the list, and then click the Options button. The Macro Options dialog box allows you to change the macro's shortcut key assignment and its description.

3. You want to assign Ctrl-Shift-C as the shortcut key. If necessary, click in the box below the Shortcut key label and press Shift-C.

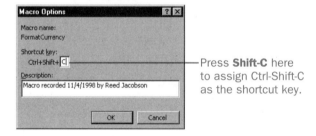

Press **Shift-C** here to assign Ctrl-Shift-C as the shortcut key.

Important Excel uses many Ctrl key combinations as built-in shortcuts. For example, Ctrl-C is Copy and Ctrl-Z is Undo. If you assign one of these shortcuts to your macro, pressing the shortcut runs your macro rather than the built-in command. If you always assign a Ctrl-Shift key combination for your macros, you'll be much less likely to override a built-in shortcut.

You can also assign a shortcut key at the time you first record a macro.

4. Click OK to return to the Macro dialog box, and then click Cancel to get back to the worksheet.

5. Select cells D11:F13, and press Ctrl-Shift-C to run the macro.

6. Save the Chapter1 workbook.

Now you've successfully recorded, run, and enhanced a macro—all without seeing anything of the macro itself. Aren't you burning with curiosity to see what you've just created?

Look at the macro

The macro is actually hidden away in the workbook, but you need to open the Visual Basic Editor to be able to see it.

1. On the Visual Basic toolbar, click the Run Macro button.

2. Click FormatCurrency, and then click Edit. The Visual Basic Editor window appears. The Visual Basic Editor appears to be a separate program, but it is "owned" by Excel. If you quit Excel, Visual Basic automatically shuts down. Inside the Visual Basic Editor, a window captioned Module1 appears as well.

3. Maximize the Module1 window so that it fills the Visual Basic Editor, and then resize the Visual Basic Editor window so that you can see the Excel workbook in the background.

4. If any other windows are visible in the Visual Basic Editor, close them now.

Run Macro button

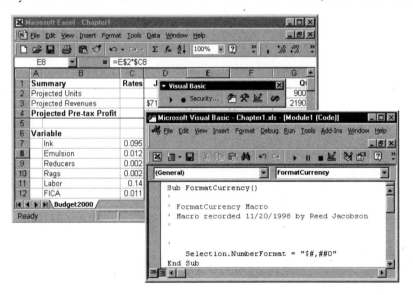

The window captioned Module1, a *module*, is the place where the recorder puts macros. Your macro is in the Module1 module. The macro looks like this:

```
Sub FormatCurrency()
'
' FormatCurrency Macro
' Macro recorded 11/15/98 by Reed Jacobson
'


    Selection.NumberFormat = "$#,##0"
End Sub
```

For details about number format codes, ask the Assistant for help, using the words "user-defined numeric formats."

The five lines that start with apostrophes at the beginning of the macro are *comments*. The apostrophe at the beginning of the line indicates that the following text is a comment. (The blank line among the comments, without even an apostrophe, is where the recorder would have put the shortcut key combination if you had assigned it when you recorded the macro.) The recorder puts in the comments partly to remind you to add comments as you write a macro. You can add to them, change them, or delete them as you wish without changing how the macro runs. Comments are green to help you distinguish them from statements that do something.

The macro is written in VBA and follows standard Visual Basic rules. The macro itself begins with *Sub*, followed by the name of the macro. (Is *Sub* used because a macro is typically hidden, out of sight, like a *sub*marine? Or does it stand for *sub*routine, for reasons you'll learn at the end of Chapter 2? Stay tuned.) The last line of a macro is always *End Sub*.

The *Selection.NumberFormat* statement does the real work. It is the body of the macro. *Selection* stands for "the current selection." *NumberFormat* refers to an attribute—or *property*—of the selection. To interpret a VBA instruction, read the statement from right to left, like this: "Let '$#,##0' be the number format of the selection."

Note   Some people wonder why the word *NumberFormat* comes after the word *Selection* if you read *Selection.NumberFormat* as "number format of the selection." In an Excel worksheet, you don't use the English language convention of stating an action first and then the object. ("Copy these cells. Put the copy in those cells.") Instead, on an Excel worksheet you select the object first and then perform the action. ("These cells—copy. Those cells—paste.") Selecting the object first in the worksheet makes carrying out multiple actions more efficient.

Macro statements in Visual Basic work backward, the same as actions do in an Excel worksheet. In a macro statement, you state what you're going to work on, and then you do something to it.

Changing Multiple Properties at Once

The FormatCurrency macro changes a single attribute of the current selection—the number format. In Excel macros, an attribute is called a *property*. In the FormatCurrency macro, *NumberFormat* is a property of a cell. Many macro statements assign a value to a property. Whenever the macro recorder creates a statement containing an equal sign, the word in front of the equal sign is a property. Sometimes when you record an action, the macro changes multiple properties at the same time.

Merge text vertically with a command

Excel has a toolbar button that can merge and center several cells in a horizontal row: the Merge And Center button. But sometimes you might want to merge cells vertically along the edge of a report. Excel doesn't have a toolbar button that merges cells vertically along the edge and adjusts the position of text in those cells, but you can record a macro that does.

To better understand what's required, first walk through the steps to create this format using menu commands.

1. Activate the Budget2000 window.

2. Select the range A6:A12. The label, Variable, is at the top of the selected range.

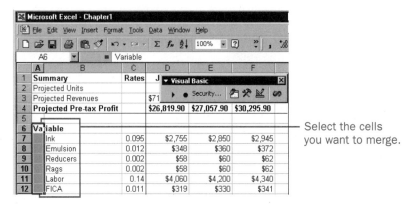

Select the cells you want to merge.

3. On the Format menu, click Cells, and then click the Alignment tab. The Alignment tab has several controls that control alignment, wrapping, orientation angle, shrinking, and merging.

4. Click the Merge Cells check box, and drag the red diamond in the orientation control up to the top of the arc to set the orientation to 90 degrees.

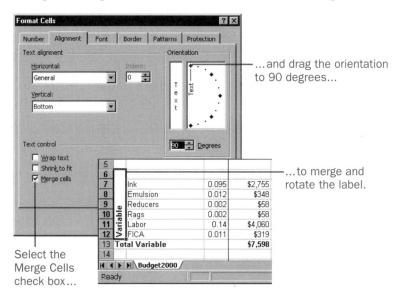

...and drag the orientation to 90 degrees...

...to merge and rotate the label.

Select the Merge Cells check box...

5. Click OK to merge and tilt the label.

Putting a label to the side of a block of cells is extremely powerful. You can make it easy to do by recording a macro.

Record a macro to merge cells vertically

1. Rearrange your windows as necessary so that you can see both the Module1 window and the Excel window.

Tip To rearrange the windows, minimize all the applications you have open except Excel and the Visual Basic Editor. Then right-click the taskbar, and click Tile Vertically from the shortcut menu.

Record Macro button

2. Select the range A15:A20, and then click the Record Macro button.

3. In the Record Macro dialog box, replace the default macro name with **MergeVertical,** replace the default description with **Merge cells vertically**, and set Ctrl-Shift-M as the shortcut key.

Important If you assign the same shortcut key to two macros, the one that appears first in the Run Macro list is the one that runs. A shortcut key is valid only while the workbook containing the macro is open.

---

4. Click OK. In the module window, you can see that the recorder immediately puts the comment lines, the keyboard shortcut, and the Sub and End Sub lines into the macro.

5. On the Format menu in the Excel window, click Cells. In the Format Cells dialog box on the Alignment tab, select the Merge Cells check box, set the alignment to 90 degrees, and click OK. The recorder puts several lines into the macro all at once.

6. Click the Stop Recording button.

Stop Recording button

7. Save the Chapter1 workbook. The new macro in the Module1 window looks like this:

```
Sub MergeVertical()
'
' MergeVertical Macro
' Merge cells vertically
'
' Keyboard Shortcut: Ctrl+Shift+M
'
    With Selection
        .HorizontalAlignment = xlGeneral
        .VerticalAlignment = xlBottom
        .WrapText = False
        .Orientation = 90
        .AddIndent = False
        .ShrinkToFit = False
        .MergeCells = True
    End With
End Sub
```

The macro shows seven different property settings for the cell alignment. Each property is followed by an equal sign. These properties correspond exactly to the controls you saw in the Format Cells dialog box.

Each of the property settings affects the current selection, just as the *Number-Format* property setting does in the FormatCurrency macro. In the Format-Currency macro, however, the property name is attached directly to *Selection* with a period, to show that the property affects the cells in the current selection. In this macro, however, each property name just "hangs there," preceded only by a period.

A pair of statements beginning with *With* and ending with *End With* is called a *With structure*. It means that every time there is a period with nothing in front of it, you pretend that the word that followed the *With* is there. With structures make the code easier to read because you can tell instantly that all the properties relate to the current selection. You'll often see With structures in macros that you record.

Eliminate unnecessary lines from the macro

In many dialog boxes, the macro recorder records all the possible properties, even though you might change the values of only one or two of them. You can make your macro easier to understand if you eliminate unnecessary properties.

In the MergeVertical macro, you need to change the values of only the *Orientation* and *MergeCells* properties. You can therefore delete the other lines from the macro.

1. Activate the Visual Basic Editor window, and click as far to the left of the *HorizontalAlignment* statement as you can within the Editor window. (Your mouse pointer should turn into a right-pointing arrow before you click.) This action selects the entire line, including the indent that precedes the text.

2. Press the Delete key.

3. Repeat steps 1 and 2 for each of the properties except *Orientation* and *MergeCells*. If you delete too much, click the Undo button to restore what

Undo button

Where Do New Macros Go?

The first time you record a macro, Excel creates a new module. Each time you record an additional macro, Excel adds the new macro to the end of the same module. When you close and reopen the workbook, the macro recorder starts recording macros into a new module. There is no way for you to control where the recorder puts a new macro.

Having macros in multiple modules shouldn't be a problem. When you use the Macro dialog box to select and edit a macro, it automatically takes you to the appropriate module.

you deleted. The simplified macro (ignoring the comment lines, which you can delete if you want) should look like this:

```
Sub MergeVertical()
    With Selection
        .Orientation = 90
        .MergeCells = True
    End With
End Sub
```

4. Activate the Excel window, and select cells A25:A30.

5. Press Ctrl-Shift-M. The macro adjusts the label.

6. Save the Chapter1 workbook.

Now you've not only recorded a macro, but you've also deleted parts of it—and it still works. Next you'll record a macro and make additions to it.

Editing a Recorded Macro

A typical Excel worksheet has light gray gridlines that mark the boundaries of the cells. Sometimes, you might want to remove the gridlines. First walk through the process to remove the gridlines with menu commands, and then record a macro to make the change.

Remove gridlines with a command

1. On the Tools menu, click Options, and then, if necessary, click the View tab.

2. Clear the Gridlines check box at the bottom of the Window Options group.

3. Click OK. The gridlines disappear.

4. Repeat step 1, and select the Gridlines check box to turn the gridlines back on. Then click OK.

Gridlines are a property of the window. You can select the Gridlines check box so that the value of the property is True and the window displays the gridlines, or you can clear the check box so that the value of the property is False and the window doesn't display the gridlines. Now see how the recorder turns off the gridlines.

Record a macro to remove gridlines

1. Click the Record Macro button.

2. Replace the default macro name with **RemoveGrid**, and click OK. The recorder puts the shell of the macro (the comments and the Sub and End Sub lines) into the module.

3. On the Tools menu, click Options, clear the Gridlines check box on the View tab, and then click OK. The gridlines disappear.

Record Macro button

4. Click the Stop Recording button, and then save the Chapter1 workbook.

Stop Recording
button

5. Click the Run Macro button, select RemoveGrid, and then click Edit to look at the resulting code. Ignoring the comment lines, here's what it looks like:

```
Sub RemoveGrid()
    ActiveWindow.DisplayGridlines = False
End Sub
```

Run Macro
button

This macro is similar to the FormatCurrency macro. You can read it as "Let 'False' be the *DisplayGridlines* property of the active window." This time you're not changing the selection but rather the active window. In both cases, you're changing an *object*, an Excel element that you can control with macros. However, this time the object isn't a range of cells, but a window.

You'll learn
more about
objects in Part 2.

Run the macro from the Visual Basic Editor

You can easily change the macro to make it restore the gridlines.

1. In the RemoveGrid macro, replace *False* with **True**. You can't use a shortcut key while you're in the Visual Basic Editor, but the Visual Basic Editor has its own shortcut for running whatever macro you're currently editing.

2. Press F5 to run the macro. The gridlines reappear in the current Excel worksheet. Pressing F5 from the Visual Basic Editor is a fast way to run a macro while you're testing it.

> **Tip**   If you're in VBA and want to display the Macro dialog box so that you can select a macro, click outside of any macro before you press F5.

Toggle the value of a property with a macro

You could create one macro to turn the gridlines off and a second macro to turn them back on, but somehow, letting a single macro toggle the value of the property seems more natural. To toggle the value of a property, you first ask Excel for the current value, which you can store in a special container called a *variable*. You then change the value as you assign the variable back to the property. Here's how:

1. Insert a new blank line after the comments.

2. Select *ActiveWindow.DisplayGridlines*, and press and hold the Ctrl key as you drag it up to the blank line. This makes a copy of the statement.

3. At the beginning of the new line, type **myGrid =** ; the resulting statement is *myGrid = ActiveWindow.DisplayGridlines*. This statement stores the current value of *DisplayGridlines*, whether True or False, in the variable *myGrid*.

Note   You can use any name you want as a variable name, but you should avoid names already used by Excel or Visual Basic. If you add a prefix such as *my* to the variable name, you'll most likely avoid any potential conflict.

---

4. Double-click *True* in the original statement, and replace it with **Not myGrid**. The VBA keyword *Not* turns the value True into False and False into True.

5. Change the name *RemoveGrid* to **ToggleGrid**, to better reflect the macro's new capabilities. This is what the macro should look like now:

```
Sub ToggleGrid()
    myGrid = ActiveWindow.DisplayGridlines
    ActiveWindow.DisplayGridlines = Not myGrid
End Sub
```

Tip   If *Option Explicit* appears at the top of the module, delete it before running this macro.

---

6. Save the Chapter1 workbook, reactivate the Module1 window, and then press F5 several times to test the macro.

The macro reads the old value of the property, changes it to the opposite with the keyword *Not,* and assigns the newly inverted value back to the property.

Recording Actions in a Macro

By now, you should see a pattern to creating a simple convenience macro: Try out an action interactively. Once you know how to do the task, start the recorder. Do the task with the recorder on. Then stop the recorder.

So far, all the macros you've recorded have changed the value of one or more properties of an object. Some actions that you can record don't change the value of a property. Let's see what a macro looks like when it doesn't change a property.

Suppose you want to freeze the formulas of some cells in the Budget2000 worksheet at their current values. First change the formulas to values using menu commands, and then create a macro that can change any formula to a value.

Convert a formula to a value using menu commands

1. Activate the Budget2000 window, and then select cell D4.

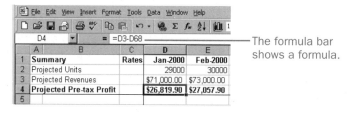

The formula bar shows a formula.

Notice the formula in the formula bar: =D3-D68.

2. On the Edit menu, click the Copy command.

3. Don't change the selection. On the Edit menu, click the Paste Special command. The Paste Special dialog box appears.

4. Select the Values option from the Paste group, and click OK. Excel pastes the value from the cell over the top of the existing cell, eliminating the formula that was in it. The moving border is still visible around the cell, indicating that you could paste the value again somewhere else if you wanted.

5. Press the Esc key to get out of copy mode and clear the moving border.

	A	B	C	D	E
1	Summary		Rates	Jan-2000	Feb-2000
2	Projected Units			29000	30000
3	Projected Revenues			$71,000.00	$73,000.00
4	Projected Pre-tax Profit			$26,819.90	$27,057.90
5					

——— The formula bar now shows a value.

Look at the formula bar: cell D4 now contains the value 26819.9.

As you carry out the copy and paste actions with the menus, notice that the Copy command doesn't bring up a dialog box. You see a moving border around the cells and a message in the status bar, but you don't need to tell Excel how to do the copying. The Paste Special command, on the other hand, does require additional information from you to carry out its job, so it displays a dialog box. Some actions in Excel require additional information about how to carry out the action, and some don't.

Convert a formula to a value with a macro

Watch how the macro recorder handles actions that display a dialog box, compared with how it handles actions that don't.

1. On the Budget2000 worksheet, select cell E4. Notice the formula in the formula bar: =E3-E68.

2. On the VBA Toolbar, click Record Macro.

Record Macro button

3. Replace the default name with **ConvertToValues**.

4. Set the shortcut key to Ctrl-Shift-V, and click OK.

5. On the Edit menu, click Copy.

6. On the Edit menu, click Paste Special, click the Values option, and click OK.

7. Press the Esc key to get rid of the moving border.

8. Click the Stop Recording button, and save the Chapter1 workbook. Look at the formula bar. Cell E4 now contains the value 27057.9.

Stop Recording button

9. Switch to VBA to look at the recorded macro.

```
Sub ConvertToValues()
    Selection.Copy
    Selection.PasteSpecial Paste:=xlValues, Operation:=xlNone, _
        SkipBlanks:=False, Transpose:=False
    Application.CutCopyMode = False
End Sub
```

The basic structure of this macro is the same as that of the other macros you've seen in this chapter. The last line, for example, sets the value of the *CutCopyMode* property in much the same way that the ToggleGrid macro changed the *DisplayGridlines* property setting of the active window. The two lines that begin with *Selection*, however, are something new. Neither has a simple equal sign in it.

Selection.Copy looks similar to *Selection.NumberFormat* from the Format-Currency macro. In that macro, *NumberFormat* was a property of the selection and you were assigning a new value to the *NumberFormat* property. *Copy,* however, isn't a property. That's why it doesn't have an equal sign after it. You don't assign anything to *Copy;* you just do it. Actions that don't use an equal sign to set the value of a property—that is, actions like *Copy*—are called *methods*. Like the names of properties, the names of methods are recorded by Excel and displayed at the end of the object's name.

When you use the Copy command from the menu, Excel doesn't ask you for any extra information. In the same way, when you use the *Copy* method in a macro, you don't give any extra information to the method.

PasteSpecial is also a method in Excel. *PasteSpecial* doesn't have an equal sign after it; it isn't a property that you assign a value to. The Paste Special command on the Edit menu displays a dialog box, but the dialog box doesn't show you properties to change; it just asks how to carry out the paste special action. When you execute the *PasteSpecial* method in a macro, you give the extra information to the method. The extra pieces of information you give to a method are called *arguments*.

Using a method with an object is like giving instructions to your nine-year-old. With some instructions—like, "Come eat"—you don't have to give any extra information. With other instructions—like, "Go to the store for me"—you have to tell what to buy (milk), how to get there (on your bike), and when to come home (immediately). Giving these extra pieces of information to your child is like giving arguments to an Excel method. (You call them arguments because whenever you tell your child how to do something, you end up with one.)

The four arguments you give to *PasteSpecial* correspond exactly to the four option groups in the Paste Special dialog box. Each argument consists of a name for the argument (for example, *Paste*) joined to the argument value (for example, *xlValues*) by a colon and an equal sign (:=).

Don't confuse an *argument* with a *property*. When you assign a new value to a property, you separate the value from the property with an equal sign, as in this statement:

```
ActiveWindow.DisplayWorkbookTabs = False
```

You read this statement as "Let 'False' be the *DisplayWorkbookTabs* property of the active window."

Assigning a value to a property can appear superficially similar to using a named argument with a method. When you use a named argument with a method, you separate the method name from the argument name with a space, and you separate the argument name from the argument value with a colon and an equal sign. You must never confuse an equal sign with a colon and equal sign, any more than you would confuse beer with root beer.

When you have more than one argument, separate each one from the next with a comma and a space, as in this statement:

```
Selection.PasteSpecial Paste:=xlValues, Operation:=xlNone
```

An argument looks a lot like a property, but an argument always follows a method name, whereas a property follows an object. Also, a property is followed by an equal sign, but an argument is followed by a colon and an equal sign.

Make a long statement more readable

When one of the statements in a macro gets to be longer than about 70 characters, the macro recorder puts a space and an underscore (_) after a convenient word and continues the statement on the next line. The underscore tells the macro that it should treat the second line as part of the same statement. You can manually break long statements into several lines, as long as you break the line after a space. You can also indent related lines with tabs, to make the macro easier to read.

1. In the ConvertToValues macro, put each argument of the *PasteSpecial* statement on a separate line, using a space and an underscore character at the end of each line except the last.

```
Sub ConvertToValues()
    Selection.Copy
    Selection.PasteSpecial _
        Paste:=xlValues, _
        Operation:=xlNone, _
        SkipBlanks:=False, _
        Transpose:=False
    Application.CutCopyMode = False
End Sub
```

Splitting a statement into several lines doesn't change the way the macro runs; it just makes it easier to read.

2. In Excel, select cell F4 and press Ctrl-Shift-V to run the macro. Look at the formula bar to make sure the formula changed to a value.

3. Save the Chapter1 workbook.

Most of the macros in this chapter change the settings of object properties, but this macro executes object methods. Properties and methods look very similar: both are separated from objects by periods. However, you assign new values to properties, whereas you execute methods, sometimes giving the method arguments along the way.

Create a personal signature

Included with your Microsoft Office 2000 CD is a program that you can use to create a personal signature.

1. On the Windows Start menu, click Find, and then click Files Or Folders. In the Named box, type **selfcert**. In the Look In list, select the drive containing the Microsoft Office 2000 CD or the network folder containing the Office installation files. Then click Find Now.

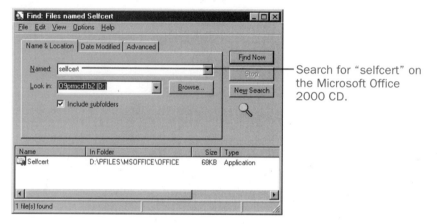

Search for "selfcert" on the Microsoft Office 2000 CD.

2. When the program file Selfcert appears at the bottom of the dialog box, double-click its name to run the program.

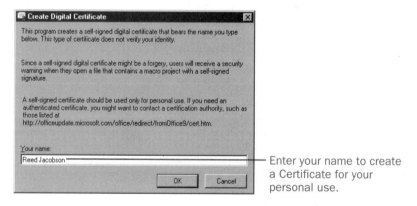

Enter your name to create a Certificate for your personal use.

3. In the Your Name box, type your name, and click OK. Click OK to close the confirmation box.

4. Close the Find dialog box.

You've now created a personal signature that you can use to sign your macro projects.

Signing Personal Macros

When you open a workbook that contains a macro, Excel displays a message warning you that macros can contain viruses that can harm your computer.

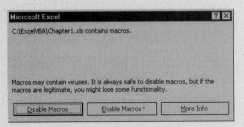

You certainly don't want to see this message every time you open a workbook. One way to avoid the message is to change Excel's security level to Low, but then if someone e-mails you a workbook that happens to contain a macro virus, you wouldn't have any warning at all.

If you have Microsoft Internet Explorer version 4 or later installed on your computer (even if it isn't your default browser), you can *digitally sign* your VBA project to avoid the warning message. Before you can sign a project, you need a digital signature. You might work at a company that can issue you a digital signature, or you can obtain a digital signature from a certificate authority such as VeriSign or Thawte, or you can create a self-signature for your own macros.

Tip For information about how to get a digital certificate, ask the Answer Wizard for information using the words "Digital Certificate."

Add a signature to your project

You add a signature to the VBA project part of your workbook. If a virus—or anyone else—changes the VBA project, the signature becomes invalid. The signature applies only to the VBA project, not to the workbook data, so anyone can change the worksheets without invalidating the signature.

1. With the Chapter1 workbook open, activate the Visual Basic Editor, and on the Tools menu, click Digital Signature.

2. In the Digital Signature dialog box, click Choose.

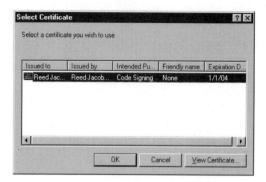

3. In the Select Certificate dialog box, select the certificate with your name and click OK.

4. Click OK to close the dialog box. Switch to Excel, and save and close the workbook.

The project in the Chapter1 workbook is now signed. If you need to modify a macro, as long as you do it on the machine that contains your digital signature, VBA automatically reapplies the signature. But no one else can reapply your signature to the project.

Trust a signature

Now that you have a workbook containing a signed project, you can tell Excel to trust workbooks that contain macros you have signed.

1. Open the Chapter1 workbook.

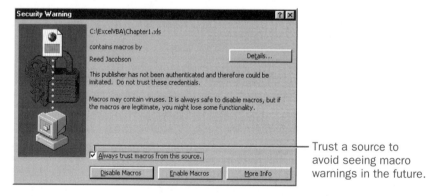

Trust a source to avoid seeing macro warnings in the future.

A message asks if you want to enable macros, and also if you want to trust macros from this source in the future.

Note When you create your own digital signature, Excel can't be certain that the signature is authentic, so it displays a warning message. If you obtain your signature from a certifying agency, no caution message appears.

2. Select the Always Trust Macros From This Author check box, and click the Enable Macros button.

3. Close the Chapter1 workbook, and then reopen it. No warning message appears. Excel recognizes you as a trusted source for macros.

4. Close the Chapter1 workbook, and quit Excel.

Security is important when you create any programs, including macros. Security is especially important when you share applications with others. If you create macros for others to use, you'll probably want to obtain a properly authenticated digital signature to protect your work.

Chapter Summary

To	Do this	Button
Show the Visual Basic toolbar	Right-click any toolbar, and click the Visual Basic Editor from the menu.	
Turn on the recorder	On the Visual Basic toolbar, click the Record Macro button.	
Turn off the recorder	Click the Stop Recording button.	
Run a macro	Click the Run Macro button, select the name of the macro, and click Run.	
Look at a macro	Click the Run Macro button, select the name of the macro, and click Edit.	
Add a shortcut key	Click the Run Macro button, select the name of the macro, and click Options.	
Save the value of a property	Make up a variable name and assign the property value to it.	
Change the value of a property	Change the value that the recorded macro assigns to the property.	
Split a long statement into multiple lines	Break lines after convenient words and put a space and an underscore (_) at the end of each line except the last.	
Create a digital signature for yourself	Run the Selfcert program, and type the name you want to use.	
Apply a digital signature to a VBA project	In the VBA editor, on the Tools menu, click Digital Signatures. Click Choose, select your signature, and click OK.	

For online information about	Ask the Assistant for help using the words
Recording macros	"Recording Macros"

Preview of the Next Chapter

In the next chapter, you'll learn how to combine small macros to automate whole tasks. You'll also learn how to find and fix problems when your macros don't work quite the way you want.

Chapter 2

Make a Macro Do Complex Tasks

Estimated time: 45 minutes

Chapter Objectives

In this chapter, you'll learn how to:

- Break a complex project into manageable pieces.

- Watch a macro run one statement at a time.

- Enter values into a macro while it's running.

- Record movements relative to the active cell.

- Create a macro that runs other macros.

Rube Goldberg was famous for inventing intricate contraptions with hundreds of parts that made something that would seem to be straightforward appear wildly complex. For example, in his cat "alarm clock," a ball drops into a bucket and the weight of the bucket lifts a lever that releases a spring that wakes up a cat. Rube Goldberg contraptions are fun to look at. Milton Bradley has been successful for years with the Mousetrap game, which is based on a Rube Goldberg concept. Boston's Logan International Airport has two massive, perpetually working Rube Goldberg contraptions in the lobby that entertain irritated travelers for hours.

Entertainment is one thing. Getting your job done is another. Sometimes the list of steps you have to go through to get out a monthly report can seem as complicated as a Rube Goldberg invention. First you import the monthly order file and add some new columns to it. Then you sort it and print it and sort it a different way and print it again. Then you paste it onto the end of the cumulative order-history file, and so forth. Each step has to be completed just right before the next one is started, and you start making sure you don't schedule your vacation during the wrong time of the month because you'd never want to have to explain to someone else how to get it all done correctly. Right?

One good use for macros is putting together all the steps to turn a cumbersome Rube Goldberg monthly report into a mouse click. This chapter will help you learn how to do it.

Start the lesson

1. Start Microsoft Excel, and save the blank default workbook as Chapter2 in the folder that contains the practice files for this book. (If you installed the practice files using the default settings, then on the toolbar, click the Save button, select the Favorites group, double-click the Excel VBA Practice folder, type **Chapter2** as the filename, and click Save.)

2. Display the Visual Basic toolbar.

Divide and Conquer

The secret to creating a macro capable of handling a long, intricate project is to break the project into small pieces, create a macro for each separate piece, and then glue the pieces together. If you just turn on the recorder, carry out 400 steps, and cross your fingers hoping for the best, you have about a 1-in-400 chance of having your macro work properly. Let's look at a hypothetical example.

As the bookkeeper at Miller Textiles' Screen Printing division, you have an elaborate month-end project you'd like to automate so that you can delegate it to subordinates when you go on vacation. Currently, you get a monthly summary report of orders for the previous month from the order-processing system.

```
                    Miller Textiles
              Order Summary for November 2000

State    Channel    Price  Category        Qty    Dollars
======== ========== ====== =============== ====== =========
WA       Retail     Mid    Kids                9      40.5
                    Low                      143    434.06
                    High   Art                17      93.5
                    Mid                        23     103.5
                    High   Sports             26       143
                    Mid                         6        27
                    Low                         4        14
                    High   Seattle            13      71.5
                    Mid                         7      31.5
                    Low                        25      87.5
                    Mid    Dinosaurs          22        99
                    Low                        22        77
                    Mid    Humorous          143    554.32
                    Low                        13      45.5
                    Mid    Environment        35     157.5
                    Low                        40       140
         Wholesale  Mid    Kids               30      67.5
                    Low                        10      17.5
                    High   Art               410  1,062.13
                    Mid                       900  1,848.48
                    High   Sports             25     68.75
                    Mid                         30      67.5
                    Low                         5      8.75
                    High   Seattle           910  2,134.83
                    Mid                        60       135
                    Low                       405     687.6
                    Mid    Dinosaurs         660  1,401.08
                    Low                       345     586.6
                    Mid    Humorous           65    146.25
                    Low                        25     43.75
```

The report shows sales information for each state, channel, category, and price combination. The order-processing system exports the report as a text file.

You prepare the file and add the new month's orders to a cumulative order-history database.

This chapter shows you how to record the tasks that make up this large, complex project and then combine these small macros into one comprehensive macro. Along the way, you might learn some useful techniques for completing everyday tasks as well.

Task One: Opening the Report File

The orders for the most recent month, November 2000, are in the text file Nov2000.txt. The first task is to open the file, splitting it into columns as you do, and move the file into the workbook with the macro.

> **Open the report file**

Note   You might want to carry out steps 3 through 6 as a dry run before recording the macro.

---

1. If the Chapter2 workbook window is maximized, click the Restore Window button.

Restore Window button

2. On the Visual Basic toolbar, click the Record Macro button, type **ImportFile** as the macro name, and then click OK.

Record Macro button

3. Click the Open button, type **Nov2000.txt** in the File Name box, and then click Open. Step 1 of the Text Import Wizard appears.

Open button

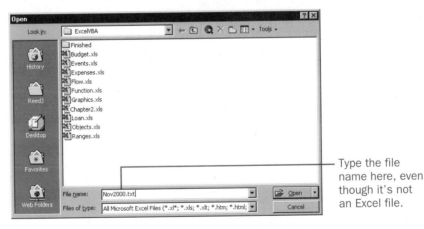

Type the file name here, even though it's not an Excel file.

4. The first three rows of the file contain the report title and a blank line, so change the Start Import At Row value to **4**. The other default options in the Text Import Wizard are suitable for this file, so click Finish. The text file opens, with the columns split into Excel columns.

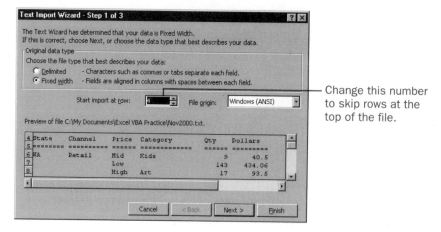

Change this number to skip rows at the top of the file.

5. Drag up the bottom of the new window so that you can see the tabs at the bottom of the Chapter2 workbook. Then drag the tab for the Nov2000 worksheet down in front of the Sheet1 tab of the Chapter2 workbook.

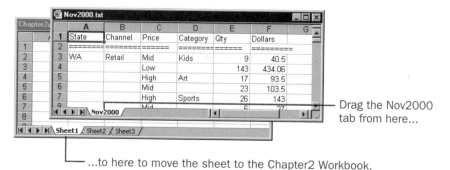

Drag the Nov2000 tab from here...

...to here to move the sheet to the Chapter2 Workbook.

The Nov2000 worksheet moves to the Chapter2 workbook, and the Nov2000.txt workbook disappears (because it lost its only worksheet, and a workbook can't exist without at least one sheet).

Note   You'll have several copies of the Nov2000 worksheet after you test this macro several times. Multiple copies will be useful as you develop the macros for the later project tasks. Because you already have a worksheet named Nov2000 in the workbook, new copies are automatically named Nov2000 (2), Nov2000 (3), and so forth.

6. Row 2 contains equal signs that you don't need. Select cell A2, choose the Edit menu and click the Delete command, select the Entire Row option in the Delete dialog box, and then click OK.

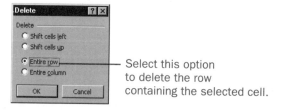

Select this option to delete the row containing the selected cell.

7. Select cell A1, and click the Stop Recording button to stop the recorder.

8. Save the Chapter2 workbook.

Stop Recording button

You should now have the imported file split into columns and stripped of extraneous rows.

Watch the ImportFile macro run

Rather than merely read the macro, you can both read and test it as you watch it work. As you step through the macro, make notes of minor changes you might want to make to it.

Whenever you step through a macro, the Visual Basic Editor window appears over the top of the workbook. The Visual Basic window displays the selected macro and allows you to see which statement will execute next.

1. Click the Run Macro button, select ImportFile from the Macro Name list, and click Step Into. The Visual Basic window appears on top of the workbook, with your recorded macro visible in the module. The statement that is ready to execute is highlighted in yellow, with a yellow arrow in the left margin.

Run Macro button

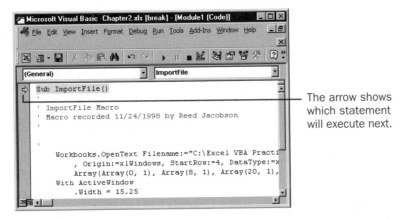

The arrow shows which statement will execute next.

The highlighted statement is the first statement in the macro, the statement that contains the macro name:

```
Sub ImportFile()
```

2. Press F8 to highlight the first statement in the body of the macro:

```
Workbooks.OpenText _
    FileName:="C:\ExcelVBA\Nov2000.txt", _
    Origin:= xlWindows, _
    StartRow:=4, _
    DataType:=xlFixedWidth, _
    FieldInfo:=Array(Array(0, 1), Array(8, 1), _
        Array(20, 1), Array(27, 1), Array(42, 1), _
        Array(49, 1))
```

This long statement opens the text file. You can probably identify the argument that specifies the filename. The *Origin* and *DataType* arguments were default values in the first step of the Text Import Wizard. The *StartRow* argument is where you specified the number of rows to skip. The *FieldInfo* argument tells how to split the text file into columns. Be grateful that the macro recorder can create this statement so that you don't have to!

The macro recorder divides this long statement into several lines by putting a space and an underscore at the end of each partial line. However, it doesn't divide the statement at the most logical places. When you edit the macro, you should redivide the statement into meaningful lines. (Dividing before each new argument usually clarifies the intent of the macro.) In your recorded macro, the line divisions will differ from those in this example. You can use the way the statement is divided in the OpenText macro above as a model.

This month, you opened the Nov2000.txt file. Next month, you'll open the Dec2000.txt file. Make a note to change the macro statement to let you select the file you want to open. You'll learn how to generalize your macro in the next section.

See Appendix A for alternatives to using F8 to step through the macro.

3. Press F8 to open the file and highlight the next statement, which is the first line of this *With* structure:

```
With ActiveWindow
    .Width = 452.25
    .Height = 254.25
End With
```

These four statements were added when you moved the window out of the way. (Your *Width* and *Height* properties might have different values, and if you moved the window, there will be statements that change the *Top* and *Left* properties as well.) When you edit the macro, you'll be able to delete these statements without harming the macro.

4. Press F8 to step through any statements that move or resize the window. Make a note to delete all of them. The next statement is now highlighted:

```
Sheets("Nov2000").Select
```

This statement makes the Nov2000 sheet into the active sheet, even though it was already the active sheet. (Macro recorders can't be too cautious, now.) You'll be able to delete this statement later also.

Note You can edit many statements while stepping through the macro. For example, you could delete the *Select* statement. Some changes, however, would force you to restart the macro. For example, you can't delete a *With* structure without restarting the macro (although you can delete individual statements inside a *With* structure). Visual Basic warns you if you try to make a change that would require you to restart the macro.

---

5. Press F8 to highlight the next statement:

```
Sheets("Nov2000").Move _
    Before:=Workbooks("Chapter2.xls").Sheets(1)
```

This statement moves the new sheet into the Chapter2 workbook. But when you run this macro next month, the sheet won't be named Nov2000. It will be Dec2000. If you change *Sheets("Nov2000")* to *ActiveSheet* in the macro, however, it will work every month.

6. Press F8 to move the worksheet and highlight the next statement:

```
Range("A2").Select
```

This statement selects cell A2 of the worksheet.

7. Press F8 to select cell A2 and highlight the next statement:

```
Selection.EntireRow.Delete
```

Because the selected cell is A2, and this statement deletes the entire row of the selected cell, this statement deletes row 2.

8. Press F8 to delete the row and highlight the next statement:

```
Range("A1").Select
```

This statement selects cell A1.

9. Press F8 to select cell A1 and highlight the final statement of the macro:

```
End Sub
```

10. Press F8 to end the macro.

In summary, this is how you want to modify the macro:

- Allow the user to decide which file to open.

- Delete unnecessary statements.

- Make the macro work with any month's file.

The next section shows you how to make these changes.

Generalize the macro

Excel provides a method that prompts the user to open a file, but Excel doesn't actually open the file. Instead it returns the name of the file, which you can turn over to the *OpenText* method.

1. Make the statement that begins with *Workbooks.Open* easier to read by dividing it into meaningful lines. Put a space and an underscore at the end of each partial line. Follow the ImportFile macro example in the "Watch the ImportFile macro run" section earlier in this chapter.

2. Insert a new line immediately before the *Workbooks.OpenText* statement, and enter this statement:

```
myFile = Application.GetOpenFilename("Text Files,*.txt")
```

As soon as you type the period after *Application*, Visual Basic displays a list of all the methods and properties that can be used with an Application object. This feature is called *Auto List Members*. (The word *Members* refers to both methods and properties.) When you type the letter *G*, the list scrolls to show methods and properties that begin with that letter. At that point, you can press the Down Arrow key to select *GetOpen-Filename* and press the Tab key to enter the method name into the macro.

When you type the opening parentheses, Visual Basic displays the possible arguments for the *GetOpenFilename* method. This feature is called *Auto Quick Info.* You can ignore it for now. Just type the words in parenthesis as they appear in step 2 above.

The *Application.GetOpenFilename* method displays the Open dialog box, just as if you had clicked the Open toolbar button. The words in parentheses tell the method to display only text files—files ending with the *.txt* extension. (Be careful to type the quotation marks just as they appear in step 2 above.) The word *myFile* at the beginning of the statement is a variable for storing the selected filename.

If Option Explicit *appears at the top of your module sheet, delete it before continuing.*

3. In the *Workbooks.OpenText* statement, select the entire filename, including the quotation marks, and delete it. In its place, type **myFile.** The first part of the statement should look like this when you finish:

```
Workbooks.OpenText _
    Filename:=myFile, _
    Origin:=xlWindows, _
    StartRow:=4, _
```

By the time this statement executes, the variable *myFile* will contain the name of the file.

4. Delete the statements that resize the window and also the statement that selects the Nov2000 sheet.

5. Change the words *Sheets("Nov2000").Move* to **ActiveSheet.Move**. When you're finished, the macro should look like this:

```
Sub ImportFile()
    myFile = Application.GetOpenFilename("Text Files,*.txt")
    Workbooks.OpenText _
        FileName:=myFile, _
        Origin:=xlWindows, _
        StartRow:=4, _
        DataType:=xlFixedWidth, _
        FieldInfo:=Array(Array(0, 1), Array(8, 1), _
            Array(20, 1), Array(27, 1), Array(42, 1), _
            Array(49, 1)
    ActiveSheet.Move
```

```
Before:=Workbooks("Chapter2.xls").Sheets(1)
     Range("A2").Select
     Selection.EntireRow.Delete
     Range("A1").Select
End Sub
```

6. Save the Chapter2 workbook.

7. Press F5 to run the macro and make sure it works. It should display the Open dialog box (displaying only text files), and then it should open the file that you select and move the worksheet to the Chapter2 workbook.

That concludes the macro for the first task of your month-end processing project. By now you should have several copies of the Nov2000 worksheet in the Chapter2 workbook. You're ready to move on to the next task.

Task Two: Filling in Missing Labels

When the order-processing system produces a summary report, it enters a label in a column only the first time that label appears. Leaving out duplicate labels is one way to make a report easier for a human being to read, but for the computer to sort and summarize the data properly, you need to fill in the missing labels.

	A	B	C	D	E	F
1	State	Channel	Price	Category	Qty	Dollars
2	WA	Retail	Mid	Kids	9	40.5
3			Low		143	434.06
4			High	Art	17	93.5
5			Mid		23	103.5
6			High	Sports	26	143
7			Mid		6	27

Fill the blank cells with the label from the cell above.

You might assume that you need to write a complex macro to examine each cell and determine whether it's empty, and if so, what value it needs. In fact, you can use Excel's built-in capabilities to do most of the work for you. Because this part of the project introduces some powerful worksheet features, you'll go through the steps before recording the macro.

Select only the blank cells

Look at the places where you want to fill in missing labels. What value do you want in each empty cell? You want each empty cell to contain the value from the first nonempty cell above it. In fact, if you were to select each empty cell in turn and put into it a formula pointing at the cell immediately above it, you would have the result you want. The range of empty cells is an irregular shape, however, which makes the prospect of filling all the cells with a formula daunting. Fortunately, Excel has a built-in tool for selecting an irregular range of blank cells.

1. In the Chapter2 workbook, select cell A1.

2. Choose the Edit menu and click the Go To command. The Go To dialog box appears.

See Appendix B for alternative ways to display the Go To dialog box.

3. In the Go To dialog box, click Special.

Click here to open
the Go To Special dialog box.

*You also can
press Ctrl-Shift-*
to select the
current region.
Press and hold
the Ctrl key
while pressing *
on the numeric
keypad or Shift-8
on the regular
keyboard.*

4. In the Go To Special dialog box, click the Current Region option, and then click OK.

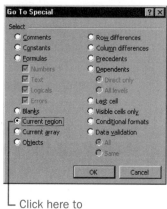

Click here to
select the current region.

Excel selects the *current region*—the rectangle of cells including the active cell that is surrounded by blank cells or worksheet borders.

5. Choose the Edit menu, click Go To, and then click Special.

6. In the Go To Special dialog box, click the Blanks option, and then click OK. Excel subselects only the blank cells from the selection. These are the cells that need new values.

Go To Special, Blanks selects just the cells you need to fill.

Excel's built-in Go To Special feature can save you—and your macro—a lot of work.

Fill the selection with values

You now want to fill each of the selected cells with a formula that points at the cell above. Normally when you enter a formula, Excel puts the formula into only the active cell. You can, however, if you ask politely, have Excel put a formula into all the selected cells at once.

1. With the blank cells selected and D3 as the active cell, type an equal sign (=) and then press the Up Arrow key to point at cell D2. The cell reference D2—when found in cell D3—actually means "one cell above me in the same column."

2. Press Ctrl-Enter to fill the formula into all the currently selected cells. When more than one cell is selected, if you type a formula and press Ctrl-Enter, the formula is copied into all the cells of the selection. If you press the Enter key without pressing and holding the Ctrl key, the formula goes into only the one active cell. Each cell with the new formula points to the cell above it.

	A	B	C	D	E	F
1	State	Channel	Price	Category	Qty	Dollars
2	WA	Retail	Mid	Kids	9	40.5
3	WA	Retail	Low	Kids	143	434.06
4	WA	Retail	High	Art	17	93.5
5	WA	Retail	Mid	Art	23	103.5
6	WA	Retail	High	Sports	26	143
7	WA	Retail	Mid	Sports	6	27

Use Ctrl-Enter to fill all the selected cells.

3. Press Ctrl-Shift-* to select the current region.

4. Choose the Edit menu, and click Copy. Then choose the Edit menu, click Paste Special, click the Values option, and then click OK.

5. Press the Esc key to get out of copy mode, and then select cell A1.

Now the block of cells contains all the missing-label cells as values, so the contents won't change if you happen to re-sort the summary data. In the next section, you'll select a different copy of the imported worksheet and follow the same steps, but with the macro recorder turned on.

Record filling the missing values

1. Select a copy of the Nov2000 worksheet (one that doesn't have the labels filled in), or run the ImportFile macro again.

2. Click the Record Macro button, type **FillLabels** as the name of the macro, and then click OK.

3. Select cell A1 (even if it's already selected), press Ctrl-Shift-*, choose the Edit menu, click Go To, click the Special button, click the Blanks option, and then click OK.

Record Macro button

4. Type =, press the Up Arrow key, and press Ctrl-Enter.

5. Press Ctrl-Shift-*.

6. Choose the Edit menu, and click Copy. Next choose the Edit menu, click Paste Special, click the Values option, and then click OK.

7. Press the Esc key to get out of copy mode, and then select cell A1.

8. Click the Stop Recording button, and save the Chapter2 workbook.

You've finished creating the FillLabels macro. Read it while you step through the macro.

Stop Recording button

Watch the FillLabels macro run

1. Select another copy of the imported worksheet, or run the ImportFile macro again.

2. Click the Run Macro button, select the FillLabels macro, and click Step Into. The Debug window appears, with the header statement of the macro highlighted.

Run Macro button

3. Press F8 to move to the first statement in the body of the macro:

```
Range("A1").Select
```

This statement selects cell A1. It doesn't matter how you got to cell A1—whether you clicked the cell, pressed Ctrl-Home, or pressed various arrow keys—because the macro recorder always records just the result of the selection process.

4. Press F8 to select cell A1 and highlight the next statement:

```
Selection.CurrentRegion.Select
```

This statement selects the current region of the original selection.

5. Press F8 to select the current region and move to the next statement:

```
Selection.SpecialCells(xlCellTypeBlanks).Select
```

This statement selects the blank special cells of the original selection. (The word *SpecialCells* refers to cells you selected using the Go To Special dialog box.)

6. Press F8 to select just the blank cells and move to the next statement:

```
Selection.FormulaR1C1 = "=R[-1]C"
```

For more information about R1C1 notation, ask the Assistant for help using the words "R1C1 references" (with the Excel window active).

This statement assigns =R[-1]C as the formula for the entire selection. When you entered the formula, the formula you saw was =C2, not =R[-1]C. The formula =C2 really means "get the value from the cell just above me"—only as long as the active cell happens to be cell C3. The formula =R[-1]C also means "get the value from the cell just above me," but without regard for which cell is active.

You could change this statement to *Selection.Formula = "=C2"* and the macro would work exactly the same—provided that the order file you use when you run the macro is identical to the order file you used when you recorded the macro and that the active cell happens to be cell C3 when the macro runs. If the command that selects blanks produces a different active cell, however, the revised macro will fail. The macro recorder uses R1C1 notation so that your macro will always work correctly.

7. Press F5 to execute the remaining statements in the macro:

```
Selection.CurrentRegion.Select
Selection.Copy
Selection.PasteSpecial Paste:=xlValues, Operation:=xlNone, _
    SkipBlanks:=False, Transpose:=False
Application.CutCopyMode = False
Range("A1").Select
```

These statements select the current region, convert the formulas to values, cancel copy mode, and select cell A1.

You've completed the macro for the second task of your month-end project. Now you can start a new macro to carry out the next task—adding dates.

Task Three: Adding a Column of Dates

The order summary report you're working with doesn't include the date in each row since the text file includes numbers for only a single month. Before you can append these new records to the order-history database, you'll need to add the current month to each record.

Add a constant date

First you'll create a macro that fills the range with the date *Nov-2000*, by inserting a new column A and putting the date into each row that contains data.

1. Select a worksheet that has the labels filled in, click the Record Macro button, type **AddDates** as the name of the macro, and then click OK.

2. Select cell A1, and then choose the Insert menu and click Columns. Excel inserts a new column A, shifting the other columns over to the right.

3. Type **Date** in cell A1, and then press the Enter key.

4. Press Ctrl-Shift-* to select the current region.

5. Choose the Edit menu, click Go To, and click the Special button. Click the Blanks option, and click OK to select only the blank cells. These are the cells in which the dates should go.

6. Type **Nov-2000** and press Ctrl-Enter to fill the date into all the cells. Excel fills the date into all the rows.

7. Select cell A1, and then click the Stop Recording button to stop the recorder.

Record Macro button

Excel displays the date as Nov-00, but it stores the full date.

Stop Recording button

Step through the macro

1. With cell A1 selected, choose the Edit menu, click Delete, click the Entire Column option, and then click OK.

Run Macro button

2. Click the Run Macro button, select the AddDates macro, and then click Step Into. Ignoring comments, this is what the macro should look like:

```
Sub AddDates()
    Range("A1").Select
    Selection.EntireColumn.Insert
    ActiveCell.FormulaR1C1 = "Date"
    Range("A2").Select
    Selection.CurrentRegion.Select
    Selection.SpecialCells(xlCellTypeBlanks).Select
    Selection.FormulaR1C1 = "Nov-2000"
    Range("A1").Select
End Sub
```

3. Press F8 repeatedly to step through the macro.

This macro is pretty straightforward. Notice that the statement that enters the word *Date* changes the "formula" of only the active cell, whereas the statement that enters the actual date changes the "formula" of the entire selection. When you enter a formula using the Enter key alone, the macro uses the word *ActiveCell*. When you enter a formula using Ctrl-Enter, the macro uses the word *Selection*. (If the selection is only a single cell, *ActiveCell* and *Selection* are equivalent.)

The recorder always records putting a value into a cell by using the *Formula R1C1* property—even if you enter a label—just in case you might have entered a formula.

Prompt for the date

Your recorded macro should work just fine if you always run it using the same month's data file. But the next time you actually use this macro, you'll be working with December orders, not November orders. You need to change the macro so that it asks you for the date when you run it.

1. Insert a new line after the comments in the AddDates macro, and enter this new statement:

```
myDate = InputBox("Enter the date in MMM-YYYY format")
```

InputBox is a Visual Basic function that prompts for information while a macro runs. The words in parentheses are the message it displays. The variable *myDate* stores the date until the macro is ready to use it.

Tip The *InputBox* function is a useful tool for making a macro work in slightly changing circumstances.

2. Select and delete the text "*Nov-2000*" in the macro. Be sure to delete the quotation marks.

3. Type **myDate** where the old date used to be. The revised statement should look like this:

```
Selection.FormulaR1C1 = myDate
```

4. Activate a worksheet that needs the date column added. (Delete the old date column, or run the FillLabels macro, as needed.)

5. Click the Run Macro button, select the AddDates macro, and then click Run. The macro prompts for the date and then inserts the date into the appropriate cells in column A.

Run Macro button

Note If you click the Cancel button, the macro leaves the date cells empty. In Chapter 7, you'll learn how to program the macro to determine whether the user clicked the Cancel button.

---

6. Type **Nov-2000,** and click OK.

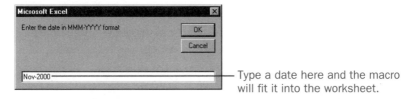
— Type a date here and the macro will fit it into the worksheet.

7. Save the Chapter2 workbook.

This completes your third task. Now you're ready to append the new data to the database.

Task Four: Appending to the Database

Now that you've added monthly dates to the imported Nov2000 worksheet, it has the same columns as the order-history database, so you can just copy the worksheet and append it to the first blank row below the database. Of course, you don't want to include the column headings.

Append a worksheet to a database

First you'll copy the data (without the headings) from the Nov2000 worksheet. Then you'll open the database, select the first blank cell below the database, rename the database range to include the new rows, and close the database file.

You might want to do steps 2 through 10 as a dry run before recording the macro.

1. Select one of the Nov2000 worksheets that has the labels filled and the dates added, click the Record Macro button, type **AppendDatabase** as the macro name, and then click OK.

Record Macro button

2. Select cell A1. Choose the Edit menu, click Delete, click the Entire Row option, and click OK. This deletes the heading row so that you won't include it in the range you copy to the database.

3. Press Ctrl-Shift-* to select the current region, and then click Copy on the Edit menu.

Open button

4. Click the Open toolbar button, type **Orders.dbf** in the File Name box, and click Open. The Orders.dbf database file opens with cell A1 selected. (The dates in the database look different from those in Nov2000 because of formatting differences.)

5. Press Ctrl-Down Arrow to go to the last row of the database.

6. Press the Down Arrow key to select the first cell below the database. (It should be cell A3301.)

	A	B	C	D	E	F
3299	10/1/00	WA	Retail	Mid	Seattle	6
3300	10/1/00	WA	Retail	Mid	Sports	5
3301						
3302						
3303						
3304						

— You want to paste into the first cells under the database.

7. Choose the Edit menu, click Paste to append the rows you previously copied, and then press the Esc key to remove the copy message from the status bar.

	A	B	C	D	E	F
3299	10/1/00	WA	Retail	Mid	Seattle	6
3300	10/1/00	WA	Retail	Mid	Sports	5
3301	Nov-00	WA	Retail	Mid	Kids	9
3302	Nov-00	WA	Retail	Low	Kids	143
3303	Nov-00	WA	Retail	High	Art	17
3304	Nov-00	WA	Retail	Mid	Art	23

8. Press Ctrl-Shift-* to select the entire new database range, including the newly appended rows.

Note When you open a dBase file in Excel, the range containing the actual database records is automatically named Database. When you save the updated Orders.dbf file as a dBase file, only the values within the range named Database are saved. Any other cell values in the file are discarded. To have the new rows saved with the file, you must enlarge the Database range definition to include them.

9. Choose the Insert menu, choose the Name submenu, and click the Define command. Type **Database** in the Names In Workbook box, and then click OK.

Important Don't select Database from the list of names. If you do, the range name will keep its current definition.

Type the name here
to redefine the database.
Don't select it from the list.

Now the entire database, including the new rows, is included in the
Database range name and will be saved with the file.

10. Choose the File menu, click Close, and then click No when asked if you
want to save changes. For now, you don't actually want to save the
database with the new records back to the Orders.dbf file because you'll
want to test the macro.

11. Select cell A1, and then click the Stop Recording button to turn off the
recorder.

*Stop Recording
button*

Step through the AppendDatabase macro

Step through the macro to see it work, and make notes of any changes you
should make.

1. Activate a worksheet with the labels filled in and the dates added. (Run
the ImportFile, FillLabels, and AddDates macros if necessary.)

2. Click the Run Macro button, select the AppendDatabase macro, and click
the Step Into button. Look at the first five lines of the macro:

*Run Macro
button*

```
Sub AppendDatabase()
    Range("A1").Select
    Selection.EntireRow.Delete
    Selection.CurrentRegion.Select
    Selection.Copy
```

These statements are similar to statements you've seen in earlier macros.

3. Press F8 five times to execute the first five statements in the macro. In the
Debug window, the statement that opens the database should be
highlighted:

```
Workbooks.Open Filename:="C:\ExcelVBA\Orders.dbf"
```

This statement opens the database.

Tip If you remove everything except Orders.dbf from the filename, the macro
looks for the file in the current folder. That would be useful if you move the project
to a new folder.

---

4. Press F8 to execute the statement containing the *Open* method and move to the next statement:

```
Selection.End(xlDown).Select
```

This statement is equivalent to pressing Ctrl-Down Arrow. It starts with the active cell, searches down to the last nonblank cell, and selects that cell.

5. Press F8 to select the last cell in the database and move to the next statement:

```
Range("A3301").Select
```

This statement selects cell A3301. That is the first cell below the database this month, but next month it will be wrong. This is the statement the recorder created when you pressed the Down Arrow key. What you wanted was a statement that moves one cell down from the active cell. You'll need to fix this statement. Make a note to do so.

6. Press F8 to select cell A3301 and move to the next statement. The next two statements work together:

```
ActiveSheet.Paste
Application.CutCopyMode = False
```

These statements paste the new rows into the database and remove the status bar message.

7. Press F8 twice. The next two statements redefine the Database range:

```
Selection.CurrentRegion.Select
ActiveWorkbook.Names.Add Name:="Database", RefersToR1C1:= _
        "=Orders!R1C1:R3478C7"
```

The first statement selects the current region, which is the correct range for the new database range. The second statement gives the name Database to the specific range R1C1:R3478C7 (A1:G3478). This isn't what you want. You want the name Database to be assigned to whatever selection is current at the time the statement executes. You'll also need to fix this statement. Make a note to do so.

8. Press F8 twice to move to the statement that closes the workbook file:

```
ActiveWorkbook.Close
```

This statement closes the active workbook. If you've made changes to the workbook, it also prompts for whether to save the changes. You can program the macro to always save changes or (while testing) to never save changes. (See the "Choose whether to save changes while closing a file" section later in this chapter.

9. Press F8 to close the database workbook. Click No when asked if you want to save changes. Only two statements remain in the macro:

```
Range("A1").Select
End Sub
```

10. Press F8 twice to end the macro.

The macro works now only because you're running it under circumstances identical to those when you recorded it, with the same current month file and the same database file. Here's a recap of the changes you'll need to make:

- Select the first row under the database.

- Give the name Database to the current selection.

- Don't prompt when closing the database.

The next few sections show you how to make these changes.

Record a relative movement

Take a closer look at the two *AppendDatabase* statements that find the first blank cell under the database. Imagine what will happen when you run this next month, when the database has more rows. The statement:

```
Selection.End(xlDown).Select
```

will select the bottom row, but then the statement:

```
Range("A3301").Select
```

will always select the absolute cell A3301 anyway.

When you select a cell, the macro recorder doesn't know whether you want the absolute cell you selected or a cell relative to where you started. For example, when you select a cell in row 1 to change the label of a column title, you always want the same absolute cell, without regard to where you started. But when you select the first blank cell at the bottom of a database, you want the macro to select a cell relative to where you started.

The macro recorder can't automatically know whether you want to record absolute cell addresses or relative movements, but you can tell the recorder which kind of selection you want. Use the recorder to record a new statement that you can use to replace the offending statement. You'll record the new statement in a new, temporary macro, and then copy the statement and delete the temporary macro.

1. Click the Record Macro button, type **DeleteMe** as the macro name, and click OK.

Record Macro button

2. On the Stop Recording toolbar, click the Relative Reference button. When this button is activated, the recorder makes all new cell selections *relative* to the original selection. Now you need to replace the statement that selects cell A3301 with one that makes a relative movement.

   You want to record the action of moving down one cell so that you can record the macro from any cell, on any worksheet.

Relative Reference button

3. Press the Down Arrow key once to record a relative movement.

4. Click the Relative Reference button to deselect it, and then click the Stop Recording button.

Stop Recording button

5. Edit the DeleteMe macro and look at the change. The new statement you recorded should look like this:

```
ActiveCell.Offset(1,0).Range("A1").Select
```

This statement means, "Select the cell below the active cell." It really does. At this point, you don't need to understand everything about how this statement works. Just trust the recorder. But you might wonder why the statement includes the words *Range("A1")* when it has nothing to do with cell A1. This statement calculates a new single-cell range shifted down one cell from the original active cell. The macro treats that new range as if it were the top left corner of an entire "virtual" worksheet and selects cell A1 of that imaginary worksheet!

6. Select the new statement and copy it.

7. Drop down the Procedures list (below the toolbars on the right side of the Module window), and select AppendDatabase.

8. Select *Range("A3301").Select*, delete it, and paste the new statement in its place.

9. Select the DeleteMe macro from the Procedures drop-down list.

10. Delete the DeleteMe macro by first selecting all the statements from *Sub DeleteMe* to *End Sub* and then pressing the Delete key.

With the Relative Reference button, you can control whether selections are absolute or relative to the current active cell. You can turn the Relative Reference button on and off as many times as you need while you're recording a macro.

Name the current selection

The statement in the AppendDatabase macro that defines the Database range name contains a potentially serious problem:

```
ActiveWorkbook.Names.Add Name:="Database", RefersToR1C1:= _
    "=Orders!R1C1:R3478C9"
```

This statement sets the name Database to the range that the database occupies at the end of this month. If you don't change this statement before next month, December orders will be discarded from the database when you save it. This is a case where the macro recorder generates a complicated statement when a simple one would work better.

1. Delete the entire recorded statement.

2. In its place, type

```
Selection.Name = "Database"
```

Name is a property of a range. By simply assigning a word in quotation marks as the value of the *Name* property, you can name the range.

Choose whether to save changes while closing a file

The statement that closes the database file looks like this:

```
ActiveWorkbook.Close
```

It triggers a prompt that asks if you want to save changes to the file, because you've made changes to it since you opened it. Sometimes when you automate a process, you know that you always will (or won't) want to save changes. The *Close* method has an optional argument that allows you to specify whether to save changes. For now, while you're testing the macro, set the statement to *not* save the changes.

1. Change the statement that closes the workbook to this:

```
ActiveWorkbook.Close SaveChanges:=False
```

The *SaveChanges* argument answers the dialog box's question before it even gets asked.

2. Save the Chapter2 workbook. Then run and test the AppendDatabase macro yourself.

3. Once you've finished testing the macro and are ready to use it regularly, change the word *False* to **True**.

Note Technically, since the active workbook happens to be a dBase file, setting the *SaveChanges* argument to *True* prevents Excel from asking if you want to save the changes, but it still displays a dialog box to ensure that you want to save the file as a dBase file. If the active workbook is a native Excel workbook, however, the *SaveChanges* argument causes Excel to save it quietly.

Here's the final version of the AppendDatabase macro:

```
Sub AppendDatabase()
    Range("A1").Select
    Selection.EntireRow.Delete
    Selection.CurrentRegion.Select
    Selection.Copy
    Workbooks.Open Filename:="C:\Excel VBA Practice\Orders.dbf"
    Selection.End(xlDown).Select
    ActiveCell.Offset(1, 0).Range("A1").Select
    ActiveSheet.Paste
    Application.CutCopyMode = False
    Selection.CurrentRegion.Select
    Selection.Name = "Database"
    ActiveWorkbook.Close SaveChanges:=True
    Range("A1").Select
End Sub
```

If you want, you can run the macro again now. It will work the same as it did before, but it's also ready for next month, when the database will have more records.

You're almost finished. The only task left is to get rid of the imported worksheet.

Task Five: Deleting the Worksheet

You imported the text file worksheet so that you could fill in the labels and add a column of dates before appending the data to the database. Once the data is safely appended, you don't need the imported worksheet any more.

Create a macro to delete the active sheet

Record Macro button

Stop Recording button

1. Activate an expendable worksheet, click the Record Macro button, type **DeleteSheet** as the macro name, and then click OK.

2. Choose the Edit menu, click Delete Sheet, and then click OK when asked to confirm.

3. Click the Stop Recording button to turn off the recorder.

4. Select another expendable worksheet, and step through the DeleteSheet macro:

```
Sub DeleteSheet()
    ActiveWindow.SelectedSheets.Delete
End Sub
```

The recorded statement refers to the "selected sheets of the active window" because it's possible to select and delete multiple sheets at the same time. (Press and hold the Ctrl key as you click several sheet tabs to see how you can select multiple sheets. Then click an unselected sheet without using the Ctrl key to deselect the sheets.) Because you're deleting only one sheet, you could change the statement to *ActiveSheet.Delete* if you wanted, but that isn't necessary.

The only problem with this macro is that it asks for confirmation each time you run it. When the macro deletes the imported sheet as part of the larger project, you would prefer not to be prompted.

Make the macro operate quietly

Run Macro button

The *Delete* method doesn't have an optional argument that eliminates the confirmation prompt. You must add a new statement to turn off the warning.

1. Click the Run Macro button, select the DeleteSheet macro, and click Edit.

2. Insert a new line after the comments following the statement *Sub DeleteSheet()* and then enter this statement:

```
Application.DisplayAlerts = False
```

DisplayAlerts is a property of the Excel application. When you set the value of *DisplayAlerts* to *False*, any confirmation prompts that you would normally see are treated as if you had selected the default answer. The *DisplayAlerts* setting lasts only until the macro finishes running; you don't need to set it back to *True*. However, you do need to be careful not to run this macro when the active sheet is something you care about. You should also, naturally, save your work often.

> **Tip** The Auto List Members feature will help you type the words *DisplayAlerts* and *False*. When you select a word in the list, press the Tab key to finish entering the word into the statement.

3. Save the Chapter2 workbook.

4. Select an expendable worksheet and run the DeleteSheet macro.

Assembling the Pieces

You have all the subordinate task macros ready for carrying out your complex monthly project:

* ImportFile opens and parses the text file.

* FillLabels makes the file look like a database.

* AddDates distinguishes one month from another in the database.

* AppendDatabase adds the new rows to the bottom of the saved database.

* DeleteSheet cleans up the temporary worksheet.

    Each piece is prepared and tested. Now you get to put them all together.

Record a macro that runs other macros

The easiest way to start gluing macros together is to record a macro that runs other macros.

1. Click the Record Macro button, type **MonthlyProject** as the macro name, and click OK.

2. Click the Run Macro button, click ImportFile, and then click Run.

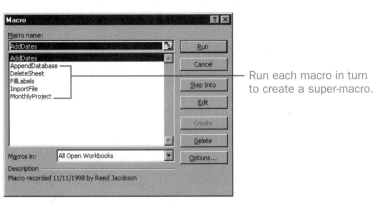

Run each macro in turn to create a super-macro.

Record Macro
button

Run Macro
button

3. Select the text file you want to import and then click Open.

4. Click the Run Macro button, click FillLabels, and then click Run.

5. Click the Run Macro button, click AddDates, and then click Run.

6. Type an appropriate date and click OK.

7. Click the Run Macro button, click AppendDatabase, and then click Run.

8. Click the Save button, and then click the Yes button to confirm that you wish to replace the Orders.dbf file.

9. Click the Run Macro button, click DeleteSheet, and then click Run.

10. Click the Stop Recording button.

Stop Recording button

Now you can look at what you created. Click the Run Macro button, select the MonthlyProject macro, and click Edit. After deleting the standard comments, here's what the macro to run other macros looks like:

```
Sub MonthlyProject()
    Application.Run "Chapter2.xls!ImportFile"
    Application.Run "Chapter2.xls!FillLabels"
    Application.Run "Chapter2.xls!AddDates"
    Application.Run "Chapter2.xls!AppendDatabase"
    Application.Run "Chapter2.xls!DeleteSheet"
End Sub
```

The MonthlyProject macro runs each of the subordinate macros in turn. The subordinate macros are known as *subroutines*. (By the way, this is the reason you start macros with the word *Sub,* so that you can turn them into subroutines simply by running them from another macro.)

Simplify the subroutine statements

The statement that the macro recorder creates for running a subroutine is somewhat unwieldy. You can simplify the statement, making it easier to read and faster to run.

1. Delete everything from each recorded subroutine statement except the name of the macro itself. Here's what the macro should look like when you're done:

```
Sub MonthlyProject()
    ImportFile
    FillLabels
    AddDates
    AppendDatabase
    DeleteSheet
End Sub
```

2. Save the Chapter2 workbook.

3. Press F5 to test the MonthlyProject macro. (You might also want to try pressing F8 to step through the main macro and each of the subroutines.)

You've worked hard and deserve a rest. Take the rest of the day off.

Chapter Summary

To	Do this	Button
Select the current region	Press Ctrl-Shift-*.	
Select blank cells in the current selection	Choose the Edit menu, click Go To, click the Special button, and then click the Blanks option.	
Fill all the selected cells at one time	Press Ctrl-Enter instead of just Enter.	
Watch a macro execute one statement at a time	Select the macro name in the Macro dialog box and click Step Into. Press F8 to execute the next statement.	
Have your macro give the name TestRange, for example, to the selected range	Use the statement *Selection.Name = "TestRange"*.	
Allow the user to select a file name from a dialog box	Use the *Application.GetOpenFilename* method.	
Prompt for a value while the macro runs	Use the *InputBox* function.	
Record movements relative to the active cell	On the Stop Recording toolbar, click the Relative Reference button.	
Create a macro to run other macros	Type the names of the other macros into one main macro shell.	

The first time you use help from Visual Basic for Applications, you might need the Excel 2000 installation media.

For online information about	Ask the Assistant for help using the words
Editing Visual Basic macros	"Edit Macros" (with Excel window active)
Stepping through a macro	"Step Into" (with Visual Basic window active)

Preview of the Next Chapter

In this chapter, you learned how to break a complex project into pieces, record and test each piece, and then pull all the pieces together into a single macro. You ended up with a macro that does a lot of work, and you used the macro recorder to create most of the macro. In the next chapter, you'll learn how to manipulate objects without relying on the macro recorder.

Review and Practice

You'll review and practice how to:

- Use the macro recorder to create utility macros.

- Use relative references when recording macros.

- Customize recorded macros.

- Add shortcut keys to macros.

- Make a macro request input when you run it.

In Part 1, you learned how to record and edit utility macros. Now you'd like to apply what you've learned to some new situations. At Miller Textiles, you have a log of expenses that you manage.

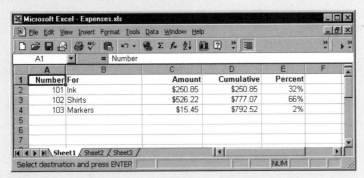

The expenses file is basically a list, with constant values in the first three columns and formulas in the last two columns. Occasionally, when you print the expenses list, you need to rearrange the order of the columns. You can create a macro that makes it easy to rearrange the columns.

Also, whenever you add a new expense, you have to increment the item number and copy the formula cells. You'd like to create one or more macros that make it easy to add a new expense item.

A completed Part1 workbook is in the Finished folder that accompanies the practice files. Your macros don't need to match the sample exactly.

Shifting a Column

Moving a column isn't particularly difficult: you simply select the column, cut it, move to the new location, and choose the Cut Cells command on the Insert menu. But it's something you do often enough that you'd like to be able to do it with a single keystroke.

Step 1: Record a Macro to Shift a Column to the Right

First you want a macro that can move the active column one column to the right. You can use the macro recorder to create this macro.

1. Save a copy of the Expenses workbook as Part1, and in it record a new macro named MoveColumnRight, with Ctrl-Shift-R as the shortcut key.

2. With the recorder set to use relative references, select the entire current column, cut it, press the Right Arrow key twice to move two columns to the right, and insert the cut cells (thus shifting the column one column to the right). Then select the original active cell.

3. Turn off the recorder and test the macro.

For more information about	See
Recording macros	Chapter 1, "Creating a Simple Macro"
Creating shortcut keys	Chapter 1, "Assign a shortcut key to the Macro"
Using relative references	Chapter 2, "Record a relative movement"

Step 2: Edit a Macro to Shift a Column to the Left

You also want to be able to shift a column to the left. Rather than record an entirely new macro, you decide to create the new macro by modifying a copy of the original. This macro will produce an error if you run it with a cell in column A selected, but that's all right for now.

1. Make a copy of the MoveColumnRight macro. Rename the copy to MoveColumnLeft and give it Ctrl-Shift-L as a shortcut key.

2. Modify the MoveColumnLeft macro to move one column to the left (rather than two columns to the right) before pasting the cut column.

Tip The Offset method takes two arguments: one for the row offset and one for the column offset. Giving a row offset a negative value moves the row up. Giving a column offset a negative value moves the column to the left.

3. Change the macro to allow the active cell to remain in the newly pasted location.

4. Test the MoveColumnLeft macro.

For more information about	See
Editing macros	Chapter 1, "Editing a Recorded Macro"
Renaming macros	Chapter 1, "Toggle the value of a property with a macro"

Adding a Row with Formulas

Appending a new expense to the list isn't difficult: you just go to the first blank cell below the list and start typing. But typing or copying formulas gets tedious, and sometimes when you enter the formula that calculates a percentage, Excel formats the number as currency. If you copy the bottom row down to the first blank row, you'll get the formulas automatically. It's easier to copy the entire row, even though you'll replace the values in the cells that contain constants.

Step 1: Append a New Row

Before working in the Expenses workbook, make sure that you have the columns set back to their original order: Number, For, Amount, Cumulative, and Percent.

Note   This step creates the first part of the AppendRow macro as it appears in the Finished folder. You'll create the last four statements in the section, "Step 4: integrating macros."

---

1. In the Part1 workbook, record a new macro named AppendRow. Use Ctrl-Shift-A as the shortcut key.

2. With Relative References turned *off*, select cell A1. Then turn on Relative References, press the End key followed by the Down Arrow key to jump to the bottom row of the list, select the entire row, copy it, move down one row, and paste a copy.

3. Cancel copy mode, turn off the recorder, and test the macro.

For more information about	See
Selecting within a list	Chapter 2, "Select only the blank cells"
Turning off copy mode	Chapter 2, "Fill the selection with values"

Step 2: Increment the Value from the Cell Above

The first column of the Expenses list is an incremental number. You could just use a formula to add 1 to the cell above, but then the numbers would change if you sort the list in a different way. You can record a macro that inserts a formula to increment the number and then converts the formula to a value.

If you click Cancel when prompted, Excel will leave the cell blank but continue the macro.

1. Record a new macro named Increment, with or without a shortcut key.

2. With Relative References still turned *on,* select the cell in the current row in column A. Add a formula to add 1 to the previous number. Convert the cell with the formula to a value.

3. Cancel copy mode, turn off the recorder, and test the macro.

For more information about	See
Recording a formula	Chapter 2, "Task Two: Filling in Missing Labels"
Converting a formula to a value	Chapter 1, "Convert a formula to a value with a macro"

Step 3: Prompt for New Values

Rather than just typing new values in the For and Amount columns, you can create macros to prompt you.

1. Start with a cell in column A selected. With Relative References turned on, record a macro named PromptFor.

2. Select the next cell to the right (in column B), type a sample value, and turn off the recorder.

3. Change the macro to prompt for a new For value. Use "Enter what the expense is for" as the prompt string.

4. Copy the PromptFor macro and rename the copy as PromptAmount. Change the prompt message in this macro to "Enter the expense amount."

5. Test both macros.

For more information about	See
Prompting for a value from a macro	Chapter 2, "Prompt for the date"

Step 4: Integrating Macros

Rather than run four separate macros when you need to add a new row, you'd like to run only one.

1. Make the AppendRow macro automatically run the other three macros.

2. Make the AppendRow macro reselect cell A1 when finished.

3. Test the combined macro. Then save and close the Part1 workbook.

For more information about	See
Running one macro from another	Chapter 2, "Assembling the Pieces"

Part 2

Exploring Objects

Chapter 3

Explore Microsoft Excel's Object Library

Chapter Objectives　　　　Estimated time: 45 minutes

In this chapter, you'll learn how to:

- Store values and objects in variables.

- Change object property values.

- Navigate to new objects.

- Use different resources in Microsoft Excel to learn about objects.

Last year, on a certain spring holiday known for having children search for candy, my wife and I put together a special hunt for our children. For example, I gave my youngest son a note that said, "Look under the armchair in the living room." When he got there, he found another note that said, "Look in the oven." When he got there, he found a note that said, "Look in your toy cupboard." When he got there, he found a basket of candy. We enjoyed the candy very much.

One of the notes—not coincidentally the last one—pointed to a basket of candy. Each of the other notes merely pointed to the location of another note. What my son cared about was the basket of candy, but he couldn't get there without following a chain of pointers.

In a macro, some methods and properties carry out actions and some point—or *refer*—to objects. Once you start modifying recorded statements, and especially when you start writing statements from scratch, you need to understand methods and properties that refer to objects. In this chapter, you'll learn how methods and properties refer to objects and how you can use the Microsoft Visual Basic tools to learn more about objects.

Start the lesson

1. Start Microsoft Excel. In the folder containing the practice files for this book, open the Objects workbook (enable macros if prompted).

2. Save a copy of the workbook as **Chapter3**.

See the Introduction to this book for more information about installing the practice files.

Using the Locals Window to Learn About Objects

Methods and properties fall into two groups. Those in one group—for example, *Copy*, *PasteSpecial*, *NumberFormat*, and *FormulaR1C1*—come at the end of a statement and carry out an action. I call these *action words*. Those in the other group—for example, *Application*, *ActiveWindow*, and *Range("A1")*—refer to objects.

Note Technically, a word such as *ActiveCell* means "a property that returns a reference to an Active Cell object." Informally, you can just call it an object, because that's what it refers to.

You can store an object—or, rather, a reference to an object—in a variable in much the same way that you store a value in a variable. Visual Basic has a powerful tool for letting you see what a variable contains: the Locals window.

Store values in variables

First let's watch the Locals window as a macro stores some simple values in a variable. This macro is a very simple one that assigns several different values to a variable.

Run Macro button

1. In the Chapter3 workbook, click the Run Macro button, select StoreValue, and click Edit. Here's the code you'll see:

```
Sub StoreValue()
    myValue = 500
    myValue = "Dog"
    myValue = True
    myValue = #5/1/99#
    myValue = 125.3
End Sub
```

2. From the View menu, select the Locals Window command. The Locals window appears, but it's empty. The Locals window shows variables only while you're stepping through a macro.

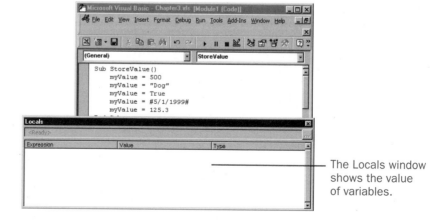

The Locals window shows the value of variables.

Tip If the Locals window is squeezed into the same area as the Module1 code window (that is, if it's *docked*), press and hold the Ctrl key as you drag the Locals title bar away from the code window. Holding the Ctrl key prevents a Visual Basic window from docking with another window.

---

3. Click the Module window, and press F8 to start stepping into the macro. The Locals window now shows Module1 (which you can ignore), and it also shows the variable *myValue*. In the Value column, it shows that *myValue* is *Empty* (which means that you haven't assigned anything to it yet). In the Type column, it shows that *myValue* is *Variant* (which means that you can assign anything to it) and that it doesn't yet have anything assigned to it.

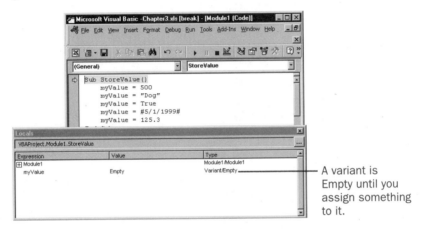

A variant is Empty until you assign something to it.

4. Press F8 twice to assign the value *500* to the variable. Now the Locals window shows that the value is 500. The Type column shows that the type is *Integer*. An Integer is a whole number, one that doesn't have any decimal places.

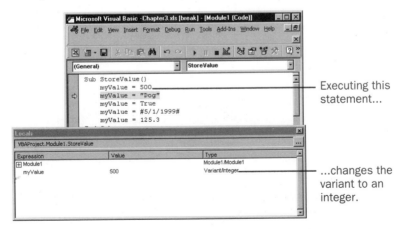

Executing this statement...

...changes the variant to an integer.

5. Press F8 again to assign the value *"Dog"* to the variable. The Locals window shows the new value and indicates that the type is *String*. A

string is any text. If you don't put quotation marks around a string, Visual Basic tries to interpret it as a variable.

6. Press F8 again to assign the value *True* to the variable. The Locals window shows that the type is now *Boolean*. Boolean is simply a fancy word for a value that can be only True or False.

7. Press F8 again to assign the value *#5/1/1999#* to the variable. The Locals window shows the type as *Date*. The number signs indicate that this is a date and not the numeral 5 divided by 1 divided by 1999. Number signs indicate dates in the same way that quotation marks indicate strings.

8. Press F8 to assign the value *125.3* to the variable. The type is now *Double*. A Double is a number with a decimal portion. In general, small numbers used for counting things are Integers, and large numbers used for serious calculations are Doubles.

9. Press F8 to end the subroutine.

When you type a two-digit year in a date, Visual Basic changes it to a four-digit year.

You usually don't need to worry about what data type a value has. As you can see, Visual Basic automatically changes *myValue* to hold whatever type of value you want to assign to it. Numbers, strings, dates, and Booleans are all different kinds of simple values. In the Locals window, you see the value in the Value column. Now let's see what a variable looks like when you assign an object reference to it.

Store objects in variables

When you assign a value to a variable, you just use an equal sign to assign the value. When you assign an object reference to a variable, however, you still use an equal sign, but you also must put the keyword *Set* at the beginning of the statement.

1. In the Procedure list on the right side above the code window, select the *StoreObject* procedure. It's a simple test procedure to let you see the difference between assigning a value and assigning an object reference.

```
Sub StoreObject()
    myObject = Range("A1")
    Set myObject = Range("A1")
End Sub
```

2. Press F8 to start stepping through the macro. Once again, you see Module1 and an empty variable.

3. Press F8 twice to assign *Range("A1")* to the variable. The value in cell A1 is the string *"Test Cell."* The Locals window shows that the variable now contains the string value *"Test Cell."* This statement didn't use the keyword *Set* to assign the range, so Visual Basic retrieved the value from the cell and assigned that value to the variable.

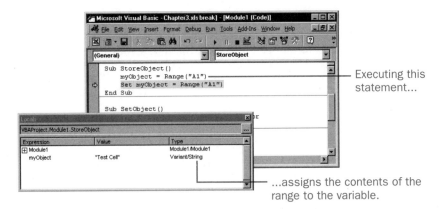

Executing this
statement...

...assigns the contents of the
range to the variable.

4. Press F8 again to assign *Range("A1")* to the variable using the *Set* keyword. The Locals window doesn't show anything as the value of *myObject*. Rather, *myObject* now has a plus sign next to it and says Variant/Object/ Range under Type. The variable now contains a reference to an object— specifically, to a Range object.

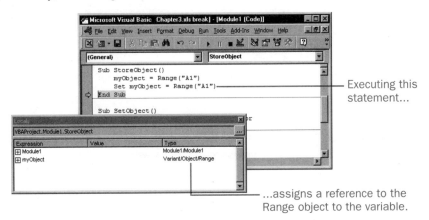

Executing this
statement...

...assigns a reference to the
Range object to the variable.

5. In the Locals window, click the plus sign next to the *myObject* variable. A list with all the properties of the cell A1 Range object appears. This list includes only properties, not methods. Each property either shows a value or has a plus sign next to it. A property that has a plus sign is a reference to another object. A property that has no plus sign is a value.

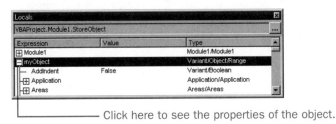

Click here to see the properties of the object.

6. Scroll down until you see the *Value* property. The value of the cell is the string *"Test Cell."* This is the property Visual Basic used when the macro assigned *Range("A1")* to the variable without using the *Set* keyword.

To assign a value to a variable, use an equal sign. To assign an object reference to a variable, use an equal sign and also put the word *Set* at the front of the statement.

Change object property values

You can change the value of a property right in the Locals window. Some properties are *read-only* so you can't change them, but other properties are available to change. Changing the property in the Locals window has exactly the same effect as changing the property in a Visual Basic statement, so you can try out properties interactively as you're trying to find the property you want.

1. In the Locals window, scroll from the *Value* property you were just looking at up to the *ColumnWidth* property. (Rearrange windows as necessary so that you can see cell A1 in Excel.)

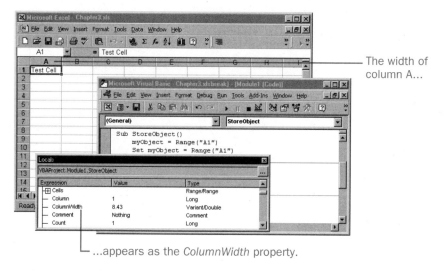

The width of column A...

...appears as the *ColumnWidth* property.

2. Click *ColumnWidth* to select the entire row. Then click *8.43* in the Value column to select just the number. This is the default width of a column.

3. Type **25** and press the Enter key. The width of the column changes. Changing the value of the property tells Excel to change the object on the screen.

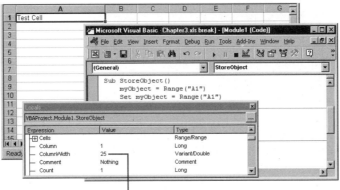

— Type a value here to change the column width in Excel.

4. To see a read-only property, click Column in the Locals window to select the row with the *Column* property. Then click the 1 in the Value column. Nothing happens. Sorry, you just can't change which column cell A1 is in by assigning a new value to the *Column* property. *Column* is a *read-only* property.

5. In the Visual Basic module window, insert a new line above the *End Sub* statement of the StoreObject macro, and type **myObject.ColumnWidth = 5**. This is the Visual Basic code equivalent of changing the value of the *ColumnWidth* property in the Locals window.

6. Drag the yellow arrow that points at the *End Sub* statement up to point at the new *ColumnWidth* statement you just typed. Dragging the arrow changes which statement will execute next.

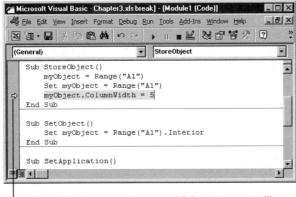

— Drag the arrow to change which statement will execute next.

7. Press F8 to execute the new statement. The column width shrinks.

The Locals window gives you a quick view of all the properties that belong to a particular object. The Locals window also makes it clear which properties contain values—the ones that have a value in the Value column—and which contain a reference to an object—the ones that have a plus sign next to them.

It also makes it easy to find out whether a value-holding property is read-only: just click the value and see if you can change it.

Next let's look at what happens when you delve into one of those properties that contains a reference to an object.

Navigate to new objects

1. With the StoreObject macro still stopped on the *End Sub* statement, click the plus sign next to *myObject*, and then click the plus sign next to the *Interior* property of *myObject*. The *Interior* property of a Range object returns a reference to a new object, an *Interior* object. The Interior object controls the color and pattern of the interior of the cell. The reason Interior is a separate object is that many different objects can have interiors—most notably, many components of a chart.

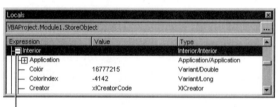

— The *Interior* property is a whole new object, with its own properties.

2. Click the *Color* property, and then click the number *16777215* in the Value column. Theoretically, a cell can have any of 16,777,216 possible values ranging from 0 (Black) to 16,777,215 (White). In practice, Excel picks out 56 of those colors to make up a palette. When you assign a number between 0 and 16,777,215 to the Color property, Excel "rounds" the number to the closest color in the palette. Fortunately, Visual Basic has some predefined names for common colors.

3. Type **vbRed** as the value of *Color,* and press the Enter key. The interior of cell A1 changes to red, the *Color* property value changes to 255 (which happens to be the color number for red), and the *ColorIndex* number changes to 3.

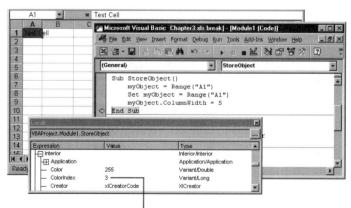

Type **vbred** to change the color of the cell interior.

Note The *ColorIndex* property is a value between 0 and 56, corresponding to the colors in Excel's palette. In Excel 5, the numbers matched the order of the boxes in the Fill Color toolbar palette on Excel's Formatting toolbar. But in more recent versions of Excel, the colors in the palette were arranged in a more logical order, while retaining the original color index numbers for the sake of backward compatibility. So there is no longer any apparent order to the numbers.

---

4. Click the *ColorIndex* property, and then click the number 3. Type **34** and press the Enter key. The cell changes to a nice pale blue.

Changing the *ColorIndex* property changes the *Color* property, too.

5. In the Code window, just above the *End Sub* statement, type **myObject.Interior.ColorIndex = 45**.

6. Drag the yellow pointer up to the new statement and press F8. The interior of the cell changes to orange.

7. Press F5 to finish executing the macro.

The purpose of this section wasn't to teach you about cell colors, but rather to show you how you can link from one object to another using properties. You can try out the properties—whether properties that refer to other objects or properties that contain values—in the Locals window as you explore ways to bend Excel to your unbridled will.

Using the Immediate Window to Learn About Objects

Each object in Excel has methods and properties that allow you to navigate to other objects. One common way to navigate between objects is to move up and down Excel's hierarchy of objects. In this hierarchy, each object in Excel has a parent object. You can move up the hierarchy by using the *Parent* property. In this section, you'll navigate up and down the Excel hierarchy using a powerful Visual Basic feature: the Immediate window.

Navigate up by using parent

1. Use the Procedure drop-down list to select the SetObject macro. It looks like this:

```
Sub SetObject()
    Set myObject = Range("A1").Interior
End Sub
```

This is a trivial macro. It simply assigns the interior of cell A1 to a variable.

2. Press F8 three times to assign the object. Look at the Locals window. The object type is listed as Variant/Object/Interior.

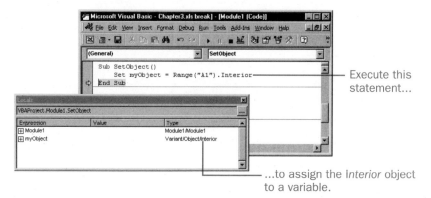

Execute this statement...

...to assign the *Interior* object to a variable.

3. From the View menu in the Visual Basic window, click the Immediate window command. (If the window docks with one of the other windows, press and hold the Ctrl key and drag it away.)

4. In the Immediate window, you can enter any statement you want and execute it immediately, without modifying the macro in the module. In the Immediate window, type **Set myObject = myObject.Parent** and press the Enter key. The description in the Type column of the Locals window shows that the object is a range, because the parent of this particular interior object is a range.

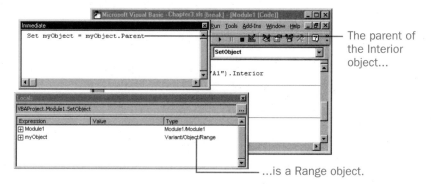

The parent of the Interior object...

...is a Range object.

5. Move the cursor back to the same statement in the Immediate window (it doesn't have to be at the end), and press the Enter key again. For some reason, the variable type shows only Object. It should say Worksheet, because the parent of a cell is a worksheet. But Excel really does know it is a Worksheet object, as you can tell when you move up one more generation.

6. Execute the statement again. This time the type changes to ThisWorkbook.

7. Execute the statement once again. The type changes to Application.

8. Just for good measure, execute the statement one more time. The type doesn't change. It's still Application.

9. Press F5 to end the macro.

Each object has a parent. (Because the top object is the Application object, the Application object is also its own parent. Wouldn't Freud have had fun with that one?) This particular chain went from Interior to Range to Worksheet to ThisWorkbook to Application.

Navigate down by using collections

When you look at an open workbook, you usually see multiple sheet tabs at the bottom. It's easy when moving up Excel's object hierarchy to tell that the workbook is the parent of any of the worksheets, but when moving down the hierarchy, you run into multiple worksheets.

The way the object library deals with this clustering of objects as you go down is to group related items in a *collection*. When you navigate down the object hierarchy, you need to select a single item from each collection. To select an item from a collection, you specify either the item number or the item name.

If you have macros in the Personal.xls workbook, close it before continuing. In Excel, click Window, Unhide. Unhide the Personal workbook and close it.

1. Select the SetApplication macro from the Procedure list. It looks like this:

```
Sub SetApplication()
    Set myObject = Application
End Sub
```

This trivial macro starts at the top of the hierarchy. It assigns the Application object to *myObject*.

2. Press F8 three times to assign the Application object.

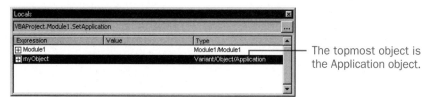
The topmost object is the Application object.

The Locals window shows that the variable contains a reference to the Application object. One of the properties of the Application object is the *Workbooks* property. The *Workbooks* property returns a reference to an object that is a collection of Workbook objects. You can specify a single item from the collection.

3. In the Immediate window, clear the previous entry, type **Set myObject = myObject.Workbooks(1),** and then press the Enter key. The Locals window shows that the variable now contains a reference to a ThisWorkbook object, which is really a Workbook object. Putting parentheses after the collection allows you to single out one item from the collection. A workbook in the collection is numbered based on the order in which the workbooks were opened. Close a workbook, and the number for each subsequent workbook changes.

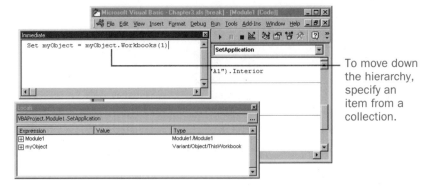

To move down the hierarchy, specify an item from a collection.

4. One of the properties of a Workbook object is the *Worksheets* property. The *Worksheets* property returns a reference to an object that contains a collection of Worksheet objects. Once again, you can specify a single item from the collection. In the Immediate window, type **Set myObject = myObject.Worksheets("Sheet2")** and press the Enter key.

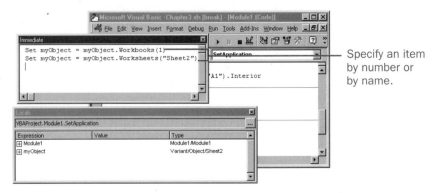

Specify an item by number or by name.

The Locals window shows that the variable now contains a reference to a Sheet2 object, which is really a Worksheet object. Once again, *Worksheets* (notice the *s* on the end) is a property that returns a collection, and the parentheses allow you to specify a single item. You can specify an item either by name (in quotation marks) or by number. The number is sometimes called an *Index*. A Worksheet in the collection is numbered based on the current position of its sheet tab. Move a worksheet, and its number in the collection changes.

5. Press F5 to end the macro.

When you specify an item from a collection, you can use either a number or a name and get a reference to the same object. Choose the method of specifying that is most convenient in a given situation.

Tip You can execute statements in the Immediate window even when you're not stepping through a macro, but you can't see variables in the Locals window unless you're stepping.

Navigate from object to object

All objects in Excel fit somewhere in the object library hierarchy—you can tell where an object is in the hierarchy by finding the object referred to by its *Parent* property—but that doesn't mean that you're limited to navigating up and down the hierarchy.

1. Select the SetApplication macro, and press F8 three times to assign the application object to the variable.

2. Click the plus sign next to *myObject*, which contains the Application object.

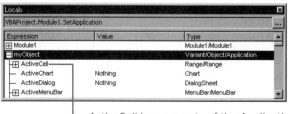

— *ActiveCell* is a property of the Application object.

The list shows the properties that belong to an Application object. The first property in the list is *ActiveCell*, which returns a reference to a Range object. You can navigate directly from the Application object to the active cell, even though the Application object isn't the parent of a Range object. (The worksheet is the parent of a range.)

3. Click the plus sign next to *ActiveCell*.

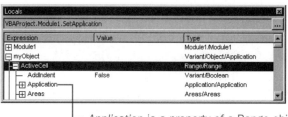

— *Application* is a property of a Range object.

This list shows the properties of a Range object. The second property in the list is *Application*. It has a plus sign and returns a reference to the Application object. Every object has an *Application* property that returns a reference directly to the top of the hierarchy.

4. Click the plus sign next to the *Application* property. The list shows another *ActiveCell* property.

5. Click the plus sign next to *ActiveCell*. Then click the plus sign next to the subsequent *Application*. (How many of these are there?)

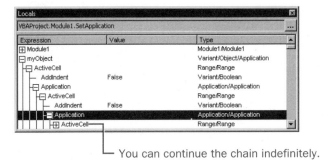

You can continue the chain indefinitely.

6. When you're bored, click the minus sign next to *myObject* to collapse everything back. (I drilled down 46 times, which is the most I could fit on the screen at 1600x1200 resolution.) Press F5 to end the macro. (You can also now close the Locals window and the Immediate window if you want to get them out of the way.)

When you get a reference to an object, regardless of how you get that reference, it's exactly the same as if you had gotten the reference by any other means. Assuming cell A1 is the active cell, *ActiveCell, Application.ActiveCell, Active-Sheet.ActiveCell, Application.ActiveWorkbook.ActiveSheet.Range("A1"), Range("A1"), ActiveSheet.Range("A1"),* and along with about 6,273 other expressions, all give you a reference to exactly the same object.

You can navigate by moving up and down the object hierarchy, or you can follow shortcut methods and properties that refer directly to an object in a different part of the family tree. Once you get an object reference, there's no way to tell how you got it. Navigating objects is like an efficient money-laundering scheme.

Using Help to Learn About Objects

You could learn about all of Excel's objects by navigating up and down the hierarchy using the Locals window and the Immediate window, but it still might be difficult to see the big picture. Fortunately, the Excel Visual Basic Reference Help file contains an overview diagram that you'll find very useful for putting all the objects into perspective.

Find the object hierarchy in Help

The first time you access Visual Basic Help, you might need access to the installation CD or network folder.

1. Click the word *Application* in the SetApplication macro, and press F1. A description of the *Application* property appears. This topic indicates that the *Application* property returns a reference to the Application object.

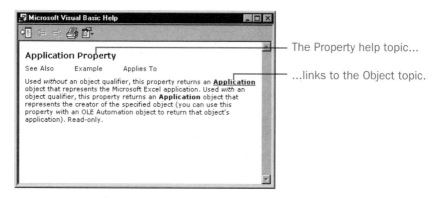

The Property help topic...

...links to the Object topic.

2. Click the word *Application* in the first sentence. A description of the Application object appears. At the top of the topic is a diagram showing the Application object in a box.

Click here to see the entire object model.

3. Click the Application box. The Microsoft Excel Objects topic appears.

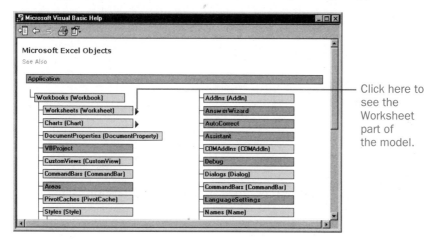

Click here to see the Worksheet part of the model.

This first page shows about one-third of the Excel Object Model. You can see the Application object at the top. (The Application object is blue because it doesn't come in a collection.) It's the parent of a Workbook object. (The Workbook's object is yellow because it does come in a collection.) A workbook is the parent of a Worksheet object (which is yellow because it also comes in a collection).

4. Click the red arrow next to the Worksheet object. This diagram shows more of the object model, starting from the Worksheet object.

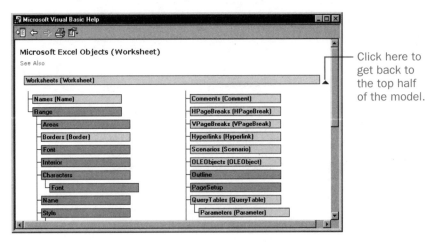

— Click here to get back to the top half of the model.

You'll learn more about Range objects and collections in Chapter 4.

A Worksheet object is the parent of a Range object. The Range object is blue because it isn't really a collection. A Range object is just weird. A Range object is the parent of an Interior object. So the parent chain goes from Interior to Range to Worksheet to Workbook to Application, as you saw in an earlier section.

5. Click the red triangle at the right of the Worksheet object to get back to the top part of the object model. On the right side of the main part of the model, you can see other objects that have the application as a parent. Most of them are objects that you'll need only in advanced situations.

Find new methods in Help

You can jump directly to the description for any object by clicking the object's box. Once you go to the topic for an object, you can learn about that object's methods and properties.

1. Click the Workbooks object box. The topic for the Workbooks collection object appears. At the top are options to show the properties and methods for the Workbooks object.

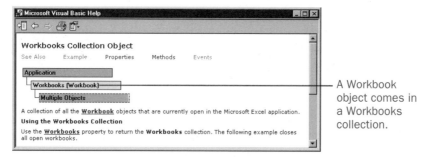

A Workbook
object comes in
a Workbooks
collection.

2. Click Properties. The dialog box shows all the properties that apply to the Workbooks collection.

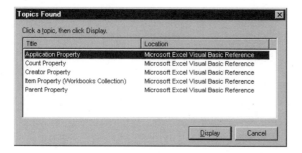

Every object has a *Parent* property, an *Application* property, and a *Creator* property. You learned about the *Parent* and *Application* properties earlier in this chapter. The *Creator* property is useful only on a Macintosh computer. All collection objects have the *Count* and *Item* properties. *Count* tells you how many items are in the collection. The *Item* property is another way of retrieving a single item from a collection.

3. Click the Cancel button, and then click the Methods option.

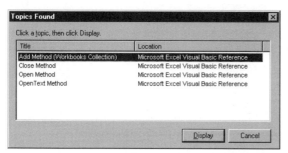

These are the methods that apply to the Workbooks collection. You can *Add* a new workbook to the collection, *Close* all the workbooks together, *Open* an existing workbook, or *OpenText* to open a text file and divide the contents into columns. (In Chapter 2, the macro recorder created a statement using the *OpenText* method. To find out what that statement means, look there.)

4. Double-click the Add Method topic.

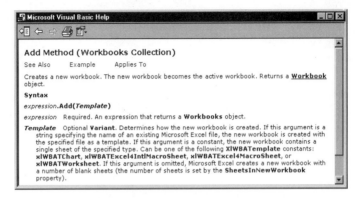

The first paragraph describes how the *Add* method creates a new
workbook (optionally using a template file) and then says that the *Add*
method "returns a Workbook object." What that means is that when you
create a new workbook using the *Add* method, you get back a reference
that you can assign to a variable using *Set*. In the next section, you'll see
how to do that.

5. The word *Workbook* is highlighted. You can jump directly to the
Workbook Object Topic. Click the Workbook link.

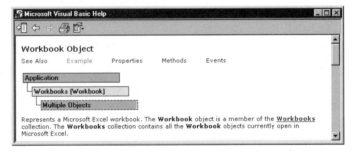

As you can see, a Workbook object is different from the Workbooks
collection object. The Workbooks Object topic has its own lists of
properties and methods. (You'll learn about Events in Chapter 9.)

6. Click the Methods link.

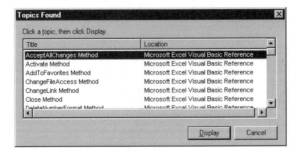

A Workbook object has many more methods available than a Workbooks collection object.

7. Double-click the Close Method topic. When you record closing a file, you'll never see arguments used with the *Close* method. As you can see from the Help topic, however, the *Close* method can take optional arguments. The most useful is the *SaveChanges* argument, which allows you to close a workbook without prompting for whether to save changes.

8. Close Help to return to the Visual Basic editor.

Help is a useful tool for learning about objects and their associated methods and properties. Help is particularly useful for discovering methods or properties that you have never used. If you vaguely recollect a method or property, but can't remember the exact name, the following section introduces you to some convenient Visual Basic tools.

Using Auto Lists to Learn About Objects

One very convenient tool for discovering or remembering methods and properties is the automatic list that Visual Basic can pop up while you're typing. You have probably noticed these lists before. In this section you'll learn more about how to take full advantage of the Auto List feature as you write macros.

Add and close a workbook

Follow these instructions to create a new macro from scratch using the methods you saw in Help.

1. At the bottom of the module, type **Sub MakeBook** and press the Enter key to create a new macro. You don't need to type the parentheses at the end; Visual Basic adds the parentheses and the *End Sub* statement for you.

2. Press the Tab key to indent the body of the macro, and then type **Workbooks.** (Be sure to type the period.) As soon as you type the period, Visual Basic displays a list of all the methods and properties available for the Workbooks collection.

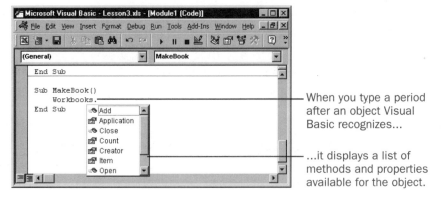

When you type a period after an object Visual Basic recognizes...

...it displays a list of methods and properties available for the object.

This list is like a combination of the two lists you saw in Help. The icon next to the name distinguishes methods and properties. The icon for a property looks like a finger pointing at a box. The icon for a method looks like a green clam hurtling through space.

3. The word *Add* is already highlighted at the top of the list. Press the Tab key to enter it into the statement, and then press the Enter key to go to the next line.

Entering the name of the *Add* method was pretty slick, right? You didn't have to type anything. You did have to type the word *Workbooks*, though. Perhaps you're too lazy to do even that much.

4. Press Ctrl-Spacebar, press the Down Arrow key until you highlight *ActiveWorkbook*, and then press the Tab key. Was that easy enough for you?

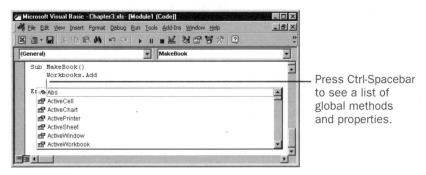

Press Ctrl-Spacebar to see a list of global methods and properties.

5. Type a period. Once again, as soon as you type the period, Visual Basic displays the list of methods and properties available for a Workbook object.

6. Type **C** to jump quickly down the list, select Close from the list, and press the Tab key. (Don't press the Enter key yet.)

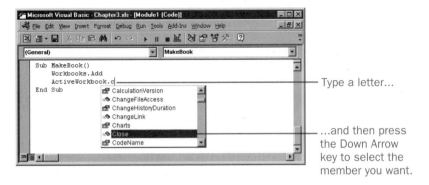

Type a letter...

...and then press the Down Arrow key to select the member you want.

7. You saw in Help that the *Close* method has optional arguments. See what happens when you get ready to type one of them: type a space. Visual Basic displays a Quick Info box showing the possible arguments for the *Close* method. You want to tell *Close* not to prompt to save changes. Because the *SaveChanges* argument is the first one in the list, you don't need to type the name of the argument, but you do want to specify a value.

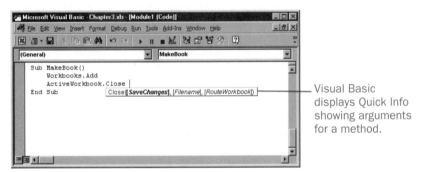

Visual Basic displays Quick Info showing arguments for a method.

8. Type **False**.

9. Test the macro by pressing F8 five times. You should see the new workbook appear and then disappear quietly.

Auto Lists not only let you know what methods and properties are available in the current context, but they also let you be lazy. What a deal!

Use Auto Lists to learn constant values

Many properties and arguments allow only a limited number of values. A limited set of values is called an *enumerated list*, because you can number each value. Visual Basic has Auto Lists that help you select a value from an enumerated list.

1. In the MakeBook macro, insert a new line after the *Workbooks.Add* statement, type (or press Ctrl-Spacebar and select) **ActiveWindow**, type a period, type (or select) **WindowState**, and then type an equal sign (=). Or, simply type **ActiveWindow.WindowState=**.

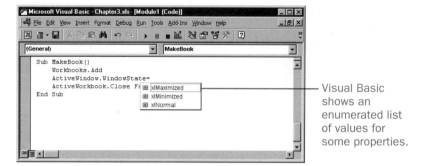

Visual Basic shows an enumerated list of values for some properties.

The *WindowState* property controls whether the window is minimized, maximized, or sizable. As soon as you finish typing the equal sign, Visual Basic displays a list enumerating the three possible values: *xlMaximized,* *xlMinimized,* and *xlNormal.*

2. Select *xlMinimized* from the list, and press the Enter key.

3. Type **Windows.Arrange** (or construct it using the Auto Lists), and then press the Spacebar. Visual Basic displays the Quick Info box, showing you the possible arguments for the *Arrange* method.

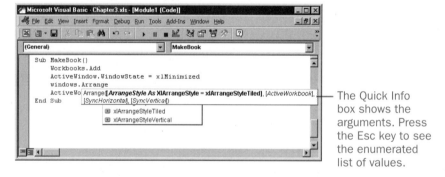

The Quick Info box shows the arguments. Press the Esc key to see the enumerated list of values.

The first argument is *ArrangeStyle.* This argument controls how the windows will be arranged. After the argument name are the words *As XlArrangeStyle = xlArrangeStyleTiled.* These words mean that Excel's object library contains a list named *XlArrangeStyle* that enumerates all the possible values for this argument. The expression = *xlArrangeStyleTiled* means that if you don't tell *Arrange* otherwise, it will tile the windows.

4. Press the Esc key to remove the Quick Info box, leaving behind the list of possible values.

5. Select *xlArrangeStyleCascade,* and press the Tab key to enter it into the statement.

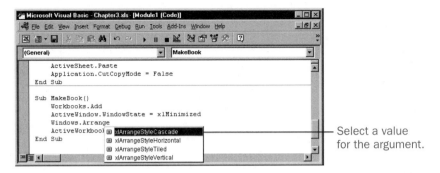

Select a value for the argument.

6. Click the Save button on the Visual Basic Standard toolbar to save the workbook, and then press F8 five times to step through part of the macro. Don't step through the statement that closes the workbook! (If you do, you'd better hope that you saved the workbook when I told you to.)

Save button

The macro creates a new workbook, minimizes it, and arranges the other workbook. If you execute the last statement now, you'll close the Chapter3 workbook rather than the workbook you just created.

7. Click the Reset button to stop the macro without closing the workbook.

Reset button

Declare variables to enable Auto Lists

When you create a new workbook, you can use ActiveWorkbook to refer to it, unless, of course, you activate a different workbook first. You need some way of storing a reference to the original workbook so that you can get back to it when you're ready. In Chapter 2, you learned how to use *Set* to store a reference in a variable. In Help, the description of the *Add* method said that the *Add* method returns a reference to the newly created workbook. You can create a workbook and store that reference in a variable at the same time.

1. Delete the *ActiveWorkbook.Close* statement from the end of the MakeBook macro.

2. At the beginning of the *Workbooks.Add* statement, insert the words **Set myBook =**. The resulting statement is *Set myBook = Workbooks.Add.* In the "Add and close a workbook" section, an automatic list appeared as soon as you typed a period after the word *ActiveWorkbook.* You now have told the macro to assign a reference to a workbook in *myBook.* Will the list automatically appear when you type a period after *myBook?*

3. Insert a new line before the *End Sub* statement, and type **myBook.** (Be sure to type the period.) Nothing happened. The list didn't appear. Why not?

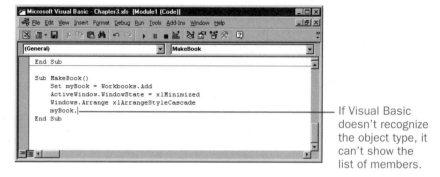

If Visual Basic doesn't recognize the object type, it can't show the list of members.

The word *myBook* acts as a variable. When you create a new word and use it as a variable, Visual Basic makes it *Variant*. Variant means that you can assign anything you want to the variable and it will change from Integer to String to Workbook to Range as fast as you can assign different values or objects to it. Visual Basic can't display the Auto List because it really doesn't know what type of value or object will be assigned to the variable at any given moment. You can, however, promise Visual Basic that you'll never, ever assign anything other than a Workbook to the *myBook* variable.

4. Delete the period you just typed. At the top of the macro, just below the *Sub MakeBook* statement, enter this statement: **Dim myBook As Workbook.** This statement *declares* the variable to Visual Basic. That is, you declare to Visual Basic that *myBook* is a variable and that the only thing you'll ever assign to it is a reference to a Workbook object. (*Dim* is an archaic term. It's short for *Dimension* and has to do with telling the computer how much space you'll need for the variable.)

5. Position the cursor at the end of the statement beginning with *myBook,* and type a period. Sure enough, the Auto List appears. Select Close, and then type **False** as an argument.

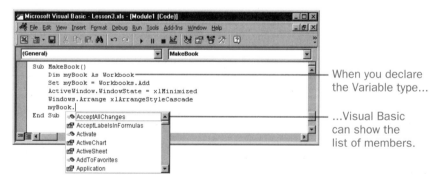

When you declare the Variable type...

...Visual Basic can show the list of members.

6. Save the workbook, and then press F8 repeatedly to step through the macro.

You can create a variable "on the fly" simply by assigning a value or an object to it, or you can use *Dim* to declare proudly to Visual Basic that you intend to use a variable of an unchanging type.

Using the Object Browser to Learn About Objects

Visual Basic has yet another tool to help you explore Excel's object library. In fact, this last tool might be the most powerful of all: the Object Browser.

> **Find a new argument for a familiar method**

There's a CopyRange macro in the Chapter3 workbook. This is what the macro recorder created when I copied cell A1 and pasted it into the D1:D6 range:

```
Sub CopyRange()
    Range("A1").Select
    Selection.Copy
    Range("D1:D6")
    ActiveSheet.Paste
    Application.CutCopyMode = False
End Sub
```

This macro first selects the source range, then copies it, then selects the target range, pastes the cells, and turns off the copy buffer. The macro recorder doesn't give you any clues about how you could make this macro simpler, but the Object Browser can.

1. Click the Object Browser button in the Visual Basic toolbar.

Object Browser button

─ The <globals> class...

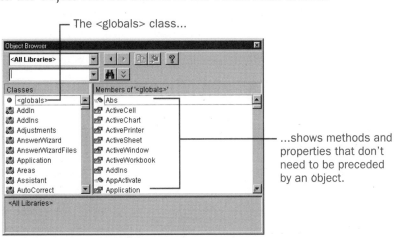

...shows methods and properties that don't need to be preceded by an object.

The Object Browser consists primarily of two lists. The one on the left is labeled *Classes*, which is a fancy name for object types, and the one on the right is labeled *Members*, which is a fancy name for methods and properties.

Note If you want to make the Object Browser float like the Locals window and the Immediate window, right-click in the middle of the Object Browser window and click the Dockable command. If it still doesn't float, press and hold the Ctrl key as you drag the caption bar off to the side.

---

2. In the list on the left, <globals> should be selected. If it's not, select it (it's at the top of the list. In the list on the right, click *ActiveCell*. The box at the bottom of the Object Browser changes to display information about *ActiveCell*.

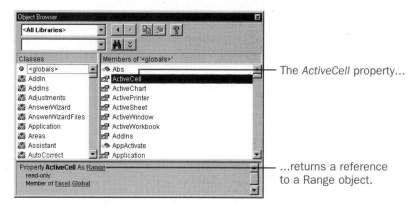

The *ActiveCell* property...

...returns a reference to a Range object.

The description, *Property ActiveCell As Range*, tells you that *ActiveCell* is a property and that it returns a reference to a Range object. In other words, the object that *ActiveCell* returns belongs to the Range class. When the word following a member name is green and underlined, it means that the member returns a reference to that kind of object. You can jump quickly to the object class.

3. Click Range. The list of classes on the left scrolls to show you the Range class. The list of members on the right now shows you all the methods and properties available for any Range object.

The Range class...

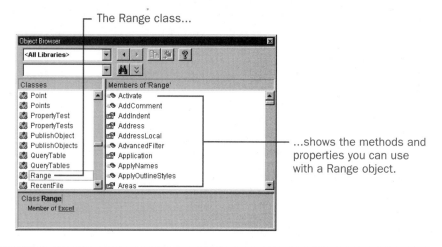

...shows the methods and properties you can use with a Range object.

Tip If all you see are properties, right-click the list and deselect the Group Members command.

The list of members on the right is exactly the same as the one that would pop up if you typed **ActiveCell** and then a period. Notice the icons showing which members are methods and which are properties. These methods and properties apply to any object that belongs to the Range class.

4. Scroll down the list of members, and click the *Copy* method. The box at the bottom of the dialog box shows a description of the *Copy* method.

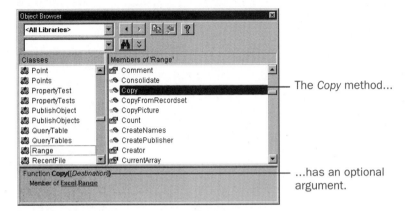

The *Copy* method...

...has an optional argument.

The macro recorder always uses the *Copy* method without arguments (which copies the cell to the clipboard), but the description at the bottom of the Object Browser shows you that you can give the *Copy* method a *Destination*. The *Destination* argument is in square brackets, indicating that it's optional.

5. Click the Close Window button to close the Object Browser.

6. In the module window, delete all the statements that form the body of the CopyRange macro (everything between the *Sub* and *End Sub* statements), and leave a blank line for the replacement statement.

7. Type **Range("A1").Copy** and press the Spacebar. The Quick Info box shows the optional *Destination* argument. Type **Range("D1:D6")** as the argument.

The finished macro looks like this:

```
Sub CopyRange()
    Range("A1").Copy Range("D1:D6")
End Sub
```

Close Window button

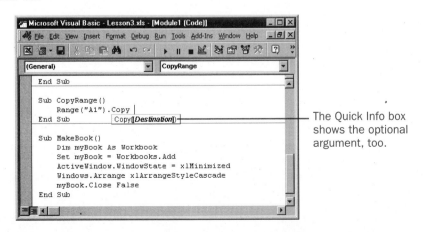

The Quick Info box shows the optional argument, too.

8. Press F5 to test the macro. The revised macro doesn't change the selection, and it's easier to read than the recorded macro. The macro recorder shows you that there is a *Copy* method, but it doesn't show you that the *Copy* method can use an argument. The Auto List displays the *Copy* method, but to see the arguments, you must enter the method into a statement. In the Object Browser, you can quickly see the arguments for all the methods simply by scrolling up and down through the list of members.

9. Save the Chapter3 workbook, and quit Excel.

The Object Browser can be an extremely powerful tool for exploring the wealth of Excel objects.

Dockable Views

The windows in the Visual Basic Editor can be confusing. You might find it easier to understand how they work if you compare them to windows in the Excel environment.

In Excel, each workbook you open has its own window. A workbook window can be either maximized to fill Excel's entire work area or sizable so that you can have more than one window visible at a time. A worksheet window can never move outside the boundary of the Excel application. It's completely owned by the main Excel window. This kind of window is a *child* window.

A toolbar, on the other hand, can be either docked or floating. A toolbar can be docked to the top, left, bottom, or right side of Excel's main window. To undock a toolbar, you drag the toolbar away from the docking position. A floating toolbar can be placed anywhere; it doesn't have to remain inside Excel's main window. A toolbar is actually a kind of window—a *dockable* window.

The Visual Basic Environment has both dockable and child windows. A module window is a child window. It can be minimized, restored, or maximized, but it can never move outside the boundaries of the Visual Basic Environment window.

The Locals window is by default a dockable window, just like toolbars in Excel. You can dock the Locals window to the top, left, bottom, or right sides of the Visual Basic window, or you can make it float by dragging it away from a docking position. You can also prevent the window from docking by pressing and holding the Ctrl key as you move the window.

Visual Basic has six dockable windows: the Locals window, the Immediate window, the Watch window, the Project Explorer window, the Properties window, and the Object Browser window. You can display any of these windows by choosing the appropriate command from the View menu.

To change a Visual Basic dockable window into a child window, right-click the window and then click the Dockable command to

Dockable Views *continued*

turn off the check mark. With the dockable setting turned off, the window behaves just like any child window; you can minimize, maximize, restore, cascade, or tile it, but you can't move it outside the main window, and it can't float above another active window.

    I usually make all windows dockable but undocked. I move, hide, and unhide windows as necessary. I also maximize the module window and keep it relatively small so that I can see the Excel window in the background.

Chapter Summary

To	Do this	Button
Watch the value of variables as you step through a macro	Click the View menu and then the LocalsWindow command.	
Undock a dockable window	Press and hold the Ctrl key as you drag the window's title bar.	
Store a reference to an object in a variable	Put the keyword *Set* at the beginning of the *Assignment* statement.	
Execute a statement without running a macro	From the View menu, click the Immediate Window command, type the statement in the Immediate window, and then press the Enter key.	
Retrieve a reference to the parent of an object	Use the *Parent* property.	
Select an item from a collection	Put the name in quotation marks or the number of the item in parentheses after the collection.	
Show the list of global methods and properties	In a module, press Ctrl-Spacebar.	
Make Auto Lists appear after a variable that contains an object reference	Declare the variable as an object using Dim. For example, type **Dim myObject As Worksheet.**	
Display the Object Browser	Click the Object Browser button.	

For online information about	Ask the Assistant for help using the words
Using objects	"Understanding Objects"
Using the Immediate window	"Immediate Window"
Using the Object Browser	"Object Browser"
Using dockable windows	"Docking"

Preview of the Next Chapter

One of the most important objects in Excel is the Range object. Because Range objects are so important, there are many different ways of working with them. The next chapter helps you see how to put Range objects to work for you.

Chapter 4

Explore Range Objects

Estimated time: 30 minutes

In this chapter, you'll learn how to:

- Simplify macros that record selections.

- Manipulate Range objects from Microsoft Visual Basic statements.

- Put formulas into cells.

- Create references dynamically as the macro runs.

The world would be much simpler if everybody were the same size. Cars wouldn't need adjustable seats; heads would never get bumped on door frames; feet would never dangle from a chair. Of course, some new complexities would probably arise. When exchanging that ghastly outfit you received for your birthday, you wouldn't be able to claim it was the wrong size.

In Microsoft Excel 2000, if your worksheets and data files are all the same size, you don't need to worry about Range objects. If you never insert new lines into a budget, if you always put yearly totals in column M, if every month's transaction file has 5 columns and 120 rows, the macro recorder can take care of dealing with ranges for you.

In the real world of humans, however, people are different sizes, and clothes and cars have to adjust to fit them. And in the real world of worksheets, models and data files are also different sizes, and you want your macros to fit them. Excel provides many properties for working with Range objects. In this chapter, you'll explore Range objects, and you'll find out several exciting ways of working with them.

Start the lesson

1. Start Excel, switch to the folder containing the practice files for this book, and open the Ranges workbook.

2. Save a copy of the workbook as **Chapter4.**

See the Intro-duction to this book for more information on how to install the practice files.

Enhancing Recorded Selections

When you carry out actions in Excel, you first select something—say, a cell—and then you do something to it—say, enter a value. The macro recorder always dutifully records both the "select" and the "do" of all your actions. Even though you can't see it, when a recorded macro runs, Excel merrily changes the selections exactly the way you did as you recorded the macro. When the macro finishes, you can see that the selection has changed. You can make a macro do less work—and make it easier to read—by eliminating unnecessary selection changes. A powerful technique for eliminating unnecessary changes to the selection begins with watching for a statement ending in *Select* followed by one or more statements beginning with *Selection* or *ActiveCell*. What you do next depends on whether a single *Selection* (or *ActiveCell*) statement follows the *Select* statement, or whether a group of them follow.

Simplify Select...Selection *pairs*

When a single *Selection* statement follows a *Select* statement, you can collapse the two statements into one. Let's record and simplify a macro that puts the names of the months across the top of a worksheet.

1. Insert a blank worksheet, and start recording a macro named **LabelMonths**.

	A	B	C	D	E
1		January	February	March	
2					
3					

Your macro might be slightly different, depending on how you entered the values into the cells.

2. Type the labels **January**, **February**, and **March** in the cells B1, C1, and D1. Turn off the recorder, and then edit the macro. The macro should look similar to this:

```
Sub LabelMonths()
    Range("B1").Select
    ActiveCell.FormulaR1C1 = "January"
    Range("C1").Select
    ActiveCell.FormulaR1C1 = "February"
    Range("D1").Select
    ActiveCell.FormulaR1C1 = "March"
    Range("D2").Select
End Sub
```

Each time you see the word *Select* at the end of one statement followed by either the word *Selection* or *ActiveCell* at the beginning of the next statement, you can delete both words, leaving only a single period. If a *Select* statement is the last one in a macro, you can delete it entirely.

3. Delete the unnecessary selections from the LabelMonths macro, as described in the preceding paragraph. The final macro should look like this:

```
Sub LabelMonths()
    Range("B1").FormulaR1C1 = "January"
    Range("C1").FormulaR1C1 = "February"
    Range("D1").FormulaR1C1 = "March"
End Sub
```

4. Insert a new blank worksheet, and test the macro. The labels appear in the cells, but the original selection doesn't change.

5. Save the Chapter4 workbook.

Why should you get rid of *Select...Selection* pairs? One reason is that doing so makes the macro run faster. Another reason is that running a macro can seem less disruptive if it doesn't end with different cells selected than when it started. But the most important reason is unquestionably that *Select...Selection* pairs in a macro are a sure sign of a neophyte macro writer.

Simplify Select groups

When you eliminate a selection change using the preceding approach, be sure that only a single statement uses the selection. If you have a single *Select* statement followed by two or more statements that use the selection, you can still avoid changing the selection, but you must do it in a different way.

1. In Excel, select a sheet with labels in the first row and start recording a macro named **MakeBoldItalic**.

2. Click cell B1, click the Bold button, click the Italic button, and then click the Stop Recording button.

Stop Recording button

	A	B	C	D	E
1		January	February	March	
2					
3					

3. Edit the macro. It will look like this:

```
Sub MakeBoldItalic()
    Range("B1").Select
    Selection.Font.Bold = True
    Selection.Font.Italic = True
End Sub
```

Obviously, if you delete the first *Select...Selection* pair, you won't be able to predict which cells will become italicized.

4. Edit the macro to assign the range to a variable named *myRange*. Then replace the Selection object with the myRange object. The finished macro should look like this:

```
Sub MakeBoldItalic()
    Dim myRange as Range
    Set myRange = Range("B1")
    myRange.Font.Bold = True
    myRange.Font.Italic = True
End Sub
```

5. Change *"B1"* to **"C1"** in the macro, and then press F8 repeatedly to step through the macro. Watch how the format of the cell changes without changing which cell is originally selected.

6. Save the Chapter4 workbook.

Eliminating the selection when there's a group might not seem like much of a simplification. With only two statements, it probably isn't. When you have several statements that use the same selection, however, converting the selection to an object variable can make the macro much easier to read.

Note   You could also replace the *Select* group with a *With* structure, like this:

```
With Range("B1")
    .Font.Bold = True
    .Font.Italic = True
End With
```

Here's what the *With* structure does secretly in the background: it creates a hidden variable, takes the object from the *With* statement and assigns that object to the hidden variable, and then puts the hidden variable in front of each "dangling" period. The *End With* statement discards the hidden variable.

Exploring Ranges

Range objects are probably the most important object class in Excel. You put values into ranges. You put formulas into ranges. You format ranges into reports. You base charts on the numbers in ranges. You put drawing objects on top of ranges. You manipulate PivotTables in ranges. You therefore need to move beyond the kind of references to ranges that the macro recorder can create.

Explore the Range *property*

Probably the most important property that returns a Range object is the *Range* property. You can use the *Range* property in either of two ways. You can use it with two arguments that give the two end points of a range, or you can use it with a single argument that gives anything that Excel can interpret as a range address.

The WatchRange macro demonstrates several uses of the *Range* property. Here's the macro in its entirety. We'll look at each statement in turn as you step through the macro.

```
Sub WatchRange()
    Range("A1", "D2").Select
    Range(ActiveCell, "B6").Select
    Range("B3:C8").Select
    Range("B2:E4").Name = "TestRange"
    Range("TestRange").Select
    Range("B2").Select
    ActiveCell.Range("B2").Select
    Range("TestRange").Range("A1").Select
End Sub
```

1. Edit the WatchRange macro, and press F8 three times to execute the *Range("A1","D2").Select* statement.

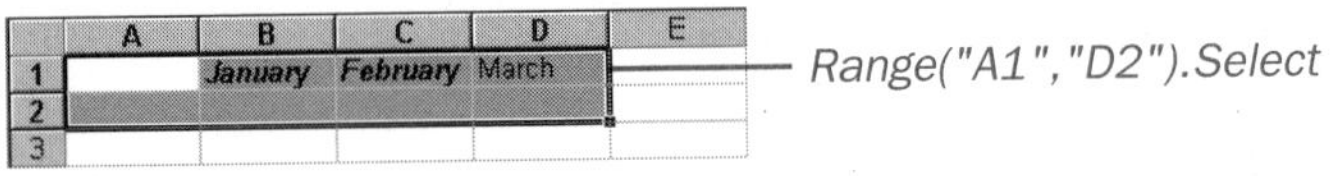

Range("A1","D2").Select

Excel selects the range A1:D2. With this form of the *Range* property, you use two arguments. Each argument can be a cell address, in A1 notation, in quotation marks. The Range object that the property returns is the rectangle formed by the two end points.

2. Press F8 to execute the *Range(ActiveCell, "B6").Select* statement.

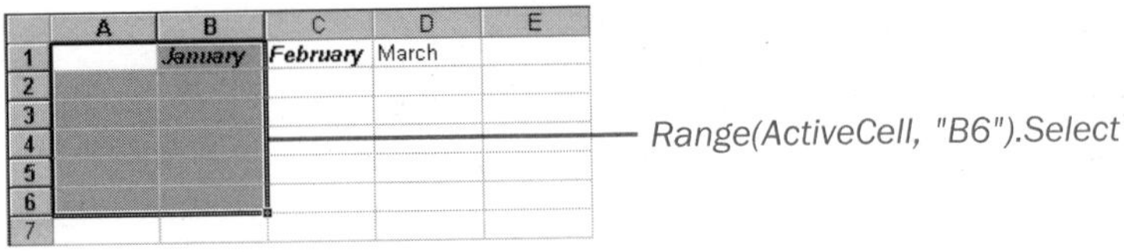

Range(ActiveCell, "B6").Select

Excel selects the range A1:B6. Each of the two arguments you give the *Range* property can be either a simple cell address or a Range object. If you assign a Range object to a variable, you can use that variable as an argument to the *Range* property.

3. Press F8 to execute the *Range("B3:C8").Select* statement.

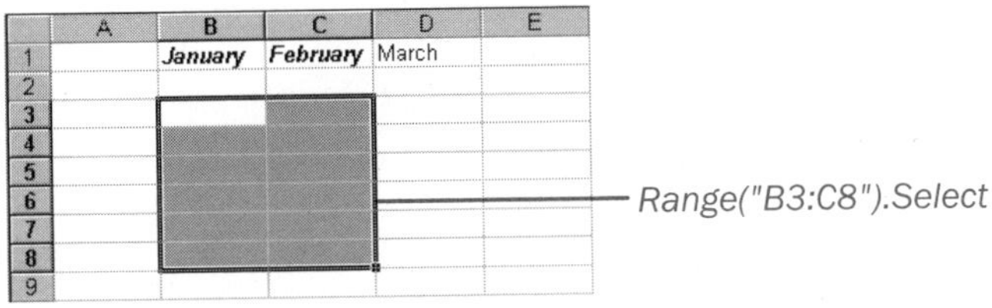

Range("B3:C8").Select

Excel selects the range B3:C8. You can also use the *Range* property with a single argument. When you use a single argument, you can put anything inside the quotation marks that Excel can interpret as a cell reference.

4. Press F8 to execute the *Range("B2:E4").Name = "TestRange"* statement. This assigns a name to the specified range.

5. Press F8 to execute the *Range("TestRange").Select* statement.

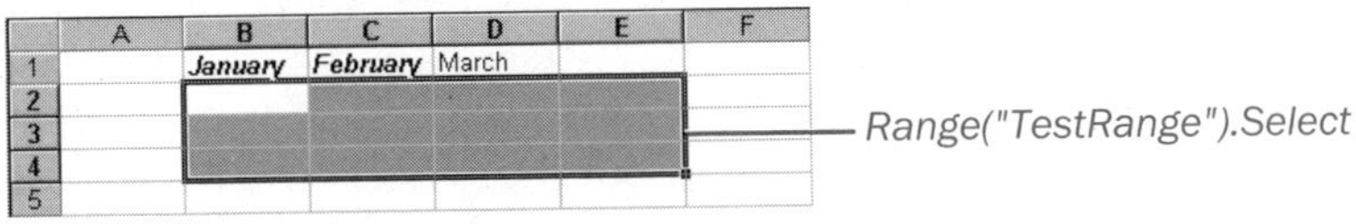

Range("TestRange").Select

Excel selects the range B2:E4. You should see the word *TestRange*, the name of the selected range, in the Reference area to the left of the formula bar. You can use a defined Excel range name as the argument to the *Range* property.

6. Press F8 to execute the *Range("B2").Select* statement.

As you might have guessed, Excel selects cell B2. The *Range* property in this example is the global *Range* property. The reference B2 means "second row, second column." In this case, Excel uses cell A1 of the worksheet as the starting point.

7. Press F8 to execute the *ActiveCell.Range("B2").Select* statement.

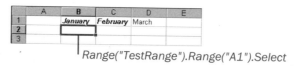

As you might *not* have guessed, Excel selects cell C3. Excel uses cell B2, the Range object returned by the *ActiveCell* property, as the starting point because the *Range* property in this example belongs to the Range object. The address B2 still means "second row, second column."

8. Press F8 to execute the *Range("TestRange").Range("A1").Select* statement.

Range("TestRange").Range("A1").Select

Excel selects cell B2, because that's the top left cell of TestRange (B2:E4).

9. Press F8 to finish the macro.

The *Range* property is a flexible way of establishing a link to an arbitrary Range object. You can use either a single text string that contains any valid reference as an argument to the *Range* property or two arguments that define a rectangular range. If you use the global *Range* property, or if you use the *Range* property with the Application object or with a Worksheet object, the addresses are relative to the top left cell of the worksheet. If you use the *Range* property with a Range object, the addresses are relative to the top left cell of that range.

Explore a range as a collection

A workbook can contain multiple worksheets, so in the Excel Object Library, Worksheets is defined as an object class. A Worksheets object has a separate list of methods and properties from a Worksheet object.

Similarly, a range can contain multiple cells. You might expect that Excel would have a Cells collection object. But a collection of cells is a little more complicated than a collection of worksheets, because cells come in two dimensions—rows as well as columns. You can think of the range A1:B3 as a collection of six cells, but you can also think of it as a collection of three rows, or as a collection of two columns.

Excel therefore has three properties that look at a range as a collection: the *Cells* property returns a collection of cells, the *Rows* property returns a collection of rows, and the *Columns* property returns a collection of columns. These are not separate classes, however. The result of any of these properties is still a Range object, and it can use any of the methods or properties of any other Range object.

The WatchCollections macro demonstrates how to use a range as a collection. Here's the macro in its entirety:

```
Sub WatchCollection()
    Dim myRange As Range
    Set myRange = Range("B2:E4")
    myRange.Interior.Color = vbYellow
    myRange.Cells(1, 4).Select
    myRange.Cells(6).Select
    myRange.Cells(myRange.Cells.Count).Select
    Cells(Cells.Count).Select
    myRange.Rows(2).Select
    myRange.Columns(myRange.Columns.Count).Select
    Columns(2).Select
End Sub
```

1. Click in the WatchCollections macro, and press F8 four times to assign the range B2:E4 to the variable *myRange* and to color the range to make it easier to see.

2. Press F8 to execute the *myRange.Cells(1,4).Select* statement.

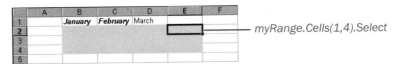

— myRange.Cells(1,4).Select

Excel selects cell E2, the fourth cell in the first row of the range. The *Cells* property treats the range as a collection of cells. You typically use two numbers with the *Cells* property, the first for the row and the second for the column.

3. Press F8 to execute the *myRange.Cells(6).Select* statement.

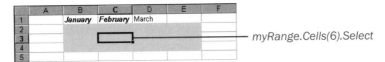

— myRange.Cells(6).Select

Excel selects cell C3, the sixth item in the collection. You can also use a single argument with the *Cells* property. If you do, the number specifies a cell in the first row. If the number is greater than the number of columns in the range, it wraps to the next row. Since *myRange* contains only four columns, the sixth item is really the second cell in the second row.

4. Press F8 to execute the *myRange.Cells(myRange.Cells.Count).Select* statement.

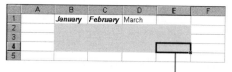

myRange.Cells(myRange.Cells.Count).Select

This one is a little bit tricky, but very useful. This statement uses the *Cells* property twice: first to find out the number of cells in the range and a second time to select the last cell. Since there are twelve cells in the range, the twelfth item in the collection is the fourth cell on the third row.

Tip Hold the mouse pointer over the expression *myRange.Cells.Count*; Visual Basic displays a box showing the value.

---

5. Press F8 to execute the *Cells(Cells.Count).Select* statement.

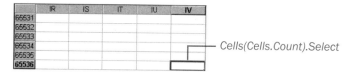

Cells(Cells.Count).Select

Excel selects the very last cell in the worksheet. If you use the *Cells* property without a Range object in front of it (that is, if you use the global *Cells* property), it returns the collection of all the cells on the active worksheet. This statement selects the 16,777,216th cell on the worksheet.

Note *Range* is both the name of the property that returns a Range object and the name of the Range object class itself. In the Object Browser, you'll find the word *Range* as a class name (on the left) and also as a property (on the right) under the <globals>, Application, Worksheet, and Range classes.

The word *Cells*, however, is only the name of a property. The *Cells* property returns a Range object. In the Object Browser, you won't find the word *Cells* in the list of object names, but you will find it as a property under the <globals>, Application, Worksheet, and Range classes.

---

6. Press F8 to execute the *myRange.Rows(2).Select* statement.

myRange.Rows(2).Select

Excel selects the range B3:E3, which is the second row of *myRange*. The *Rows* property of a range treats the range as a collection of rows. You can refer to any item you want from the collection.

The expression *myRange.Rows* refers to exactly the same range as *myRange.Cells*, which is also the same range as the variable *myRange*. Using *Rows* or *Cells* makes a difference only when you select a single item from the collection or when you look at the *Count* property of the collection.

7. Press F8 to execute the *myRange.Columns(myRange.Columns.Count).Select* statement.

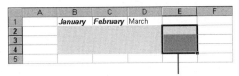

myRange.Columns(myRange.Columns.Count).Select

Excel selects the range E2:E4, which happens to be the last column of the range.

8. Press F8 to execute the *Columns(2).Select* statement.

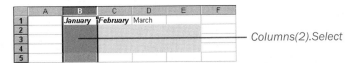

Columns(2).Select

The global *Columns* property uses the entire worksheet as a range.

Tip   Because columns have letter labels that can act as names, you can specify an item from the Columns collection using either a number—for example, *Columns(3)*—or a name in quotation marks—for example, *Columns("D")*.

---

9. Press F8 to end the macro.

A Range object is extremely important in Excel. Excel has properties that allow you to look at a range as a collection of cells, as a collection of rows, or as a collection of columns. In any case, you can use standard Range object methods and properties on the resulting object.

Explore calculated ranges

Excel has other properties that can calculate a new range based on an existing range. The *Offset* property references a range shifted down, up, left, or right from a starting range. The *Resize* property adjusts the number of rows or columns in a range. The *EntireColumn* and *EntireRow* properties extend a range to the edges of the worksheet. In this section, you'll see each of these properties in action.

The WatchCalculated macro demonstrates how to manipulate a range. Here's the macro in its entirety:

```
Sub WatchCalculated()
    Dim myRange As Range
    Sheets("Prices").Select
    Set myRange = Range("C4:E5")
    myRange.Interior.Color = vbYellow
    myRange.Offset(1, 0).Select
    myRange.Offset(0, myRange.Columns.Count).Select
    myRange.Resize(, 4).Select
    myRange.Offset(-1, -1).Resize(myRange.Rows.Count + 2, _
        myRange.Columns.Count + 2).Select
    myRange.Cells(1).EntireRow.Select
    myRange.EntireColumn.Select
    myRange.CurrentRegion.Select
End Sub
```

1. Select the WatchCalculated macro from the Procedures drop-down list, and then press F8 five times to select the Prices worksheet, assign a range to a variable, and color the range.

	A	B	C	D	E	F
1		Retail	Wholesale	Margin		
2	High	5.50	2.75	2.75		
3	Mid	4.50	2.25	2.25		
4	Low	3.50	1.75	1.75		
5						
6						

myRange.Interior.Color=vbYellow

2. Press F8 to execute the *myRange.Offset(1,0).Select* statement. Excel selects the range C5:E6, one cell down from the yellow range.

	A	B	C	D	E	F
1		Retail	Wholesale	Margin		
2	High	5.50	2.75	2.75		
3	Mid	4.50	2.25	2.25		
4	Low	3.50	1.75	1.75		
5						
6						
7						

— *myRange.Offset(1,0).Select*

The *Offset* property takes two arguments. The first is the number of rows down to shift the reference. The second is the number of columns to the right to shift it. I always think of myself as standing on the top left cell of the starting range. For the first argument, I face the bottom of the worksheet and determine the number of steps forward (or backward, if the offset is negative) that I want to take. For the second argument, I face the right side of the worksheet and do the same. Zero steps means no movement. The new range is the same size as the original range.

3. Press F8 to execute the *myRange.Offset(0,myRange.Columns.Count).Select* statement.

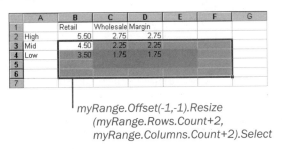

myRange.Offset(0,myRange.Columns.Count).Select

Excel selects the range F4:H5, the same size as *myRange* and adjacent to *myRange*. Imagine yourself standing in the top left cell of *myRange*. There are three columns in *myRange*, so take three steps forward. That's the starting cell for the new reference.

4. Press F8 to execute the *myRange.Resize(,4).Select* statement.

myRange.Resize(,4).Select

Excel selects the range C4:F5, one column wider than *myRange*. The *Resize* property returns a range that has been, well, resized. The first argument is the number of rows in the new reference. The second argument is the number of columns. To leave the rows or columns the same as the original range, omit the corresponding argument altogether (but leave a comma if you omit the first argument).

5. Press F8 to execute the *myRange.Offset(-1,-1).Resize(myRange.Rows.Count+2, myRange.Columns.Count+2).Select* statement.

*myRange.Offset(-1,-1).Resize
(myRange.Rows.Count+2,
myRange.Columns.Count+2).Select*

Excel selects a rectangle one cell larger in all directions than the original range. The *Offset* property shifts the starting point up one cell and left one cell. The *Resize* property makes the new range two cells taller and two cells wider than it originally was. Pretty cool, huh?

Note The combined functionality of the *Offset* and *Resize* properties is equivalent to that of the OFFSET function available on worksheets.

6. Press F8 to execute the *myRange.Cells(1).EntireRow.Select* statement.

	A	B	C	D	E	F
1		Retail	Wholesale	Margin		
2	High	5.50	2.75	2.75		
3	Mid	4.50	2.25	2.25		
4	Low	3.50	1.75	1.75		
5						
6						

myRange.Cells(1).EntireRow.Select

Excel selects all of row 4. The variable *myRange* returns a reference to the range C4:E5. The *Cells* property returns the first (that is, top left) cell of that range: C4. The *EntireRow* property extends that reference to all of row 4. Each property in the chain returns a reference to another object until you get to the final *Select* method, which does the real work.

7. Press F8 to execute the *myRange.EntireColumn.Select* statement.

	A	B	C	D	E	F
1		Retail	Wholesale	Margin		
2	High	5.50	2.75	2.75		
3	Mid	4.50	2.25	2.25		
4	Low	3.50	1.75	1.75		
5						
6						

myRange.EntireColumn.Select

Excel selects all of columns C:E. You can select the *EntireRow* or *EntireColumn* of more than a single cell. Excel simply extends whatever range you give it to the limits of the worksheet.

8. Press F8 to execute the *myRange.CurrentRegion.Select* statement.

	A	B	C	D	E	F
1		Retail	Wholesale	Margin		
2	High	5.50	2.75	2.75		
3	Mid	4.50	2.25	2.25		
4	Low	3.50	1.75	1.75		
5						
6						

myRange.CurrentRegion.Select

Excel selects the range A1:D4. The *CurrentRegion* property extends the selection to form a rectangle bounded by either blank cells or the edge of the worksheet. It always includes the top left cell of the starting range but might not include the other cells.

9. Press F8 to finish executing the WatchCalculated macro.

The *Offset* and *Resize* properties, along with the *EntireRow*, *EntireColumn*, and *CurrentRegion* properties, provide you with flexible tools for calculating new Range objects based on an original starting range.

Exploring Formulas

Selecting ranges helps you understand how to manipulate Range objects, but to get real work done, you must format cells, put values and formulas into cells, retrieve values from cells, retrieve formulas from cells, and retrieve formatted values from cells. First you should understand how references work in formulas in Excel, and then you can see how to create formulas in a macro.

Relative References

Most formulas perform arithmetic operations on values retrieved from other cells. Excel formulas use cell references to retrieve values from cells. Take, for example, the list of prices on the Prices worksheet, but without the margin formulas.

	A	B	C	D
1		Retail	Wholesale	
2	High	5.50	2.75	
3	Mid	4.50	2.25	
4	Low	3.50	1.75	
5				

Suppose you want to add a column to the list that calculates the *gross margin*—the difference between the price and the cost—for each item. You would put the label **Margin** in cell D1 and then enter the first formula into cell D2. The formula subtracts the first wholesale cost (cell C2) from the first retail price (cell B2). So you would enter **=B2-C2** into cell D2. (The formula has already been entered for you in the practice file.)

	A	B	C	D	E
1		Retail	Wholesale	Margin	
2	High	5.50	2.75	2.75	
3	Mid	4.50	2.25		
4	Low	3.50	1.75		
5					

— **=B2-C2**

You make $2.75 on the margin. Now you need to copy the formula to the other rows. The formula you typed into cell D2 refers explicitly to cells C2 and B2. When you copy the formula to cell D3, you want the formula to automatically adjust to refer to C3 and B3. Fortunately, when you copy the formulas, Excel automatically adjusts the references because, by default, references are relative to the cell that contains the formula.

	A	B	C	D	E
1		Retail	Wholesale	Margin	
2	High	5.50	2.75	2.75	
3	Mid	4.50	2.25	2.25	
4	Low	3.50	1.75	1.75	
5					
6					

— =B2-C2
— =B3-C3
— =B4-C4

If the reference =C2 is found in cell D2, it really means "one cell to my left." When you copy the formula to cell D3, it still means "one cell to my left," but now that meaning is represented by the reference =C3.

Absolute References

Sometimes you don't want relative references. Look, for example, at the prices and quantities on the Revenue worksheet. Now you'll add formulas yourself.

	A	B	C	D	E	F	G
1		Price				Discount	
2	Quantity	$5	$10	$15		10%	
3	10						
4	20						
5	30						
6	40						
7	50						
8							

You want to add formulas to calculate the revenue for each combination. To calculate the first revenue value (cell B3), you need to multiply the first price (cell B2) by the first quantity (cell A3). When you type **=B2*A3** into cell B3, you get the correct answer, $50.

	A	B	C	D	E	F	G
1		Price				Discount	
2	Quantity	$5	$10	$15		10%	
3	10	$50						→ =B2*A3
4	20						
5	30						
6	40						
7	50						
8							

But if you copy that formula to cell B4, you get the ridiculous answer of $1000. That's because the cell references are relative. You're not really referring to cells B2 and A3; you're referring to "one cell above me" and "one cell to my left." When you put the formula into cell B4, "one cell above me" now refers to cell B3, not cell B2.

You want the prices to adjust from column to column, and you want the quantities to adjust from row to row, but you always want the price to be from row 2 and the quantity to be from column A. The solution is to put a dollar sign ($) in front of the *2* in the first price reference (C$2) and in front of the *A* in the first quantity reference ($A3). The formula that should go into cell B3 is **=B$2*$A3**. The dollar sign "anchors" that part of the formula, making it absolute. When you copy the formula to the rest of B3:D7, you get correct answers.

	A	B	C	D	E	F	G
1		Price				Discount		→ =B$2*$A3
2	Quantity	$5	$10	$15		10%	
3	10	$50	$100	$150			
4	20	$100	$200	$300			
5	30	$150	$300	$450			
6	40	$200	$400	$600			
7	50	$250	$500	$750				→ =B$2*$A3
8							

The relative portion of the formula changes with the row or column of the cell that contains the formula. The absolute portion remains fixed.

If you want to modify the formula so that it also takes into account the discount value from cell F2, you must make both the row and the column of the discount reference absolute. The correct formula would be **=B$2*$A3*(1-$F$2)**.

R1C1 Notation

The reference =B3, when found in cell D3, doesn't really say what it means. What it says is "cell B3," but what it means is "two cells to my left." You don't know what the reference really means until you know which cell contains the reference.

Excel has an alternative notation for references that really does say what it means. It's called R1C1 notation. To turn on R1C1 notation, choose the Tools menu, click Options, and then click the General tab. Select the R1C1 Reference Style check box, and click OK. (To turn off R1C1 notation, clear the check box.)

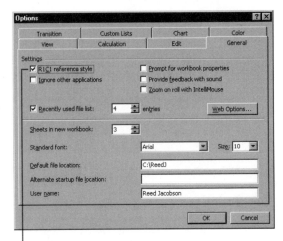

Use this option to switch between R1C1 and A1 notation.

In R1C1 notation, you specify an absolute row with the letter *R* plus the row number, and you specify an absolute column with *C* plus the column number. The reference =R1C1 refers to what is usually known as cell A1. The notation that Excel displays by default is called A1 notation.

To specify a relative reference on the same row or column as the cell with the formula, you simply use an *R* or a *C*. For example, the reference =RC3 means "the cell in column 3 of the same row as me," and the reference =R2C means "the cell in row 2 of the same column as me."

To specify a relative reference in a different row or column, you specify the amount of the difference, in square brackets, after the *R* or the *C*. For example, the reference =R[-1]C means "one cell above me," and the reference =R5C[2] means "two columns to my right in row 5."

The formula to calculate the gross margin on the Prices worksheet was =B2-C2 (but only while entered into cell D2). In R1C1 notation, the same formula is =RC[-2]-RC[-1]. The formula to calculate the discounted price on the Revenue worksheet was =B$2*$A3*(1-$F$2). In R1C1 notation, the same formula is R2C*RC1*(1-R2C6).

Note When you use A1 notation, the formula changes depending on which range you copy the formula into. When you use R1C1 notation, the formula is the same, regardless of which cell it goes into.

Put values and formulas into a range

References aren't much use until you do something with them. Typically in a spreadsheet, you put values or formulas into cells. The WatchFormulas macro demonstrates several aspects of putting values and formulas into a range. As you step through the macro and watch it work, you can learn how to use Excel formulas. Here's the macro in its entirety:

```
Sub WatchFormulas()
    Worksheets.Add
    Range("B2:B6").Select
    Selection.Formula = 100
    ActiveCell.Formula = 0
    ActiveCell.Offset(-1, 0).Formula = 1
    Selection.Formula = "=B1*5"
    MsgBox ActiveCell.Value
    MsgBox ActiveCell.Formula
    MsgBox ActiveCell.FormulaR1C1
End Sub
```

1. With the R1C1 Notation off, select the WatchFormulas macro from the Procedures drop-down list, and then press F8 three times to execute the *Worksheets.Add* statement, which creates a fresh worksheet.

2. Press F8 to execute the *Range("B2:B6").Select* statement. This selects a sample starting range of cells.

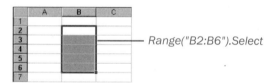
Range("B2:B6").Select

3. Press F8 to execute the *Selection.Formula = 100* statement.

Selection.Formula = 100

The number *100* fills all the cells of the selection. *Formula* is a property of the range. When you set the *Formula* property for the selection, you change the formula for all the cells in the selection.

The number 100 isn't actually a formula; it's a constant. In fact, you could just as well have used *Selection.Value = 100* to assign the constant to the cell. But the *Formula* property is equivalent to whatever you see in the formula bar when the cell is selected. The formula bar can contain constants as well as formulas, and so can the *Formula* property. When you assign a value to a cell, the Formula property and the *Value* property have the same effect.

4. Press F8 to execute the *ActiveCell.Formula = 0* statement.

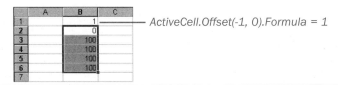

Only cell B2 changes to zero, because you changed the formula of only the active cell.

5. Suppose you want to enter a value in the first cell above the active cell, and you don't want to assume that the active cell is cell B2. Press F8 to execute the *ActiveCell.Offset(-1, 0).Formula = 1* statement.

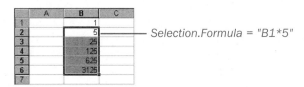

The cell B1 changes to 1. This statement starts with the active cell, uses the *Offset* property to calculate a new cell one up from that starting cell, and then sets the *Formula* property for the resulting cell.

6. Press F8 to execute the *Selection.Formula = "=B1*5"* statement.

This formula is similar to the one you created with the macro recorder in Chapter 2, except that it uses the Formula property instead of the FormulaR1C1 property

Now each of the selected cells contains a real formula, not a constant. When you entered the formula, the active cell was B2. From the point of view of cell B2, the reference B1 means "one cell above." As Excel enters the formula into all the cells of the range, it adjusts the reference as needed to always mean "one cell above."

You could have used the statement *Selection.Value = "=B1*5"* to assign a formula to the range. When you assign a value or a formula to the cell, the *Value* and *Formula* properties have the same effect.

7. Press F8 to execute the *MsgBox ActiveCell.Value* statement.

An alert box displaying the value 5 appears. The *Value* property retrieves the result of any formula in a cell. When you retrieve the contents of the cell, the *Value* property gives you the result of any formula in the cell.

8. Click OK, and then press F8 to execute the *MsgBox ActiveCell.Formula* statement.

 — ActiveCell.Formula

An alert box displaying the formula =B1*5 appears. The *Formula* property retrieves the actual formula in a cell. If the cell contains a constant, the *Formula* property retrieves it as text, even if it's a number. The *Formula* property always retrieves the formula using A1 notation references.

9. Click OK, and press F8 to execute the *MsgBox ActiveCell.FormulaR1C1* statement.

 — ActiveCell.FormulaR1C1

An alert box displaying the formula =R[-1]C*5 appears. This is the same formula as =B1*5, except that it's displayed using R1C1 notation.

10. Click OK, and then press F8 to complete the macro.

All cells have *Formula*, *FormulaR1C1*, and *Value* properties. The *Value* property and the *Formula* property are the same when you're writing to the cell. When you read the value of a cell, the *Value* property gives you the value, and the *Formula* property gives you the formula using A1 notation references. The *FormulaR1C1* property is the same as the *Formula* property, except that it uses all references in R1C1 notation, whether assigning a formula to the cell or reading the formula from a cell.

Tip The *Value* property always gives you the unformatted value of the number in a cell. A cell also has a *Text* property, which returns the formatted value of the cell. The *Text* property is read-only because it's a combination of the *Value* property and the *NumberFormat* property.

Use the address of a range to build formulas

Sometimes you need a macro to create formulas that contain references. For example, suppose you have a range of cells like the one on the Totals worksheet and you want to put a row of totals across the bottom. If the size of the range can change, you don't know until the macro runs which cells should be included in the SUM formula.

	A	B	C	D	E
1					
2		1000	100	10	
3		1500	150	15	
4		2000	200	20	
5					

Add total formulas here.

Sometimes the range of cells might extend from B2:D4, in which case the formula in cell B5 should be =SUM(B2:B4). Another time, the range of cells might extend from B2:D10, in which case the formula should be =SUM(B2:B10), this time in cell B11. Interactively, you would use the AutoSum button to create the formulas, but if you ever try clicking the AutoSum button while you're recording a macro, you'll see that the macro the AutoSum button creates isn't usually very useful. (That was a carefully restrained understatement.)

What you need to do is create a macro that behaves like a simplified version of the AutoSum button. The MakeTotals macro shows you how to do that. Some of the statements in the macro aren't necessary but are there to help you understand how the macro works. We'll step through the macro, looking at each statement. Here's the macro in its entirety.

```
Sub MakeTotals()
    Dim myRange as Range
    Dim myTotal as Range
    Set myRange = ActiveCell.CurrentRegion
    Set myTotal = myRange.Offset(myRange.Rows.Count).Rows(1)
    myTotal.Cells(1) = myRange.Columns(1).Address
    myTotal.Cells(1) = myRange.Columns(1).Address(False,False)
    myTotal.Formula = _
        "=SUM(" & myRange.Columns(1).Address(False,False) & ")"
End Sub
```

1. In Excel, select the Totals worksheet, and select cell B2.

2. In Visual Basic, select the MakeTotals macro from the Procedures drop-down list, and press F8 three times to execute the *Set myRange = ActiveCell.CurrentRegion* statement. This assigns the block of cells surrounding the active cell to the *myRange* variable.

3. Press F8 to execute the *Set myTotal = myRange.Offset(myRange.Rows.Count).Rows(1)* statement. This creates a new reference shifted down by however many rows are in the original range, but only one row tall, and then assigns that reference to the *myTotal* variable. (You could use Resize(1) instead of Rows(1) and get the same effect.) This is the range where the totals will go.

4. Press F8 to execute the *myTotal.Cells(1) = myRange.Columns(1).Address* statement.

	A	B	C	D	E
1					
2		1000	100	10	
3		1500	150	15	
4		2000	200	20	
5		$B$2:$B$4			
6					

myRange.Columns(1).Address

This statement is in the macro only to help you understand how the formula is constructed. It doesn't need to be in the final macro. It retrieves the address of the first column of the original rectangle and puts that address into the first cell of the totals row. If you put this address inside a SUM function, the total would be correct for the first cell, but the dollar signs mean that the reference is absolute. You need to make the reference relative so that it will adjust as you put it into all the columns of the totals row.

5. Press F8 to execute the *myTotal.Cells(1) = myRange.Columns(1).Address(False,False)* statement.

	A	B	C	D	E
1					
2		1000	100	10	
3		1500	150	15	
4		2000	200	20	
5		B2:B4			
6					

myRange.Columns(1).Address(False,False)

This is another statement that doesn't need to be in the final macro. The *Address* property has optional arguments that control the way the address is returned. The first two arguments determine whether the row and column parts of the reference are absolute. The default is that both parts are absolute; this statement tells the *Address* property to make both parts relative. You can now put this reference into the SUM function and fill it across the totals row.

6. Press F8 to execute the *myTotal.Formula = "=SUM(" & myRange.Columns(1).Address(False,False) & ")"* statement.

	A	B	C	D	E
1					
2		1000	100	10	
3		1500	150	15	
4		2000	200	20	
5		4500	450	45	
6					

*"=SUM("&myRange.Columns(1).
Address(False,False)&")"*

=SUM(B2:B4)

This statement constructs the final formula by joining the first part of the SUM function with the relative reference returned by the *Address* property, and then adds the closing parenthesis. An ampersand character (&) joins two pieces of text together. If the current region containing the active cell were B2:E5, the resulting formula would be =SUM(B2:B5). The totals appear in the row at the bottom, appropriately different for each column.

7. Press F8 to finish the macro, and then press F5 to run it again, adding a second row of totals. This is a little silly, but it shows how the macro automatically adjusts as new rows are added to the data. The *CurrentRegion* property includes any new rows. The *Address* property calculates the appropriate reference for the SUM function.

8. Save the Chapter4 workbook if you've made any changes to the macros or added any notes.

Ranges are a powerful tool in Excel. You can select ranges, assign them to variables, add formulas to them, name them, and retrieve their addresses. By manipulating ranges, you can build powerful, dynamic worksheet models.

Chapter Summary

To	Do this
Simplify a *Select...Selection* pair in a recorded macro	Delete from *Select* through *Selection*, leaving only a single period.
Select the range B2:C5 on the active worksheet	Use the statement *Range("B2:C5").Select*.
Select the fifth cell in the third row of the active worksheet	Use the statement *Cells(3,5).Select*.
Count the columns in the current selection	Use the expression *Selection.Columns.Count*.
Select a new range one row down from the selection	Use the statement *Selection.Offset(1,0).Select*.
Fill the cells in the selection with the value 100	Use the statement *Selection.Formula = 100*.
Enter into the active cell a formula that calculates the value of the cell above	Use the statement *ActiveCell.FormulaR1C1="=R[-1]C"*.
Retrieve a value from the active cell	Use the expression *ActiveCell.Value*.
Retrieve a formula from the active cell	Use the expression *ActiveCell.Formula* or the expression *ActiveCell.FormulaR1C1*.
Retrieve the address of a range	Use the *Address* property, with arguments to control whether the address is relative or absolute.

For online information about	Ask the Assistant for help using the words
Referencing ranges	"References," then select "How to reference cells and ranges." (A highly recommended list of topics.)
The *Selection* property	"Selection"
The *Range* property	"Range Property"
The *Address* property	"Address"

Preview of the Next Chapter

Excel is well known for its exceptional graphic output. In the next chapter you'll explore graphic objects. Graphic objects include not only circles and rectangles on the worksheet, but also text boxes and charts. Graphics can give your applications tremendous impact, and you can write macros that can simplify your work with them.

Chapter 5

Explore Graphical Objects

In this chapter, you'll learn how to:

- Manipulate drawing objects on a worksheet.
- Manipulate chart objects.
- Use the macro recorder as a reference tool.

On a warm summer day, nothing beats lying on your back in a grassy field, watching clouds float across the sky. Trees and mountains and buildings—they just sit there, attached firmly to the ground. But clouds move. Clouds change shape. They change color. Clouds can come in layers, too, with closer clouds drifting in front of the clouds in back.

On a worksheet, ranges with their formulas and formats are attached firmly to the worksheet, just as buildings are attached firmly to the ground. Cell A1 will always be in the top left corner of the worksheet. Drawing objects, however, are like clouds. They float freely above the worksheet. They can disappear and reappear. They can change color and shape.

Drawing objects—including not only shapes such as rectangles, ovals, and lines, but also charts, and even list box controls and spinner controls—add interest, information, and functionality to a worksheet. In this chapter, you'll learn how to use Microsoft Visual Basic for Applications macros to control drawing objects.

Start the lesson

1. Start Microsoft Excel, and change to the folder containing the practice files for this book.

2. Open the Graphics workbook, and save it as **Chapter5**.

For more information about installing the practice files, see the Introduction to this book.

Exploring Graphical Objects

Some people think of the macro recorder as a tool for beginners—and it is. In Part 1 of this book, you used the macro recorder to build finished macros without having to understand much about how Excel objects really work. But the macro recorder is also a powerful reference tool for advanced developers. In this chapter, you'll see how you can use the macro recorder as a reference tool for learning how to work with Excel objects.

Record a macro to create a rectangle

Graphical objects such as rectangles, ovals, text boxes, and charts can make your worksheets appealing and understandable. Microsoft Office includes an amazing collection of graphical objects. The macro recorder is an excellent tool for learning how to work with these graphical objects. Record creating a rectangle, and see how much you can learn from a simple recorded macro.

Drawing button

1. Select the Shapes worksheet in the Chapter5 workbook, and click the Drawing button on the Standard toolbar to display the Drawing toolbar.

— The Drawing toolbar

Record Macro button

2. Click the Record Macro button on the Visual Basic toolbar, replace the default macro name with **MakeRectangle**, and then click OK.

Rectangle button

3. Click the Rectangle button on the Drawing toolbar, and then click the top left corner of cell B2 and drag to the bottom right corner of cell B3.

— Drag from here...

...to here to make a rectangle.

Fill Color button

4. Click the arrow next to the Fill Color button on the Drawing toolbar, and then click the third box down in the first column. The rectangle changes to red.

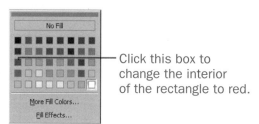

— Click this box to change the interior of the rectangle to red.

Stop Recording button

5. Click the Stop Recording button, and edit the macro. The line continuation marker in your macro might be in a different place than in the code sample below.

```
Sub MakeRectangle()
    ActiveSheet.Shapes.AddShape(msoShapeRectangle, _
        48#, 13, 48#, 25.5).Select
    Selection.ShapeRange.Fill.ForeColor.SchemeColor = 10
    Selection.ShapeRange.Fill.Visible = msoTrue
    Selection.ShapeRange.Fill.Solid
End Sub
```

This macro is short, but it does a lot. Look at the second statement:

```
ActiveSheet.Shapes.AddShape(msoShapeRectangle, _
        48#, 13, 48#, 25.5).Select
```

The statement starts by pointing at the active sheet and ends by selecting something. *Shapes* is a plural noun, so it might be a collection. To add a new item to most collections, you use the *Add* method, but *Shapes* is followed by the word *AddShape*. *AddShape* is followed by a list of arguments in parentheses. (The numbers in your list might differ somewhat. You can ignore the symbols after some numbers. The recorder adds them, but they're not necessary.) The first argument seems to tell what kind of shape you created, and the numbers seem to have something to do with the location and size of the rectangle, since nothing else in the macro sets the location.

These recorded statements give you several clues about how to create a new rectangle. Now you can build a macro on your own, using information from the recorder, coupled with the Auto Lists that Visual Basic displays.

Write a macro to create a rectangle

1. Under the recorded macro, type **Sub MakeNewRectangle** and press the Enter key. Visual Basic automatically adds the closing parentheses and the *End Sub* statement. For Visual Basic to display an Auto List of methods and properties for an object, it must know for sure which object's list to use. The properties *ActiveSheet* and *Selection* are too general: either one can refer to any of several different types of objects. The best way to let Visual Basic know what kind of object you're using is to assign the object to a variable and declare its type.

2. Type the following three statements to declare the variables and assign the active sheet to a variable:

```
Dim mySheet As Worksheet
Dim myShape As Shape
Set mySheet = ActiveSheet
```

All drawing objects belong to the Shape class. By declaring the variables, you give Visual Basic the information it needs to help you as you enter statements.

3. Type **Set myShape = mySheet.Shapes.** (including the period).

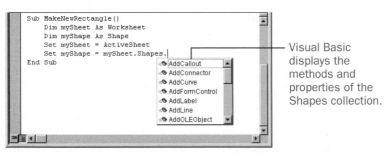

Visual Basic displays the methods and properties of the Shapes collection.

As soon as you type the period, Visual Basic shows the list of methods and properties for the Shapes collection. Apparently, you can add a lot more than just a Shape. You can add Callouts and Curves and Connectors and others. That's why the Shapes collection doesn't just use a simple *Add* method. You know from the recorded macro that you want to use the *AddShape* method to add a rectangle.

4. Type (or select) **AddShape(**, and then press the Down Arrow key.

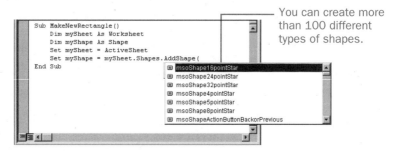

You can create more than 100 different types of shapes.

As soon as you type the opening parenthesis, Visual Basic shows you the list of possible values for the first argument. There are well over 100 different types of shapes you can add. You know from the recorded macro that you want the *msoShapeRectangle* option. (You can experiment with others later.)

A point is a unit of measurement originally used by graphic designers to lay out text for publishing.

5. Type (or select) **msoShapeRectangle,**. When you type the comma, you see that the remaining arguments are *Left, Top, Width,* and *Height.* You specify each of these values in *points.* A point is 1/72 inch.

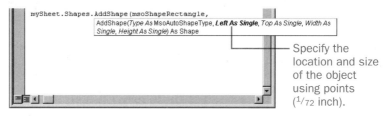

Specify the location and size of the object using points ($1/72$ inch).

6. For the remaining arguments, type **72** for *Left*, **36** for *Top*, **72** for *Width*, and **36** for *Height*. Then type a closing parenthesis and press the Enter key. The statement in the recorded macro ended with the *Select* method. When you assign an object to a variable, you don't put a *Select* method at the end of the statement.

7. Type **myShape.Fill.ForeColor.SchemeColor = 10**, and then press the Enter key. Each time you type a period, Visual Basic helps with a list of possible methods and properties. If you hadn't assigned the rectangle to a variable—if instead you'd used *Select* and *Selection* the way the recorded macro does—Visual Basic wouldn't be able to display the Auto Lists.

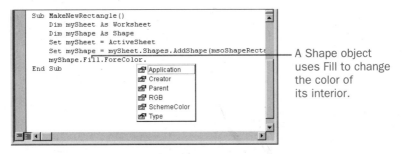

```
Sub MakeNewRectangle()
    Dim mySheet As Worksheet
    Dim myShape As Shape
    Set mySheet = ActiveSheet
    Set myShape = mySheet.Shapes.AddShape(msoShapeRectā
    myShape.Fill.ForeColor.
End Sub
```

A Shape object uses Fill to change the color of its interior.

> **Note** A shape object uses many subobjects to group formatting options. The *Fill* property returns a FillFormat object. (The object class name is different from the property name because, for chart objects, the *Fill* property returns a ChartFillFormat object.) A FillFormat object controls the formatting of the interior of the object. The *ForeColor* property returns a ColorFormat object. (This time, the object class name is different from the property name because a ColorFormat object can be returned by either the *ForeColor* property or the *BackColor* property.) Click any property name and press F1 to see the Help topic for the property and, if applicable, for its related object.

8. Press F8 repeatedly to step through the macro. A new rectangle appears on the worksheet. Depending on your screen size and resolution, the rectangle is about 1/2 inch high and 1 inch wide and is located about half an inch from the top and an inch from the left margin. The rectangle never has selection handles around its border because you never select it. You just assign a reference to a variable.

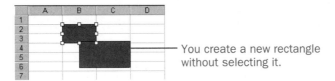

You create a new rectangle without selecting it.

In this example, you were able to create a rectangle by following the pattern given by the recorder, but you also saw how Visual Basic's Auto Lists can help you create variations of the recorded macro.

Modify an existing shape

Sometimes you'll want to modify one or more shapes that already exist on the worksheet. The macro recorder can help you see how to select a shape, and then you can use what you know about objects to convert the selection into an object variable.

1. Select the Shapes worksheet in the Chapter5 workbook. Show the Drawing toolbar, and start recording a macro named **SelectShapes**.

2. On the Drawing toolbar, click the Select Objects button, and then click the first, smaller rectangle you created.

3. Next, drag a rectangle to encompass the large rectangle and the Sun object off to the right. Turn off the recorder, select cell A1, and then click the Select Objects button to turn it off.

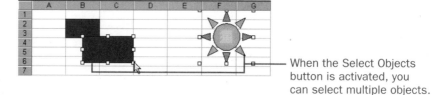

When the Select Objects button is activated, you can select multiple objects.

4. Edit the macro. It should look something like this:

The names in quotation marks might be different in your macro, depending on how many rectangles you created and how you selected them.

```
Sub SelectShapes()
    ActiveSheet.Shapes("Rectangle 2").Select
    ActiveSheet.Shapes.Range(Array("Rectangle 3", _
        "Shape3")).Select
End Sub
```

The *Shapes* property returns a collection of all the Shape objects on a worksheet. You must specify the sheet that contains the shapes. To select a single shape, you simply select a single item from the Shapes collection, using the name or the number of the item, the same as selecting an item from any other collection. This action returns a Shape (singular) object, which you can select or assign to a variable. For more information about selecting an item from a collection, see the "Navigate down by using collections" section in Chapter 3.

When you need to refer to more than one shape object, Excel has a different collection—the ShapeRange collection. A ShapeRange is just like a Shape, except that a ShapeRange can include more than one object. To create a ShapeRange object from a Shapes collection, you use the *Range* property with Visual Basic's *Array* function. The *Array* function allows you to group a list of items.

5. At the top of the macro, insert these two declaration statements:

```
Dim myShape as Shape
Dim myShapeRange as ShapeRange
```

6. Convert the first selection to assign the object to the *myShape* variable, rather than select it. Don't change the name inside the quotation marks. The resulting statement should look something like this:

```
Set myShape = ActiveSheet.Shapes("Rectangle 2")
```

7. Insert a second statement to change the RGB value of the foreground color of the fill of the shape to yellow. The final statement should look like this:

```
myShape.Fill.ForeColor.RGB = vbYellow
```

8. Convert the second selection to assign the ShapeRange object to the *myShape* variable, rather than select it. The resulting statement should look like this, with the possible exception of the names inside quotation marks:

```
Set myShapeRange = ActiveSheet.Shapes.Range(Array("Rectangle 3",
    "Shape 3"))
```

9. Insert another statement to change the RGB value of the foreground color of the fill of the shape range to blue. The final statement should look like this:

```
myShapeRange.Fill.ForeColor.RGB = vbBlue
```

10. Step through the macro, watching the objects change color.

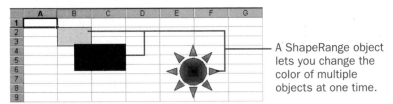

A ShapeRange object lets you change the color of multiple objects at one time.

Shapes allow you to create extremely powerful graphical effects. But keeping the different types of objects straight can be a bit confusing at first.

- **Shapes collection** Use the Shapes collection object for selecting all the shapes or a single shape, and for adding new shapes. You can't use the Shapes collection object to format multiple objects.

- **Shape object** Use the Shape object for formatting a single shape.

- **ShapeRange collection** Use the ShapeRange collection for formatting multiple objects at the same time.

Rename shapes

When you create a new shape on the worksheet, Excel gives it a default name, usually something like Rectangle 2 or Oval 5. When you record a macro that refers to the shape, the recorder puts that same name into the macro. You'll make your macros easier to read and less likely to have errors if you change the shape names to something meaningful.

1. On the Excel worksheet, click the first, smaller rectangle you created. It has a name like Rectangle 2. You can see the name in the Name box to the left of the formula bar.

This box shows the name of...

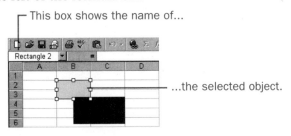

...the selected object.

Shapes and DrawingObjects

Shapes are a relatively new feature for Excel. Shapes are shared by all Microsoft Office applications and replace the earlier graphical objects that Excel used. Earlier graphical objects belonged to an object class called DrawingObjects, and you can still see some relics of DrawingObjects in Excel today.

For example, Shape objects format the interior of an object using the *Fill* property. DrawingObjects referred to the interior of an object using the *Interior* property. Shapes refer to colors that represent the red, green, and blue components of the color using the *RGB* property. DrawingObjects referred to the same type of color using the *Color* property. Shapes refer to colors from a palette using the *SchemeColor* property, whereas DrawingObjects used the *ColorIndex* property. As you might recognize, the Range object still uses all the formatting properties that the old DrawingObjects used: *Interior, Color,* and *ColorIndex.*

To maintain backward compatibility, Excel didn't remove the old DrawingObjects. They're still there, but they're hidden. Occasionally, you might see vestiges of these old graphical objects.

2. Click in the Name box, and type **Box** as a new name for the rectangle. Press the Enter key, or Excel won't recognize that you've changed the name.

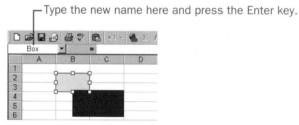

Type the new name here and press the Enter key.

3. Click the second, larger rectangle you created, and give it the name **BigBox**. Then give the sun shape the name **Sun**. Be sure to press the Enter key after typing each name in the Name box.

4. In the SelectShapes macro, change *Rectangle 2* to **Box**, *Rectangle 3* to **BigBox**, and *Shape 3* to **Sun**.

5. Change the colors in the macro from *vbYellow* to **vbGreen** and from *vbBlue* to **vbMagenta**, and then run the macro to test it. Here's what the final macro should look like:

```
Sub SelectShapes()
    Dim myShape as Shape
    Dim myShapeRange as ShapeRange
    Set myShape = ActiveSheet.Shapes("Box")
    MyShape.Fill.ForeColor.RGB = vbGreen
    Set myShapeRange =
ActiveSheet.Shapes.Range(Array("BigBox", _
        "Sun"))
    MyShapeRange.Fill.ForeColor.RGB = vbMagenta
End Sub
```

In the same way that you can give worksheets meaningful names (rather than keeping the default Sheet1, Sheet2, and so forth), you can give meaningful names to shapes on the worksheet, even though these names are less noticeable. Your macros will thank you for it.

Excel can create hundreds of different types of shapes. All these shapes work in much the same way that rectangles do. Embedded charts are also shapes in Excel. You add, manipulate, and delete Chart objects in much the same way you do rectangles. Chart objects, of course, have additional properties that are unique to charts; the macro recorder is an effective tool for finding out what they are.

Exploring Chart Objects

Chart objects have hundreds of properties and methods. Many of the attributes of a chart are themselves separate objects. Learning how to create and manipulate charts by reading a reference manual is difficult because charts have so many objects and properties. But creating and manipulating a chart is easy to record, and even though you might see many new methods, properties, and objects, the new objects work according to the same principles as other objects in Excel.

Record a macro that creates a chart

1. Activate the ChartData worksheet in the Chapter5 workbook, and select cell A1.

	A	B	C	D
1	Price	Units	Net	
2	High	6,443	22,600	
3	Mid	12,599	22,800	
4	Low	8,670	19,401	
5				

2. Click the Record Macro button on the Visual Basic toolbar, type **MakeChart** as the name for the macro, and then click OK.

Record Macro
button

3. Click the ChartWizard button on the Standard toolbar, and then click the Finish button to create the default chart.

Chart
Wizard
button

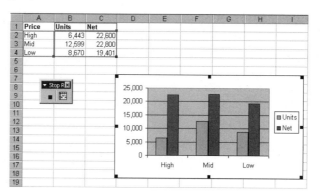

*Stop Recording
button*

4. Click the Stop Recording button, delete the chart, and then edit the
recorded macro. Here's what it looks like:

```
Sub MakeChart()
    Charts.Add
    ActiveChart.ChartType = xlColumnClustered
    ActiveChart.SetSourceData _
        Source:=Sheets("ChartData").Range("A1:C4")
    ActiveChart.Location _
        Where:=xlLocationAsObject, _
        Name:="ChartData"
End Sub
```

The macro creates an embedded chart in four steps. First, it uses the *Add*
method to create a new, blank chart (as a stand-alone sheet). Second, it uses the
ChartType property to set the type of the chart. Third, it uses the *SetSourceData*
method to assign a data range to the chart. And finally, it uses the *Location*
method to move the chart onto the worksheet.

Modify the macro that creates a chart

Once you've recorded the macro to create a chart, you can make modifications
to it to instantly create exactly the type of chart you want.

1. Click the word *xlColumnClustered* in the macro. This is one of an
enumerated list of values that can be assigned to the *ChartType* property.

2. Choose the Edit menu and the List Constants command. Excel displays
the entire list of possible chart types.

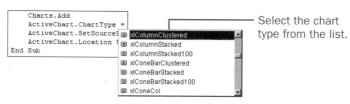

Select the chart
type from the list.

Tip Visual Basic is able to display the list of possible values because it knows that ActiveChart can return only a Chart object. Visual Basic doesn't display the list of methods and properties when ActiveSheet or Selection is the object because Visual Basic can't be sure what kind of object might currently be selected. If you declare an object variable and assign the object to the variable, Visual Basic will be able to display the helpful lists.

---

3. Select *xlConeBarStacked* from the list, and double-click it to insert it into the code.

4. Type a comma, a space, and an underscore at the end of the statement that sets the source data. Then press the Enter key to create a new line.

5. Add **PlotBy:=xlRows** as an additional argument to the statement, to make the column headings into the category labels. Here's what the revised macro looks like:

```
Sub MakeChart()
    Charts.Add
    ActiveChart.ChartType = xlConeBarStacked
    ActiveChart.SetSourceData _
        Source:=Sheets("ChartData").Range("A1:C4"), _
        PlotBy:=xlRows
    ActiveChart.Location Where:=xlLocationAsObject, _
        Name:="ChartData"
End Sub
```

6. Press F8 repeatedly to step through the modified macro. Watch how Excel creates the chart as a separate sheet first, then adds the data, and finally moves it onto the worksheet.

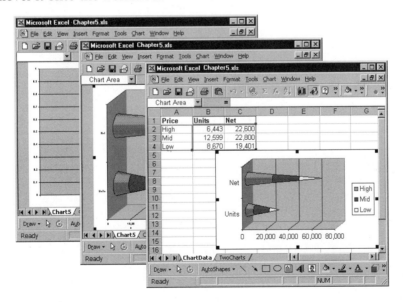

An Excel chart can exist in either of two locations. It can exist as a separate sheet in the workbook, or it can be embedded in a worksheet. Regardless of where a chart is located, it behaves the same way. There are some differences, however, in how you refer to each type of chart.

Refer to an existing embedded chart

When you create a new chart, Excel automatically selects the chart, so you can use *ActiveChart* to refer to it. If a chart already exists, you have to refer to it differently. A chart that's on a separate sheet is easy to refer to: simply select a single item from the Charts collection. Referring to a chart that's embedded on a worksheet, however, can be confusing. Fortunately for you, this section will make it all clear.

1. In Excel, if the Chart is selected, press the Esc key to deselect the chart. (If you had selected an object inside the chart, you may need to press the Esc key more than once.)

2. In Visual Basic, at the bottom of the open module, type **Sub SelectChart** and press the Enter key. Add these three declaration statements to the top of the macro:

```
Dim myShape As Shape
Dim myObject As ChartObject
Dim myChart As Chart
```

You'll assign objects to these variables to see how Excel handles charts embedded on a worksheet.

3. Press F8 twice to step down to the *End Sub* statement in the new macro. From the View menu, click the Immediate Window command to display the Immediate window.

4. In the Immediate window, type **Set myShape = ActiveSheet.Shapes(1)** and press the Enter key to assign a reference to the chart's container to the *myShape* variable.

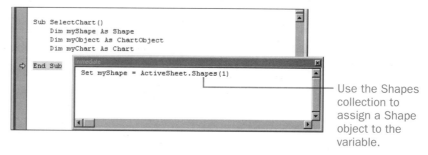

Use the Shapes collection to assign a Shape object to the variable.

5. In the Immediate window, type **Set myObject = ActiveSheet.Chart-Objects(1)** and press the Enter key to assign a reference to the chart's container to the *myObject* variable. (Both myShape and myObject refer to the same chart container object, but myShape refers to the chart as a Shape object, and myObject refers to the chart as a ChartObject object.)

6. In the Immediate window, type **?myObject.Name** and press the Enter key. The name of the chart appears.

Use a question mark in the Immediate window to show a value.

Note In the Immediate window, if you type a question mark in front of an expression that returns a value and then press the Enter key, you'll see the value displayed immediately.

---

7. In the Immediate window, type **?myShape.Name** and press the Enter key. The same name appears again. Both myObject and myShape refer to the same object.

Both the ChartObject object and the Shape object refer to the same chart container.

8. In the Immediate window, type **myObject.Left = 0** and press the Enter key. Then type **myShape.Left = 50** and press the Enter key. In each case, the chart shifts. You can use either container object to move and resize the chart.

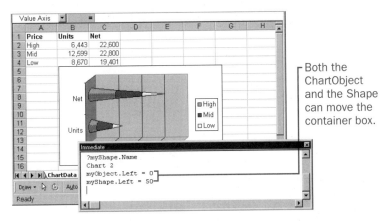

Both the ChartObject and the Shape can move the container box.

9. In the Immediate window, type **myObject.Select** and press the Enter key. Then type **myShape.Select** and press the Enter key. In both cases, the statement works and you see white boxes at the corner of the chart. The white handles show that you selected the container object, and not the chart inside.

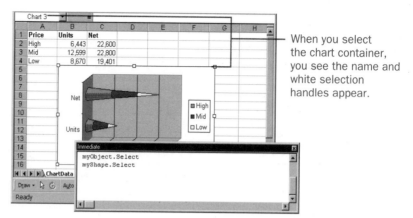

When you select
the chart container,
you see the name and
white selection
handles appear.

*Select Objects
button*

Note Interactively, when you click in an embedded chart, you immediately select the portion of the chart that you clicked. For example, if you click around the edge of a chart, you select the Chart Area portion of the chart, which has black handles. In order to select the container object interactively, you must first click the Select Objects button on the Drawing toolbar. When the container is selected, you can't select any of the chart objects inside.

10. In the Immediate window, type **myObject.Activate** and press the Enter key. When you activate the ChartObject, you see the boxes at the corners of the chart turn black, indicating that you have now selected the Chart Area inside the chart. As soon as you typed the period, Visual Basic displayed the *Activate* method in the Auto List, showing that *Activate* is a method of the ChartObject object.

11. In the Immediate window, type **myShape.Activate** and press the Enter key. (Click OK to close the error message.)

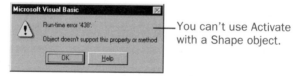

You can't use Activate
with a Shape object.

When you try to activate the Shape object, you get an error because the Shape object doesn't have an *Activate* method. (When Visual Basic displayed the Auto List for the Shape object, the *Activate* method wasn't in the list.)

12. In the Immediate window, type **Set myChart = myObject.Chart** and press the Enter key. In this statement, the *Chart* property assigns to the variable *myChart* a reference to the chart that is contained in the ChartObject object. In the same way that a Shape object doesn't have an *Activate* method, it doesn't have a *Chart* property either.

Note The ChartObjects collection is left over from the old-style Excel drawing objects. It couldn't be hidden like the other old graphical object collections because the Shape object doesn't have an *Activate* method or a *Chart* property for working with charts.

---

13. In the Immediate window, type **myChart.ChartArea.Interior.Color = vbRed** and press the Enter key. The interior of the chart changes to red. Once you have a reference to the chart, you can manipulate the objects inside it.

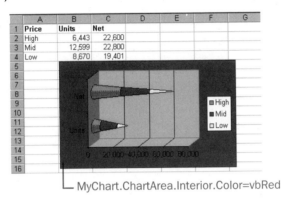

└─ MyChart.ChartArea.Interior.Color=vbRed

14. Close the Immediate window, and press F8 to finish the macro.

A chart that's embedded in a worksheet consists of two parts: the container box (a ChartObject object) and the chart inside (a Chart object). You can refer to the container box using either the Shapes collection (which returns a Shape object) or the ChartObjects collection (which returns a ChartObject object), but to get to the chart inside, you must use the ChartObjects collection, not the Shapes collection. For example, you can move and resize the container using either the Shapes collection or the ChartObjects collection, but to change the color of the chart area, you must get to the chart inside using the ChartObjects collection.

Record a macro that modifies chart attributes

Now that you understand how Excel refers to the chart container and the chart inside, you can record a macro that changes a chart and learn what methods and properties you use to control a chart.

1. On the ChartData worksheet, select cell A1. Start recording a macro named **ChangeChart**.

2. Click the edge of the chart you created in the section "Modify the macro that creates a chart." This activates the chart.

3. Double-click one of the numbers along the bottom of the chart. Doing this selects the value axis and displays the Format Axis dialog box. Select the Scale tab.

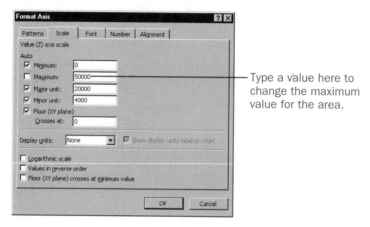

Type a value here to change the maximum value for the area.

4. Change the Maximum value to **50,000**. (Entering a value clears the Auto check box.) Click OK.

5. Turn off the recorder, and edit the macro. It looks similar to this:

The chart name inside quotation marks will probably be different in your macro.

```
Sub ChangeChart()
    ActiveSheet.ChartObjects("Chart 15").Activate
    ActiveChart.ChartArea.Select
    ActiveChart.Axes(xlValue).Select
    With ActiveChart.Axes(xlValue)
        .MinimumScaleIsAuto = True
        .MaximumScale = 50000
        .MinorUnitIsAuto = True
        .MajorUnitIsAuto = True
        .Crosses = xlAutomatic
        .ReversePlotOrder = False
        .ScaleType = xlLinear
    End With
End Sub
```

The macro first activates the chart, using the ChartObjects collection. (If you want to refer to the chart inside the embedded container without activating it, you must use the *Chart* property of the ChartObject object.) The macro then selects the ChartArea. This statement is superfluous because the statement after it selects the Value Axis. The macro then changes several properties of the Value Axis, even though you only changed one in the dialog box.

You could simplify this entire macro to a single statement:

```
ActiveSheet.ChartObjects("Chart 15").Chart.Axes(xlValue) _
    .MaximumScale = 50000
```

You can be grateful, however, that the recorder included everything it did, because you can learn the names of a lot of properties very quickly. In the next section, we'll put some of those properties to work in a very useful macro.

Write a macro that modifies a chart

On the TwoCharts worksheet are two charts that show total orders for two different regions.

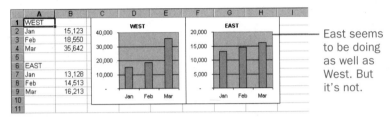

East seems to be doing as well as West. But it's not.

Based on a quick glance at the charts, you might conclude that the performance of the two regions was roughly equal. But that would be wrong. The East region is substantially lower than the West, but Excel automatically scales the axes to fit the data. Let's create a macro that will change the value axis on the East chart to match the axis on the West chart.

1. Name the charts so that you can refer to them by descriptive names: on the Drawing toolbar, click the Select Objects button, click the West chart, and then enter **West** in the Name box. Follow the same steps to give the name **East** to the East chart. Then click the Select Objects button again to deselect it.

Select Objects button

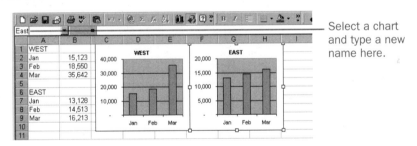

Select a chart and type a new name here.

2. In Visual Basic, at the bottom of the module, type **Sub SynchronizeCharts** and press the Enter key. Then enter the following two variable declarations:

```
Dim myWest As Chart
Dim myEast As Chart
```

You'll store a reference to a chart in each of these variables.

3. Next enter the following two statements to assign the charts to the variables:

```
Set myWest = ActiveSheet.ChartObjects("West").Chart
Set myEast = ActiveSheet.ChartObjects("East").Chart
```

You must include the *Chart* property to move from the container to the chart inside. If you hadn't renamed the charts, you'd have to use either the default "Chart 1" and "Chart 2" or the numbers 1 and 2 (and determine which was which by trial and error). Giving the charts explicit, meaningful names makes your code easier to read and less likely to contain errors.

4. Add the following statement to make sure that the value axis on the West chart is automatic:

```
myWest.Axes(xlValue).MaximumScaleIsAuto = True
```

The expression *Axes(xlValue)* was in the recorded macro. That's how you know how to refer to the value axis. The *MaximumScaleIsAuto* property didn't appear in the recorded macro, but the *MinimumScaleIsAuto* property did, and you can guess the rest.

5. Add the following statement to make the axes have the same maximum scale:

```
myEast.Axes(xlValue).MaximumScale = _
    myWest.Axes(xlValue).MaximumScale
```

Even though the maximum scale of the West chart is set to automatic, you still can read the current value from it.

6. Press F8 repeatedly to step through the macro. The difference between the two regions is much more obvious now.

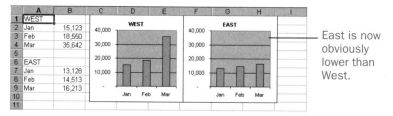

East is now obviously lower than West.

7. On the worksheet, change the *March* value for the West region to **15,000**. Then run the SynchronizeCharts macro again.

You could add still other synchronization tasks to this macro as well. For example, you could make the minimum value for each axis the same. You could make it so that if you interactively changed the color of the background on the West chart, running the macro would make the East chart the same color. For each enhancement, you simply record a macro to learn what you need to change, and then add it to your macro.

Formatting Charts

Charts are an interesting hybrid of Excel's older DrawingObjects and Office's Shapes. Charts have been around since the first version of Excel, so all of the features that can be controlled with old properties, such as *Interior*, still use those properties. For example, to set red as the color of the ChartArea of a chart assigned to the *myChart* variable, you could use the statement *myChart.Interior. Color = vbRed*.

Office Shape objects are newer than Chart objects, but Charts can still take advantage of the fancy formatting that's part of a Shape object. To get to those newer features, you must use the *Fill* property. For example, to create a gradient background for the ChartArea, you could use the statement *myChart-.Fill.TwoColorGradient msoGradientHorizontal, 1*.

The formatting properties that can be set using the *Interior* property can't be set using the *Fill* property. For example, you can set the fill color of a shape using the statement *myShape.Fill.ForeColor.RGB = vbRed*, but with a chart, the *RGB* property is read-only. You can find out the color using the new property, but you have to change it using the old one. Because the properties and methods of the fill for a chart are somewhat different from those for a shape, the *Fill* property for a chart object returns a ChartFillFormat object, whereas the *Fill* property for a shape returns a FillFormat object.

Chapter Summary

To	Do this
Create an approximately 1-inch rectangle in the top left corner of the active sheet	Use the statement *ActiveSheet.Shapes .AddShape(msoShapeRectangle, 0,0,72,72).Select.*
Change the color of the selected shape to red	Use the statement *Selection.ShapeRange.Fill. ForeColor.RGB = vbRed.*
Select a shape named *Square*	Use the statement *ActiveSheet.Shapes("Square").Select.*
Select two shapes named *Square* and *Sun*	Use the statement *ActiveSheet.Shapes.Range (Array("Square","Sun")).Select.*
Create a chart	Use the statement *Charts.Add.*
Assign a data range to a chart	Use the chart's *SetSourceData* method.
Specify a chart's location	Use the chart's *Location* method.
Assign an embedded chart named *West* to a variable *myChart*	Use the statement *Set myChart =ActiveSheet.ChartObjects("West").Chart.*
Rename a shape or a chart in the Name box.	Click the Select Objects button on the Drawing toolbar (to select a chart), and then click the object and enter a new name in the Name box.

For online information about	Ask the Assistant for help using the words
Using shapes	"Working with Shapes"
Using charts	"Charts"
Visual Basic colors	"Colors" (or click a sample color constant, such as vbRed, and press F1)

Preview of the Next Chapter

Charts and other graphical shapes can add clarity and impact to information that you have to present. Excel has another powerful tool for analyzing information: the PivotTable. In the next chapter, you'll learn how to manipulate PivotTables using VBA.

Chapter 6

Explore PivotTable Objects

Estimated time: 30 minutes

In this chapter, you'll learn how to:

- Build a PivotTable.

- Manipulate fields and items in a PivotTable.

Since the turn of the century, one of the mainstays of medical technology has been X-ray photography. One of the problems with an X-ray photograph, however, is that it shows you only the angle at which it was taken. If the bones or organs aren't properly aligned, the photograph might not reveal the problem. In 1974, the British company EMI Ltd. used the money it had made selling Beatles records to develop computerized axial tomography (CAT) scan technology. A CAT scan doesn't suffer from the blind spots of conventional X-rays.

A database report is like an X-ray photograph. It's an image, but it's a static image. If the rows and columns aren't properly defined, the person reviewing the report might miss important relationships. A PivotTable, in contrast, is like a CAT scan. It's a multidimensional view of the data that enables you to find the most meaningful perspective.

Start the lesson

1. In Microsoft Excel, open a new, empty workbook.

2. Save the workbook with the name **Chapter6** in the folder that contains the practice files for this book.

For more information about installing the practice files, see the Introduction to this book.

Building PivotTables

In Excel, each object class has its own list of methods and properties that you can use to manipulate objects belonging to that class. Many objects belong to collections or link to other objects. The objects that support PivotTables are an elegant example of how objects work.

Create a default PivotTable

1. With the Chapter6 workbook active, click the Run Macro button, type **MakePivot** in the Macro Name box, and then click Create. The Microsoft Visual Basic Editor window opens with a new, empty macro.

2. Insert the following variable declaration statements at the beginning of the macro:

```
Dim myPivot As PivotTable
Dim myField As PivotField
Dim myItem As PivotItem
Dim myRange As Range
```

Assigning objects to these variables enables Visual Basic to display Auto Lists that help you see methods and properties.

Tip To make the Immediate window fill the main Visual Basic Editor window, make it undockable by right-clicking the window and then clearing the check mark next to Dockable. When you want to see both the Immediate window and the Code window at the same time, make the Immediate window dockable again.

3. Press F8 twice to step to the *End Sub* statement. From the View menu, click the Immediate Window command. Move and size the Immediate window so that you can see the Excel window in the background.

4. In the Immediate window, type **Workbooks.Open "Orders.dbf"**, and then press the Enter key to open the database workbook. In a few seconds, the database appears. The active sheet in the database workbook is a worksheet that contains a range named Database. The Worksheet object's PivotTableWizard can create a PivotTable from a range named Database.

If the Orders.dbf file doesn't open, click the Open toolbar button, change to the folder containing the practice files for this book, and then click Cancel before executing the statement.

Workbooks.Open "Orders.dbf"

	A	B	C	D	E	F	G	H
1	DATE	STATE	CHANNEL	PRICE	CATEGORY	UNITS	NET	
2	11/1/97	WA	Wholesale	High	Seattle	40	110.00	
3	11/1/97	WA	Wholesale	High	Art	25	68.75	
4	11/1/97	WA	Retail	High	Art	3	16.50	
5	11/1/97	WA	Retail	Low	Environment	50	175.00	
6	11/1/97	WA	Wholesale	Low	Dinosaurs	40	70.00	
7	11/1/97	WA	Wholesale	Low	Seattle	35	61.25	
8	11/1/97	WA	Wholesale	Low	Environment	30	52.50	

5. In the Immediate window, type **Set myPivot = ActiveSheet.Pivot-TableWizard**, and then press the Enter key. The status bar momentarily displays the message "Reading Data," and then a PivotTable appears.

	A	B	C
1			
2			
3			

Set myPivot = ActiveSheet.PivotTableWizard

6. Because you won't be using the PivotTable toolbar, close it.

Congratulations! You've just used Microsoft Visual Basic for Applications commands to create a PivotTable. You've also assigned a reference to the PivotTable object to the *myPivot* variable.

Manipulate pivot fields

You did create a PivotTable, but it's not particularly informative. You still need to display data from the database in the PivotTable. A database usually consists of a list with a lot of rows and a few columns. Each column is called a *field*, and the label at the top of the column is the name of the field. The database in Orders.dbf has seven fields. Date, State, Channel, Price, and Category are fields that contain words. Units and Net are fields that contain numbers. A PivotTable typically summarizes the number fields, sorting and grouping them by the fields that contain words.

1. In the Immediate window, type **Set myField = myPivot.Pivot-Fields("Units")**, and then press the Enter key. This action assigns the Units pivot field to a variable.

2. Type **myField.Orientation = xlDataField**, and then press the Enter key. The label "Sum of UNITS" and a number appear in the body of the PivotTable. Because the Units field contains values, the PivotTable adds all the numbers in the Units column.

The PivotFields collection contains one item for each of the seven fields in the database. You refer to a single item from the collection in the standard way—by name or by number. In this case, it's easier to remember the name of the Units field than it is to recall where it happens to fall in the database. Assigning *xlDataField* to the *Orientation* property summarizes the data in that field.

3. Now format the Units total. Type **myField.NumberFormat = "#,##0"**, and then press the Enter key. The number in the PivotTable looks much better with a comma. *NumberFormat* is a property of a PivotField object. It works in the same way as the *NumberFormat* property of a Range object.

4. Type **Set myField = myPivot.PivotFields("State")**, and then press the Enter key. This action assigns the State pivot field to the variable.

5. Type **myField.Orientation = xlRowField**, and then press the Enter key. Row headings appear, adding appropriate subtotals to the grand total that was already there. The gray box containing the word *State* is called a *field button*. It serves as a visible heading for the pivot field.

	A	B	C
1	Sum of UNITS		
2	STATE	Total	
3	AZ	25,341	
4	CA	112,385	
5	ID	1,860	
6	NV	51,634	
7	OR	179,516	
8	UT	40,068	
9	WA	154,017	
10	Grand Total	564,821	
11			

Set myField = myPivot.PivotFields("State")
myField.Orientation = xlRowField

6. By now, you can probably guess how to turn the State field items into column headings. Type **myField.Orientation = xlColumnField**, and then press the Enter key. The state codes move from the side to the top of Sheet1. The field button moves above the state codes.

myField.Orientation = xlColumnField

	A	B	C	D	E	F	G	H	I
1	Sum of UNITS	STATE							
2		AZ	CA	ID	NV	OR	UT	WA	Grand Total
3	Total	25,341	112,385	1,860	51,634	179,516	40,068	154,017	564,821
4									

7. Row and column fields group the data in the PivotTable. In the same way that you change pages in a magazine to select which part you want to see, you can filter the data in a PivotTable by using a *page field*. Type **myField.Orientation = xlPageField**, and then press the Enter key. The State field button moves up to the top left corner of the worksheet.

The CurrentPage property works only with page fields.

8. To filter the data (by state, for example), assign a state code to the *CurrentPage* property of the State page field. Type **myField.CurrentPage = "WA"**, and press the Enter key. Then type **myField.CurrentPage = "CA"**, and press the Enter key. The numbers change as you filter by different states.

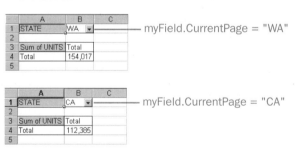

	A	B	C
1	STATE	WA	
2			
3	Sum of UNITS	Total	
4	Total	154,017	
5			

myField.CurrentPage = "WA"

	A	B	C
1	STATE	CA	
2			
3	Sum of UNITS	Total	
4	Total	112,385	
5			

myField.CurrentPage = "CA"

9. To remove a field from one of the visible areas of the PivotTable, assign it to the *hidden* orientation. Type **myField.Orientation = xlHidden**, and then press the Enter key. The State field button disappears. The PivotTable still contains a pivot field named State, but the field button is no longer visible. The *Orientation* property of PivotFields is what makes the PivotTable "pivot."

	A	B	C
1			
2			
3	Sum of UNITS	Total	
4	Total	564,821	
5			

myField.Orientation = xlHidden

Make multiple changes to a PivotTable

The PivotTable object also has a shortcut method that can assign several fields to the different PivotTable areas all at once.

1. Type **myPivot.AddFields "Category", "State", "Channel"**, and then press the Enter key. The Category field becomes the row field, the State field becomes the column field, and the Channel field becomes the page field. The arguments of the *AddFields* method always appear in *Row, Column, Page* order.

myPivot.AddFields"Category","State","Channel"

	A	B	C	D	E	F	G	H	I
1	CHANNEL	(All)							
2									
3	Sum of UNITS	STATE							
4	CATEGORY	AZ	CA	ID	NV	OR	UT	WA	Grand Total
5	Art	5,292	28,787	295	14,275	53,185	6,080	26,263	134,177
6	Dinosaurs	8,192	16,575	250	6,160	10,950	5,990	27,207	75,324
7	Environment	3,356	14,685	170	5,070	35,965	5,345	22,500	87,091
8	Humorous	1,577	6,970	290	1,784	7,466	8,140	1,423	27,650
9	Kids	3,020	37,733	226	11,490	53,288	2,402	15,067	123,226
10	Seattle					11,375		58,895	70,270
11	Sports	3,904	7,635	629	12,855	7,287	12,111	2,662	47,083
12	Grand Total	25,341	112,385	1,860	51,634	179,516	40,068	154,017	564,821
13									

2. To add more than one field to an orientation, you need to use multiple field names as a single argument. The *Array* function allows you to treat multiple field names as a single argument. Type **myPivot.AddFields Array("State","Channel"), "Price", "Date"**, and then press the Enter key. Both State and Channel become row fields, Price becomes the column field, and Date becomes the page field.

myPivot.AddFieldsArray("State","Channel"),"Price","Date"

	A	B	C	D	E	F	G
1	DATE	(All)					
2							
3	Sum of UNITS		PRICE				
4	STATE	CHANNEL	High	Low	Mid	Grand Total	
5	AZ	Retail	783	2,869	3,789	7,441	
6		Wholesale	2,940	6,140	8,820	17,900	
7	AZ Total		3,723	9,009	12,609	25,341	
8	CA	Retail	6,152	5,229	10,414	21,795	
9		Wholesale	4,970	26,275	59,345	90,590	
10	CA Total		11,122	31,504	69,759	112,385	
11	ID	Retail	193	493	1,174	1,860	
12	ID Total		193	493	1,174	1,860	

3. When you have more than one field in a given area, you can swap the order of the fields using the *Position* property. The State field is still assigned to the *myField* variable. Type **myField.Position = 2**, and then press the Enter key to swap the order of the State and Channel fields.

	A	B	C	D	E	F	G
1	DATE	(All) ▾					
2							
3	Sum of UNITS		PRICE ▾				
4	CHANNEL ▾	STATE ▾	High	Low	Mid	Grand Total	
5	Retail	AZ	783	2,869	3,789	7,441	
6		CA	6,152	5,229	10,414	21,795	
7		ID	193	493	1,174	1,860	
8		NV	13,419	8,785	15,305	37,509	
9		OR	6,336	22,291	30,094	58,721	
10		UT	380	1,376	1,867	3,623	
11		WA	3,341	12,489	17,072	32,902	
12	Retail Total		30,604	53,532	79,715	163,851	

————— myField.Position = 2

In summary, use the *AddFields* method of the PivotTable object to make major changes to a PivotTable; use the *Orientation, Position,* and *CurrentPage* properties of the PivotField objects to fine-tune the table.

Note In addition to the PivotFields collection, the PivotTable object has subcollections that contain only PivotFields of a particular orientation. For example, the RowFields collection contains only the fields whose *Orientation* property is set to *xlRowField*. The subcollections are RowFields, ColumnFields, PageFields, DataFields, and HiddenFields. These collections don't have corresponding object classes. A member of the RowFields collection is still a PivotField object, not a RowField object. You never need to use any of these subcollections, but you might find them convenient. For example, if you know that there's only one row field, you can refer to it as RowFields(1), without worrying about its name or what its number is in the entire PivotFields collection.

Refining PivotTables

Once you've created a PivotTable with rows and columns in the proper orientation, you can make many additional refinements to the table. You can manipulate specific details within a field, or change the appearance of the data, or even modify the worksheet ranges that contain portions of the PivotTable.

Manipulate pivot items

The unique values that appear in a PivotField are called *items*. You can manipulate individual items within a PivotField.

1. Type **Set myItem = myField.PivotItems("WA")**, and then press the Enter key to assign the pivot item for Washington State to a variable.

2. Now that *myItem* refers to an individual pivot item, you can manipulate that item using its properties. Type **myItem.Position = 1**, and then press the Enter key. A pivot item has a *Position* property, just as a PivotField does.

	A	B	C	D	E	F	G
1	DATE	(All) ▼					
2							
3	Sum of UNITS		PRICE ▼				
4	CHANNEL ▼	STATE ▼	High	Low	Mid	Grand Total	
5	Retail	WA	3,341	12,489	17,072	32,902	
6		AZ	783	2,869	3,789	7,441	
7		CA	6,152	5,229	10,414	21,795	
8		ID	193	493	1,174	1,860	

Set myItem = myField.PivotItems ("WA")
myItem.Position = 1

3. Type **myItem.Name = "Washington"**, and then press the Enter key.

	A	B	C	D	E	F	G
1	DATE	(All) ▼					
2							
3	Sum of UNITS		PRICE ▼				
4	CHANNEL ▼	STATE ▼	High	Low	Mid	Grand Total	
5	Retail	Washington	3,341	12,489	17,072	32,902	
6		AZ	783	2,869	3,789	7,441	
7		CA	6,152	5,229	10,414	21,795	
8		ID	193	493	1,174	1,860	

myItem.Name = "Washington"

The name of the pivot item displays in the PivotTable. If you don't like the way the database designer abbreviated state names, you can fix the problem in the PivotTable. Of course, sometimes it's better to leave conventions alone. Fortunately, the PivotItem object remembers for you what its original name was.

4. Type **myItem.Name = myItem.SourceName**, and then press the Enter key. The name changes back to the original. For obvious reasons, the SourceName property is read-only.

	A	B	C	D	E	F	G
1	DATE	(All) ▼					
2							
3	Sum of UNITS		PRICE ▼				
4	CHANNEL ▼	STATE ▼	High	Low	Mid	Grand Total	
5	Retail	WA	3,341	12,489	17,072	32,902	
6		AZ	783	2,869	3,789	7,441	
7		CA	6,152	5,229	10,414	21,795	
8		ID	193	493	1,174	1,860	

myItem.Name = myItem.SourceName

5. Perhaps changing the spelling of the state name isn't enough. Perhaps you don't like Washington state (I really do feel sorry for you) and want to eliminate it entirely. Type **myItem.Visible = False**, and then press the Enter key.

	A	B	C	D	E	F	G
1	DATE	(All) ▼					
2							
3	Sum of UNITS		PRICE ▼				
4	CHANNEL ▼	STATE ▼	High	Low	Mid	Grand Total	
5	Retail	AZ	783	2,869	3,789	7,441	
6		CA	6,152	5,229	10,414	21,795	
7		ID	193	493	1,174	1,860	
8		NV	13,419	8,785	15,305	37,509	

myItem.Visible = False

6. Perhaps, however, you suddenly realize how foolish you are not to like Washington. Fortunately, you can put it back, the same way you got rid of it. Type **myItem.Visible = True**, and then press the Enter key.

7. Another useful thing you can do with a pivot item is to hide or show the detail to the right of a field. Try hiding the detail for the Retail channel. Type **Set myItem = myPivot.PivotFields("Channel").PivotItems("Retail")**, and then press the Enter key. This action assigns the pivot item to the *myItem* variable.

8. Type **myItem.ShowDetail = False**, and then press the Enter key. All the states for the Retail channel collapse into a single row.

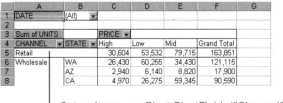

```
Set myItem = myPivot.PivotFields("Channel").PivotItems("Retail")
myItem.ShowDetail = False
```

Manipulating pivot items isn't generally as dramatic as manipulating PivotFields, but you can use the *Position*, *Name*, *SourceName*, *Visible*, and *ShowDetail* properties to refine the effect of the PivotTable.

Manipulate data fields

Data fields do the real dirty work of the PivotTable. This is where the numbers get worked over. Data fields are like other PivotFields in many ways, but they do have a few unique twists of their own. You can see how data fields are different from other fields when you add a second data field.

1. Type **Set myField = myPivot.PivotFields("Net")**, and then press the Enter key to assign the Net field to the *myField* variable.

2. Type **myField.Orientation = xlDataField**, and then press the Enter key to add a second data field.

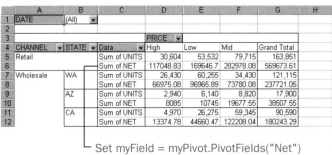

```
Set myField = myPivot.PivotFields("Net")
myField.Orientation = xlDataField
```

As soon as you have two data fields in the PivotTable, you get a new field button, labeled Data. The Data field is not a field from the database. It's a temporary field that allows you to manipulate multiple data fields. The Data field begins as a row field, but you can change it into a column field.

3. Type **Set myField = myPivot.PivotFields("Data")**, and then press the Enter key. This action assigns the temporary Data field to a variable. The statement works only if you have more than one data field.

4. Type **myField.Orientation = xlColumnField**, and then press the Enter key.

Set myField = myPivot.PivotFields("Data")
myField.Orientation = xlColumnField

	A	B	C	D	E	F
1	DATE	(All) ▼				
2						
3			PRICE ▼	Data ▼		
4			High		Low	
5	CHANNEL ▼	STATE ▼	Sum of UNITS	Sum of NET	Sum of UNITS	Sum of NET
6	Retail		30,604	117048.83	53,532	169646.7
7	Wholesale	WA	26,430	66975.08	60,255	96965.89
8		AZ	2,940	8085	6,140	10745
9		CA	4,970	13374.78	26,275	44660.47
10		NV	4,440	11759.64	4,540	7945

When you made the State field into a row field, a button labeled "State" appeared on the PivotTable. The same was true for the other row, column, and page fields. But when you made Units and Net into data fields, you didn't see buttons labeled "Units" and "Net." Rather, you saw the labels "Sum of UNITS" and "Sum of NET." These summary fields are new, derived fields that have been added to the PivotTable. To refer to one of these fields, you must use the new name.

5. Type **Set myField = myPivot.PivotFields("Sum of NET")**, and then press the Enter key.

6. Type **myField.Orientation = xlHidden**, and then press the Enter key. The Sum of NET column disappears—along with the Data button— because there's now only one data field. To create a data field, you change the orientation of the database field. To remove a data field, you change the orientation of the derived field.

Set myField = myPivot.PivotFields("Sum of NET")
myField.Orientation = xlHidden

	A	B	C	D	E	F	G
1	DATE	(All) ▼					
2							
3	Sum of UNITS		PRICE ▼				
4	CHANNEL ▼	STATE ▼	High	Low	Mid	Grand Total	
5	Retail		30,604	53,532	79,715	163,851	
6	Wholesale	WA	26,430	60,255	34,430	121,115	
7		AZ	2,940	6,140	8,820	17,900	
8		CA	4,970	26,275	59,345	90,590	
9		NV	4,440	4,540	5,145	14,125	

7. Type **Set myField = myPivot.PivotFields("Sum of UNITS")**, and then press the Enter key to assign the data field to a variable.

8. The default calculation for a number field is to sum the values. The *Function* property of a data field allows you to change the way the PivotTable aggregates the data. Type **myField.Function = xlAverage**, and then press the Enter key. The values change to averages, and the label changes to "Average of UNITS."

```
Set myField = myPivot.PivotFields("Sum of UNITS")
myField.Function = xlAverage
```

	A	B	C	D	E	F	G
1	DATE	(All)					
2							
3	Average of UNIT		PRICE				
4	CHANNEL	STATE	High	Low	Mid	Grand Total	
5	Retail		111	92	111	104	
6	Wholesale	WA	287	354	167	259	
7		AZ	72	66	77	72	
8		CA	106	237	430	306	
9		NV	159	69	64	81	

9. If you don't want the label switching around on you, you can use the *Name* property to control it yourself. Type **myField.Name = "Avg Units"**, and then press the Enter key. The label changes to "Avg Units."

```
myField.Name = "Avg Units"
```

	A	B	C	D	E	F	G
1	DATE	(All)					
2							
3	Avg Units		PRICE				
4	CHANNEL	STATE	High	Low	Mid	Grand Total	
5	Retail		111	92	111	104	
6	Wholesale	WA	287	354	167	259	
7		AZ	72	66	77	72	
8		CA	106	237	430	306	
9		NV	159	69	64	81	

Tip   Once you replace the default name for the derived data field, Excel won't automatically change the name, even if you change the *Function* property. To have Excel automatically adjust the name, change the *Name* property to what the automatic name would be for the current function. For example, if the data field currently displays averages for the Units field, change the name to "Average of Units."

When you assign *xlDataField* to a field's *Orientation* property, you don't actually change the *Orientation* property for that field; rather, you create a new, derived field that has *xlDataField* as its *Orientation* property. These derived fields allow you to create multiple data fields from a single source field. Then you can set one derived data field to show sums, another derived field to show averages, and so forth.

The umbrella Data field, which exists only when the PivotTable has more than one data field, acts like an ordinary PivotField except that it can be assigned only to the row or column orientation.

Find PivotTable ranges

A PivotTable resides on a worksheet. It doesn't use ordinary worksheet formulas to perform its calculations, but it does take up worksheet cells. If you want to apply a special format to a specific part of a PivotTable, or if you want to add formulas to cells outside the PivotTable that align with cells in the PivotTable, you need to know which cells contain which parts of the PivotTable. Fortunately, all the objects relating to PivotTables have properties to help you find the cells that contain the various parts of the PivotTable.

1. In the Immediate window, type **Set myRange = myPivot.DataBody-Range**, and then press the Enter key. When you type the period after the word *myPivot*, Visual Basic displays the list of methods and properties. Several of the properties have names with the suffix *-Range*. For example, *ColumnRange*, *DataBodyRange*, *DataLabelRange*, and *PageRange*. All these properties that end in *-Range* return a range object of some kind.

2. Type **myRange.Select**, and then press the Enter key. Excel selects the range containing the body of the data, that is, the DataBodyRange.

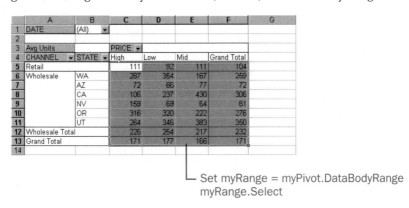

```
Set myRange = myPivot.DataBodyRange
myRange.Select
```

3. You can also go the other way: you can find a PivotTable element that resides in a particular cell in Excel. Type **Range("D4").Select**, and then press the Enter key to select cell D4.

Range("D4").Select

4. Type **Set myItem = ActiveCell.PivotItem**, and press the Enter key. The Low item from the Price field is assigned to the variable.

5. Type **myItem.DataRange.Select**, and then press the Enter key to select the data cells "owned" by the Low Price item.

Set myItem = ActiveCell.PivotItem
myItem.DataRange.Select

	A	B	C	D	E	F	G
1	DATE	(All) ▾					
2							
3	Avg Units		PRICE ▾				
4	CHANNEL ▾	STATE ▾	High	Low	Mid	Grand Total	
5	Retail		111	92	111	104	
6	Wholesale	WA	287	354	167	259	
7		AZ	72	66	77	72	
8		CA	106	237	430	306	
9		NV	159	69	64	81	
10		OR	316	320	222	276	
11		UT	264	346	383	350	
12	Wholesale Total		226	254	217	232	
13	Grand Total		171	177	166	171	
14							

When you see a property for a PivotTable object with the suffix -*Range*, you know that it returns a Range object of some kind. When you see a property for a Range object with the prefix *Pivot-*, you know that it returns an object that's in that cell.

Save your work

You've done a lot of exploring in the Immediate window. When you quit Excel, everything you've done will evaporate. You can save your explorations from the Immediate window by copying them into the MakePivot macro.

1. Press F8 to finish the macro.

2. Press Ctrl-A to select the entire contents of the Immediate window.

3. Press Ctrl-C to copy the contents of the Immediate window.

If you made the Immediate window undockable, you might want to make it dockable again now.

4. Click in the Module window, at the beginning of the *End Sub* statement. Press Ctrl-V to paste the contents of the Immediate window.

```
Sub MakePivot()
    Dim myPivot As PivotTable
    Dim myField As PivotField
    Dim myItem As PivotItem
    Dim myRange As Range
    Workbooks.Open "Orders.dbf"
Set myPivot = ActiveSheet.PivotTableWizard
Set myField = myPivot.PivotFields("Units")
myField.Orientation = xlDataField
myField.NumberFormat = "#,##0"
Set myField = myPivot.PivotFields("State")
myField.Orientation = xlRowField
```

Paste the contents
of the Immediate
window into the
macro.

5. The new lines are not indented the way proper statements in a macro should be. Click in the middle of the first line that needs indenting, scroll to the bottom, and press and hold the Shift key as you click in the middle of the last line that needs indenting. Then press the Tab key to indent them all at once.

Save button

6. Save the Chapter6 workbook by clicking the Save button in the Visual Basic Editor. Close the Orders.dbf workbook without saving changes.

7. With the insertion point anywhere in the MakePivot macro, press F8 repeatedly to repeat (and review!) everything you did in this chapter.

Note In this exploration, you assigned several different objects in turn to each of the object variables. You might find your macros easier to read if you create a unique variable with a descriptive name each time you need to assign an object to a variable.

Here, for your reference, is the entire macro that you created in this chapter:

```
Sub MakePivot()
    Dim myPivot As PivotTable
    Dim myField As PivotField
    Dim myItem As PivotItem
    Dim myRange As Range

    Workbooks.Open "Orders.dbf"
    Set myPivot = ActiveSheet.PivotTableWizard
    Set myField = myPivot.PivotFields("Units")
    myField.Orientation = xlDataField
    myField.NumberFormat = "#,##0"
    Set myField = myPivot.PivotFields("State")
    myField.Orientation = xlRowField
    myField.Orientation = xlColumnField
    myField.Orientation = xlPageField
    myField.CurrentPage = "WA"
    myField.CurrentPage = "CA"
    myField.Orientation = xlHidden
    myPivot.AddFields "Category", "State", "Channel"
    myPivot.AddFields Array("State", "Channel"), "Price", "Date"
    myField.Position = 2

    Set myItem = myField.PivotItems("WA")
    myItem.Position = 1
    myItem.Name = "Washington"
    myItem.Name = myItem.SourceName
    myItem.Visible = False
    myItem.Visible = True
    Set myItem = _
        myPivot.PivotFields("Channel").PivotItems("Retail")
    myItem.ShowDetail = False
    Set myField = myPivot.PivotFields("Net")
    myField.Orientation = xlDataField
    Set myField = myPivot.PivotFields("Data")
    myField.Orientation = xlColumnField
    Set myField = myPivot.PivotFields("Sum of Net")
    myField.Orientation = xlHidden
    Set myField = myPivot.PivotFields("Sum Of Units")
    myField.Function = xlAverage
    myField.Name = "Avg Units"
```

(continued)

```
      Set myRange = myPivot.DataBodyRange
      myRange.Select
      Range("D4").Select
      Set myItem = ActiveCell.PivotItem
      myItem.DataRange.Select
End Sub
```

This macro might not do much useful work, but now you understand how PivotTables work and how you can manipulate them using Visual Basic.

Chapter Summary

To	Do this
Create a new default PivotTable and save a pointer to it	Use the statement *Set myPivot = ActiveSheet.PivotTableWizard.*
Make a field appear in the row, column, or page areas of a PivotTable	Assign xlRowField, xlColumnField, or xlPageField to the *Orientation* property of the PivotField object.
Change the field that appears first within an area	Assign a number to the *Position* property of the PivotField object.
Change the name of a PivotField or a pivot item	Assign a new text string to the *Name* property of the object.
Restore a PivotField or pivot item to the name that appears in the database	Assign the value of the *SourceName* property to the *Name* property.
Refer to a data field that sums the value in the Units field	Use the expression *myPivot.PivotFields("Sum of Units").*
Refer to the range where the body of data from a PivotTable is located	Use the expression *myPivot.DataBodyRange.*
Refer to a PivotTable element in the active cell	Use the expression *ActiveCell.PivotItem.*

For online information about	Ask the Assistant for help using the words
Working with PivotTables	"PivotTables"
Working with PivotFields	"PivotFields"
Working with pivot items	"Pivot Items"

Preview of the Next Chapter

In the last four chapters, you've explored a variety of Excel objects. You've used Visual Basic to control Excel, but for all practical purposes, Visual Basic has done nothing but execute Excel methods and properties. In the next part of this book, you'll learn additional programming features that let you control how the Visual Basic statements run, which will make your macros even more powerful.

Review and Practice

You'll review and practice how to:

- Use a macro to create formulas.

- Use a macro to change the format of ranges.

- Use a macro to modify a PivotTable.

- Use a macro to modify a chart.

In Part 2, you learned how to work with Microsoft Excel objects, particularly PivotTables, ranges, graphical objects, and charts. Now you would like to apply what you've learned to some new tasks. Some of the steps in this review section require methods or properties that you haven't seen before. To find a new, appropriate method or property, you can use Auto Lists, Help, the Object Browser, or the macro recorder.

A completed Part2 workbook is in the Finished folder. Your macros don't need to match the sample exactly.

Add Totals to a Table

Each week, one of your associates gives you sales report information in an Excel worksheet. The tables have headings for the rows and columns, but they never have totals.

	A	B	C	D	E	F
1		High	Low	Mid		
2	Art	58866	0	75311		
3	Dinosaurs	0	36869	38455		
4	Environment	0	46605	40486		
5	Humorous	0	11026	16624		
6	Kids	0	67114	56112		
7	Seattle	26527	39359	4384		
8	Sports	14746	14839	17498		
9						

You want to create a macro that adds row and column totals to the table and formats the table to make it easier to read.

Step 1: Create a Macro That Adds Row Totals

First, create a macro that adds totals to the right side of each row.

1. Save a copy of the Tables workbook as **Part2**, and in it create a new macro named **AddTotals** with Ctrl-Shift-T as the shortcut key combination.

2. Declare two variables, one named **myTable** and one named **myTotals**, as Range objects.

3. Assign the current region around the active cell to **myTable.**

4. Assign the range that is the first column to the right of myTable to **myTotals.**

5. Assign a formula to the myTotals range that sums all the values from each row. Use the *Address* property with relative row and column references.

Tip You can assign a formula to all the rows of a range—including the place where the label will go—because your macro will later replace the formula with a label. You can include the labels within the range that the SUM formula calculates because the SUM function ignores cells containing labels.

---

6. Assign the label **Total** to the topmost cell of the myTotals range.

7. Make a copy of the Table worksheet, and test the macro. When testing, make sure the active cell is within the range of the table.

For more information about	See
Declaring variables as objects	Chapter 3, "Store objects in variables"
Selecting the current region	Chapter 2, "Select only the blank cells"
Creating formulas with a macro	Chapter 4, "Exploring Formulas"

Step 2: Extend the Macro to Add Column Totals

Next, add similar statements to the macro to create totals for each column. The easiest way to create a grand total cell that calculates the sum of the row totals is to redefine the myTable range to include the extended current region.

1. Add a blank line to the AddTotals macro. Then assign the (enlarged) current region around the active cell to myTable.

2. Assign the first row below the table to myTotals.

3. Assign a formula to the myTotals range that sums the values from each column.

4. Assign the label **Total** to the leftmost cell of the row of totals.

5. Test the macro on a copy of the Table worksheet.

Step 3: Format the Table with a Macro

Finally, add some additional formatting to the table to make it easier to read. You want the headings to be bold, and you want alternate rows of the table to be shaded light gray. For this macro, you know that the table will always contain nine rows (including the heading and totals rows).

1. Create a new macro named **FormatTable.**

2. Declare a variable named **myRange** as a Range object, and then assign the current region around the active cell to it.

3. Assign the number format "#,##0" to the entire table. Set the font of the first row of the table to Bold. Set the font of the first column of the table to Bold.

4. Set the cell shading color of the second row of the table to Light Gray. (The ColorIndex value 15 corresponds to Light Gray.)

5. Set the cell shading color of the fourth, sixth, and eighth rows of the table to Light Gray. (Make three copies of the previous statement.)

6. Test the macro on a copy of the Table worksheet.

7. Add a statement to the end of the TotalTable macro to run the FormatTable macro, and test the combined macro.

For more information about	See
Changing a number format with a macro	Chapter 1, "Creating a Simple Macro"
Changing the background color of a cell	Chapter 4, "Explore a range as a collection"
Running one macro from another	Chapter 2, "Record a macro that runs other macros"

Synchronize Two PivotTables

You have a worksheet that contains two PivotTables that share the same underlying data. Both PivotTables have Category and Date as page fields. Both reports have States down the side, but one shows the Price field for the columns and the other shows the Channel field for the columns.

	A	B	C	D	E	F	G	H	I
1	CATEGORY	(All)				CATEGORY	Seattle		
2	DATE	11/1/99				DATE	11/1/99		
3									
4	Sum of UNITS	PRICE				Sum of UNITS	CHANNEL		
5	STATE	High	Low	Mid		STATE	Retail	Wholesale	
6	AZ	185	493	626		AZ			
7	CA	570	1376	3221		CA			
8	ID					ID			
9	NV	300	360	355		NV			
10	OR	695	2990	1166		OR	130	210	
11	UT					UT			
12	WA	1454	2738	2121		WA	56	2010	
13	Grand Total	3204	7957	7489		Grand Total	186	2220	
14									

Sometimes you intentionally select different page values for the two PivotTables—for example, when you want to compare the Seattle category to All categories. But many times, you want to change the page fields on the first PivotTable and make the second PivotTable's page fields change to match. Create a macro that synchronizes the page fields of the second PivotTable with those of the first.

Step 1: Create a PivotTable Synchronization Macro

1. Activate the Pivots worksheet. To make the macro clearer, assign the name **Master** to the PivotTable on the left, and assign the name **Slave** to the PivotTable on the right. (To change the name, right-click in the PivotTable and click Table Options.)

2. Create a macro named **SynchTables** with Ctrl-Shift-S as the shortcut key combination.

3. Declare two variables, one named **myMaster** and one named **mySlave**, as PivotTable objects.

4. On the active sheet, assign the PivotTable named Master to myMaster, and assign the one named Slave to mySlave.

5. Assign the value of the current page from the first page field of myMaster to the corresponding property of mySlave.

Tip When you retrieve the value of the current page, use the expression *CurrentPage.Value*, but when you change the value of the current page, omit the *Value* property.

---

6. Do the same for the second page field of the two PivotTables.

7. Change the page field values of the PivotTable on the left, and test the macro.

For more information about	See
Modifying a PivotTable with a macro	Chapter 6, "Refining PivotTables"

Chart a Row from a PivotTable

You have a PivotTable and want to be able to chart any single row from the table.

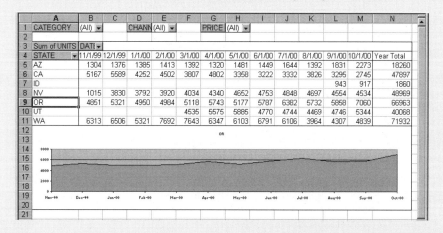

The trickiest part of this task is creating a chart that plots only one row. When you create a chart that refers to a PivotTable, Excel automatically converts it into a PivotChart report, which not only plots all the visible rows, but also puts the row labels from the PivotTable across the bottom of the chart.

Step 1: Set Up the Chart

First, create a chart that displays a single row from the PivotTable. If you create a blank chart, you can add data from a single row of the PivotTable to the chart. You can create the chart interactively; you don't need a macro.

1. Activate the Chart worksheet. Click anywhere outside the PivotTable, and click the ChartWizard button. Select Area as the Chart Type, and then click Finish to create a blank chart.

2. Position the chart over the range A12:N20. (Press and hold the Alt key as you drag a sizing handle to snap the corners to the grid.)

3. Select the range A8:M8 (the data for Nevada, not including the total column), and drag the border of the selection onto the chart.

4. Select the range B4:M4 (the date headings), and drag the border of the selection onto the chart.

5. Delete the legend from the chart.

Now you have an ordinary chart that refers to a single row from the PivotTable.

Step 2: Make a Macro Point the Chart at the Active Cell

Next, create a macro that makes the chart plot whichever state has the active cell. First, give a name to the chart to make it easier to reference from the macro.

1. Give the chart container the name **RowChart**. (Click off the chart, and then press and hold the Ctrl key as you click the chart to select the container object.)

2. Create a macro named **ChartRow**, and assign the shortcut key combination Ctrl-Shift-C.

3. Declare two variables, **mySeries** (declared as a Series object) and **myItem** (declared as a PivotItem object).

4. Assign the first series of the chart to the *mySeries* variable. (Remember to specify the Chart object to get from the chart container object to the actual chart object.)

5. From the PivotTable, assign the item associated with the active cell to the *myItem* variable.

6. Assign the data range of the item as the value of the chart's series.

7. Assign the label range of the item as the name of the chart's series.

8. Select the item for various states, and press the shortcut key combination to test the macro.

For more information about	See
Manipulating a chart from a macro	Chapter 5, "Record a macro that modifies chart attributes"
Finding the range associated with a PivotTable object	Chapter 6, "Find PivotTable ranges"

Step 3: Make the Macro Work from Any Cell on a Row

If you select any cell other than a cell from the first column, the macro will fail. You can make the macro easier to use by letting the active cell be any cell on the same row as the state you want.

1. Change the statement in the ChartRow macro that assigns an object to the *myItem* variable so that it now gets the item from the first cell in the row that contains the active cell.

2. Test the macro again, this time selecting any cell from a row.

The macro still requires that you select a row within the PivotTable, but you don't have to worry about staying in the first column.

For more information about	See
Finding an entire row from a macro	Chapter 4, "Explore a range as a collection"

Part 3

Exploring
Visual Basic

Chapter 7

Controlling Visual Basic

Estimated time: 30 minutes

In this chapter, you'll learn how to:

- Use conditional statements.

- Create loops using three different structures.

- Retrieve the names of files in a folder.

- Create breakpoints to debug long loops.

- Show progress while a macro executes a loop.

Walk outside and stand in front of your car. Look down at the tread on the right front tire. See that little piece of gum stuck to the tread? Well, imagine you're that little piece of gum. Imagine what it feels like when the car first starts to move. You climb up, higher and higher, as if you were on a Ferris wheel. Then you experience the pure thrill as you come back down the other side. (Who needs Disneyland, anyway?) But don't you think that by the five millionth revolution, you might start to get a little bored? Thwack, thwack, thwack, thwack. It really could get old after a while.

Just about anything you do is interesting—the first few times you do it. Repetition, however, can bring boredom. When you start doing the same task over and over, you start wanting somebody—or something—else to take it off your hands. This chapter will teach you how to record a repetitive task as a macro and then turn it into a little machine that works relentlessly to improve your life.

Start the lesson

1. Start Microsoft Excel, and change to the folder containing the practice files for this book.

2. Open the Flow workbook, and save a copy as **Chapter7**.

For more information about installing the practice files, see the Introduction to this book.

Using Conditionals

Recorded macros are, to put it bluntly, dumb. They can repeat what you did when you recorded the macro, but they can't behave differently in different circumstances. They can't make decisions. The only way that you can make your macros "smart" is to add the decision-making ability yourself.

Make a decision

The Chapter7 workbook contains a macro named MoveRight. The MoveRight macro looks like this:

```
Sub MoveRight()
    ActiveCell.Offset(0, 1).Select
End Sub
```

This macro simply selects the cell to the right of the active cell. It has the keyboard shortcut Ctrl-Shift-R assigned to it. This macro works fine—most of the time.

1. With cell A1 selected, press Ctrl-Shift-R. The macro selects cell B1.

2. Press Ctrl-Right Arrow to select cell IV1, the rightmost cell on the first row, and press Ctrl-Shift-R. Microsoft Visual Basic displays an error.

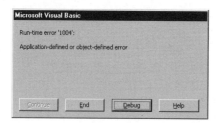

You can't select the cell to the right of the rightmost cell. An ugly error message appears. You'd rather have your macro simply do nothing if it can't move to the right.

3. Click the Debug button to jump to the code, and then click the Reset button to stop the macro.

Reset button

4. Insert the statement **If ActiveCell.Column < 256 Then** after the *Sub* statement, indent the main statement, and insert the statement **End If** before the *End Sub* statement. The revised macro should look like this:

```
Sub MoveRight()
    If ActiveCell.Column < 256 Then
        ActiveCell.Offset(0, 1) .Select
    End If
End Sub
```

An *If* statement (a statement that begins with the word *If*) pairs with an *End If* statement. The group of statements from the *If* to the *End If* are called, collectively, an *If structure*.

Visual Basic looks at the expression immediately after the word *If* and determines whether it's true or false. This true-or-false expression is called a *conditional expression*. If the expression is true, then in a simple *If* structure such as this example, Visual Basic executes all the statements between the *If* statement and the *End If* statement. If the expression is false, Visual Basic jumps directly to the *End If* statement. You must always put the word *Then* at the end of the *If* statement.

5. Switch back to Excel, select cell IS1, and then press Ctrl-Shift-R four or five times. The macro moves the active cell to the right until it gets to the last cell. After that it does nothing, precisely according to your instructions.

You can make your macro smart enough to avoid an error.

You can't use the macro recorder to create an *If* structure. This kind of decision is pure Visual Basic and you must add it yourself. Fortunately, adding an *If* structure is easy.

6. Figure out a question with a "yes or no" answer. In this example, the question is, "Is the column of the active cell less than 256?" You can then turn this question into the true-or-false conditional expression in an *If* statement.

7. Put the word *If* in front of the conditional expression, and put the word *Then* after it.

8. Figure out how many statements you want to execute if the conditional expression returns a *True* value.

9. Put an *End If* statement after the last statement that you want controlled by the *If* structure.

Using *If* structures makes your macro smart.

Make a double decision

Sometimes—such as when you're preventing an error—you want your macro to execute only if the conditional expression is true. Other times, you want the macro simply to behave differently depending on the answer to the question.

For example, suppose that you want a macro that moves the active cell to the right, but only within the first five columns of the worksheet. When the active cell gets to the fifth column, you want it to move back to the first cell of the next line, like a typewriter. In this case, you want the macro to carry out one action if the cell column is less than five (move to the right) and a different action if it isn't (move down and back). You can make the macro choose between two options by adding a second part to the *If* structure:

1. Switch to the Visual Basic Editor, and change the number 256 to **5** in the *If* statement.

2. Add the statement **Else** before the *End If* statement, and press the Enter key. Then press the Tab key and add the statement **Cells(ActiveCell. Row+1,1).Select** after the *Else* statement. The revised macro should look like this:

```
Sub MoveRight()
    If ActiveCell.Column < 5 Then
        ActiveCell.Offset(0, 1).Select
    Else
        Cells(ActiveCell.Row + 1, 1).Select
    End If
End Sub
```

The *Else* statement simply tells Visual Basic which statement(s) to execute if the conditional expression is false.

3. Press F5 repeatedly to execute the macro. You see it move to the right and then scroll back to column A, much as a typewriter would do.

After you move here...
...the macro moves here.

If structures can contain a single part, executing statements only when the conditional expression is true, or they can have two or more parts, executing one set of statements when the conditional expression is true and a different set when it's false.

Note *If* structures can also become much more complex than either of these two alternatives. Ask the Office Assistant for information using the words "if then" to find out more about *If* structures.

Ask yourself a question

In Chapter 2, you created a macro that asked you to enter a date. You used Visual Basic's *InputBox* function to do that. The *InputBox* function is excellent for asking a question, but you must be careful about what happens when you click the Cancel button.

The Chapter7 workbook contains a macro named TestInput that prompts for the date. The code in this macro should look familiar:

```
Sub TestInput()
    Dim myDate As String
    myDate = InputBox("Enter Month in MMM-YYYY format")
    MsgBox "Continue the macro"
End Sub
```

The macro prompts for a date. It then displays a simple message box indicating that it's running the rest of the macro.

1. Click in the TestInput macro. Press F5 to run the macro, type **Nov-2000** for the date, and then click OK. The message box appears, simulating the rest of the macro.

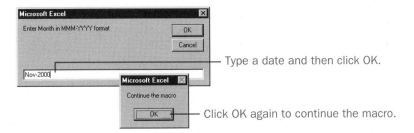

Type a date and then click OK.

Click OK again to continue the macro.

2. Click OK to close the message box.

3. Press F5 to run the macro again, but this time click Cancel when prompted to enter the date. The message box still appears, even though your normal expectation when you click Cancel is that you'll, uh, cancel what you started.

4. Click OK to close the message box. You need a question to which the answer is "yes" if you want the macro to continue. An appropriate question is, "Did you enter anything in the box?" Clicking Cancel is the same as leaving the box empty. In either case, the *InputBox* function returns an empty string (equivalent to two quotation marks with nothing between them). The operator <> (a less than sign followed by a greater than sign) means "not equal"; it's the opposite of an equal sign.

5. Before the *MsgBox* statement, enter the statement **If myDate <> ""** **Then**. Before the *End Sub* statement, enter **End If**. Indent the statement inside the *If* structure. The revised macro should look like this:

```
Sub TestInput()
    Dim myDate As String
    myDate = InputBox("Enter Month in MMM-YY format")
    If myDate <> "" Then
        MsgBox "Continue the macro"
    End If
End Sub
```

6. Press F5 to run the macro. Type a date, and click OK. The macro "continues."

7. Click OK to close the message box.

8. Now run the macro again, but this time click Cancel when prompted for a date. The macro stops quietly.

9. Run it again, but this time type **hippopotamus** in the input box and click OK. The macro continues, just as if you had entered a date.

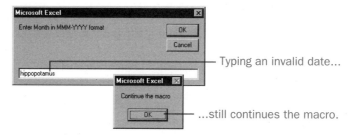

Typing an invalid date...

...still continues the macro.

10. Click OK to close the message box. This could be a problem. You need to check for whether the box is empty, but you also need to check for a valid date. Visual Basic has an *IsDate* function that will tell you whether Visual Basic can interpret a value as a date. However, you want to check for a date only if the user didn't click Cancel. This calls for super-duper, special-deluxe, *nested If* structures.

11. Change the macro to look like this:

```
Sub TestInput()
    Dim myDate As String
    myDate = InputBox("Enter Month in MMM-YY format")
    If myDate <> "" Then
        If IsDate(myDate) Then
            MsgBox "Continue the macro"
        Else
            MsgBox "You didn't enter a date"
        End If
    End If
End Sub
```

Be sure to indent each statement in such a way as to make it clear which statement is governed by which *If* or *Else* statement. Visual Basic doesn't require proper indentation, but indentation is critical to help you (or someone following after you) interpret the macro the same way that Visual Basic does.

Try different date formats, such as 11/00, to see which formats Visual Basic interprets as a date.

12. Run the macro at least three times. Test it with a valid date, an invalid entry, and by clicking Cancel. The valid and invalid entries should display the appropriate messages. Clicking Cancel or leaving the box empty should display no message.

Using the *InputBox* function can be a valuable way of making a macro useful across a wide range of circumstances. You must be careful, however, to check the result of the *InputBox* before you continue the macro. Typically, you need to check for three possibilities: valid input, invalid input, and Cancel. An *If* structure—and sometimes a nested *If* structure—can make your macro smart enough to respond to all the possible options.

Visual Basic's *MsgBox* function is handy for displaying simple messages. As its name implies, this function displays a message box. The *MsgBox* function can do much more than that, however. It can ask questions, too. Many times, when a macro needs to ask a question, all it needs is a simple yes-or-no answer. The *MsgBox* function is perfect for yes-or-no answers.

Suppose that you have two macros. One is a long, slow macro named PrintMonth, and the other is a short, quick macro named ProcessMonth. You find that you often accidentally run the slow one when you meant to run the quick one. One solution might be to add a message box to the beginning of the slow macro that asks you to confirm that you really did intend to run the slow one.

The Chapter7 workbook includes a macro named CheckRun. You'll enhance this macro to see how to use a *MsgBox* function to ask a question. The macro looks like this before you start:

```
Sub CheckRun()
    MsgBox "This takes a long time. Continue?"
    MsgBox "Continue slow macro..."
End Sub
```

1. Click in the CheckRun macro, and press F5 to run it. Click OK twice to close each of the message boxes. The first message box appears to ask a question, but it has only a single button. To ask a question, you must add more buttons.

The original macro displays two message boxes.

2. Move the cursor to the end of the first *MsgBox* statement. Immediately after the closing quotation marks, type a comma. As soon as you type the comma, Visual Basic displays the Quick Info for the *MsgBox* function. The first argument is named *Prompt*. That's the one where you enter the message you want to display. The second argument is named *Buttons*. This is an enumerated list of values. The default value for Buttons is *vbOKOnly*, which is why you saw only a single OK button when you ran the macro before.

The *Buttons* argument allows you to specify which buttons to display.

Along with the Quick Info box, Visual Basic also displays the Auto List of possible values for the *Buttons* argument. You want the buttons to ask the question in terms of yes or no.

3. Scroll nearly to the bottom of the list, select vbYesNo, and then press the Tab key.

4. Press F5 to run the macro. The first message box now has two buttons.

The message box asks a question, but it totally ignores your answer. You need to get the answer from the *MsgBox* function and then use that answer to control the way the macro runs.

5. Click Yes, and then click OK to close both message boxes. Then type the statement **Dim myCheck As VbMsgBoxResult** at the beginning of the macro. When you know a variable will contain only the value from an enumerated list, you can use the name of the list when you declare the variable. When you later test the value of the variable, Visual Basic will display the list of possible values for you.

6. At the beginning of the first *MsgBox* statement, type **myCheck =** , and then put parentheses around the argument list of the *MsgBox* function. The revised statement should look like this:

```
myCheck = MsgBox("This takes a long time. Continue?",vbYesNo)
```

Important When you use the return value of a function such as *MsgBox*, you must put parentheses around the argument list. When you don't use the return value, you must not use parentheses.

---

7. Insert these three statements before the second *MsgBox* statement:

```
If myCheck = vbNo Then
    Exit Sub
End If
```

When you create a conditional expression using the result of the *MsgBox* function, you must not check for True or False. *MsgBox* has many different types of buttons it can display, so it has many different types of answers. If you use vbYesNo as the Buttons type, *MsgBox* will always return either vbYes or vbNo.

The *Exit Sub* statement causes Visual Basic to stop the current macro immediately. To avoid making your macros hard to understand, you should use *Exit Sub* sparingly. One good use for *Exit Sub* is when you cancel the macro right at the beginning, as in this case.

8. Test the macro. Run it and click Yes, and then run it and click No. Make sure the rest of the macro runs only when you click Yes.

A message box is a powerful tool for asking simple questions. Be very careful to compare the answer to the correct constant rather than to True or False. Declaring a variable with the name of the enumerated list makes it easy to choose the correct constant. The *MsgBox* function is also a good example of when and when not to use parentheses around argument lists: use the parentheses if you use the return value of the function, and don't if you don't.

Creating Loops

In his classic book *The Wealth of Nations*, economist Adam Smith asked how much it would cost to make a single straight pin compared with how much it would cost to make 10,000 straight pins. The cost of one pin is almost as great as the cost of all 10,000 pins. Similarly, writing a macro that runs once is almost as much work as writing a macro that runs thousands of times in a loop.

Loop through a collection using a For Each loop

Excel allows you to protect a worksheet so that nobody can change anything in any cells that aren't specifically unlocked. You must, however, protect each sheet individually. Suppose that you have a workbook containing budgets for ten different departments and that you want to protect all the worksheets.

The Chapter7 workbook includes a macro named ProtectSheets. Here's what it looks like:

```
Sub ProtectSheets()
    Dim mySheet As Worksheet
    Set mySheet = Worksheets(1)
    mySheet.Select
    mySheet.Protect "Password", True, True, True
End Sub
```

This macro assigns a reference to the first worksheet to the *mySheet* variable, selects that sheet, and then protects it. (Selecting the sheet really isn't necessary, but it makes it easier to see what the macro is doing.) Now see how you can convert this macro to protect all the worksheets in the workbook.

1. Click in the ProtectSheets macro, and press F8 repeatedly to step through the macro. Make sure you understand everything that the original macro does.

2. In the third line, replace *Set* with **For Each**, replace the equal sign with **in**, and remove the parentheses and the number between them.

3. Indent the next two statements, add a line break at the end of the second one, and then type the statement **Next mySheet**. The revised macro should look like this:

```
Sub ProtectSheets()
    Dim mySheet As Worksheet
    For Each mySheet In Worksheets
        mySheet.Select
        mySheet.Protect "Password", True, True, True
    Next mySheet
End Sub
```

For Each acts just like *Set*. It assigns an object reference to a variable. But instead of assigning a single object to the variable, it assigns each object from a collection to the variable. Then, for each (get it?) object in the collection, Visual Basic executes all the statements down to the *Next* statement. Statements beginning with *For Each* and ending with *Next* are called *For Each structures* or *For Each loops*. (Technically, you don't need to put the variable name after *Next*. If you do use it, Visual Basic requires that it match the variable name after *For Each*. Always using a variable after *Next* can help you keep the right *Next* with the right *For*.)

4. Press F8 repeatedly to step through the macro, watching as it works on each worksheet in turn.

5. Switch to Excel, and try typing a value into a cell on any worksheet. (Close the error message box.)

6. Create a new macro named **UnprotectSheets** that unprotects all the worksheets. (Hint: You'll need to use the *Unprotect* method of the worksheet object, with a single argument that gives the password.) Here's what your macro should look like:

```
Sub UnprotectSheets()
    Dim mySheet As Worksheet
    For Each mySheet In Worksheets
        mySheet.Select 'This statement is optional
        mySheet.Unprotect "Password"
    Next mySheet
End Sub
```

7. Save the workbook, press F5 to test the UnprotectSheets macro, and try changing a value on a worksheet.

Looping through a collection is as easy as assigning a single value to an object. Just replace *Set* with *For Each*, specify the collection, and add a *Next* statement.

Tip A *For Each* loop is a handy way of browsing collections in the Immediate window. However, in the Immediate window, everything you type must be on a single line. You can put multiple statements on a single line by separating the statements with colons. For example, here's what you'd type in the Immediate window to see the names of all the Worksheets in the active workbook: **For Each x in Worksheets: ?x.Name: Next x**. (In the Immediate window, it's all right to use short, meaningless names for variables.)

Loop with a counter using a For loop

Sometimes you want to do actions repeatedly but can't use a *For Each* loop. For example, *For Each* loops only act on a single collection. If you want to compare two parallel collections—such as two ranges—you can't use a *For Each* loop. In that situation, Visual Basic has another, more generalized way to loop: a *For loop*.

The Compare worksheet in the Chapter7 workbook contains two named ranges. The one on the left is named Old, and the one on the right is named New. You can think of these as being an original forecast and a revised forecast. The cells in the Old range contain values. The cells in the New range contain a formula that will calculate a random number each time you press F9 to recalculate the workbook. (The formula is =ROUND(RAND()*50+100,0), which tells Excel to calculate a random number between 0 and 1, multiply it by 50, add 100, and round to the nearest whole number.)

Because these numbers are randomly generated, the numbers you see will be different from the ones shown here.

	A	B	C	D	E	F	G	H
1								
2	Old				New			
3	143	116	110		116	140	133	
4	133	136	114		140	133	108	
5	123	113	120		147	146	112	
6	103	148	129		148	119	115	
7								

The New numbers are random sample numbers.

The Chapter7 module in the Visual Basic Editor contains a macro named CompareCells, which looks like this:

```
Sub CompareCells()
    Dim i As Integer
    Calculate
    i = Range("New").Cells.Count
    If Range("New").Cells(i) > Range("Old").Cells(i) Then
        Range("New").Cells(i).Interior.Color = vbYellow
    Else
        Range("New").Cells(i).Interior.Color = vbCyan
    End If
End Sub
```

The macro first executes the *Calculate* method, which is like pressing the F9 function key. It calculates new values for all the cells in the New range. Then the macro compares only the last cell in the New range with the last cell in the Old range. If the New value is greater than the Old, it turns yellow; otherwise, it turns blue. The macro assigns the Count of cells in the range to the variable *i*. The macro uses that number several times, and *i* requires less typing than *Range("New").Cells.Count*.

If you're not comfortable with any of the Range methods and properties, review Chapter 4. If you're not comfortable with If structures, review the first half of this chapter.

Now see how you can convert this macro to compare all the cells at once.

1. Click in the CompareCells macro, and press F8 repeatedly to step through the macro. Make sure you understand everything the original macro does.

	A	B	C	D	E	F	G	H
1								
2	Old				New			
3	143	116	110		116	140	133	
4	133	136	114		140	133	108	
5	123	113	120		147	146	112	
6	103	148	129		148	119	115	
7								

The original macro compares the last cell of each range and flags the difference with a color change.

2. In the statement that assigns the Count to the variable, insert the word **For** in front of the variable, and then insert **1 To** after the equal sign.

3. Type **Next i** before the *End Sub* statement, and indent all the statements between *For* and *Next*. The revised macro should look like this:

```
Sub CompareCells()
    Dim i As Integer
    Calculate
    For i = 1 To Range("New").Cells.Count
        If Range("New").Cells(i) > Range("Old").Cells(i) Then
            Range("New").Cells(i).Interior.Color = vbYellow
        Else
            Range("New").Cells(i).Interior.Color = vbCyan
        End If
    Next i
End Sub
```

The keyword *For* works just like a simple assignment statement. It assigns a number to the variable. (The *For* keyword assigns a number to a variable, and *For Each* assigns an object reference to a variable.) The variable that gets assigned the number is called a *loop counter*. You specify the first value *For* should assign (in this case, 1) and the last value it should assign (in this case, the number of cells in the range).

Each time *For* assigns a number to the loop counter, Visual Basic executes all the statements down to the *Next* statement. Then *For* adds 1 to the loop counter and executes all the statements again, until the loop counter is greater than the value you specified as the last value.

4. Press F8 repeatedly to watch the macro work. Step through at least two or three loops, and then press F5 to finish the macro.

	A	B	C	D	E	F	G	H
1								
2	Old				New			
3	143	116	110		108	119	147	
4	133	136	114		120	103	113	
5	123	113	120		119	124	117	
6	103	148	129		132	118	125	
7								

A *For* loop allows you to loop through two collections at once.

In many cases, using a *For Each* loop is more convenient than using a *For* loop. However, a *For* loop is a more general tool in that you can always use a *For* loop to reproduce the behavior of a *For Each* loop. For example, here's how you could write the ProtectSheets macro without using *For Each*:

```
Sub ProtectSheets()
    Dim mySheet As Worksheet
    Dim i as Integer
    For i = 1 to Worksheets.Count
        Set mySheet = Worksheets(i)
        mySheet.Select
        mySheet.Protect "Password", True, True, True
    Next i
End Sub
```

If you were going to be marooned on a desert island and could take only one of these two looping structures with you, you'd probably be better off choosing *For*. Fortunately, however, you don't have to make the choice. In the many cases where *For Each* loops can work, use them happily. In cases where you need a counter, use *For* loops.

Loop indefinitely using a Do loop

A *For Each* loop works through a collection. A *For* loop cycles through numbers from a starting point to an ending point. In some situations, however, neither of these options works. For example, Visual Basic has a function that tells you the names of files in a folder. The function is named *Dir*, after the old MS-DOS operating system command of the same name. The first time you use *Dir*, you give it an argument that tells which kind of files you want to look at. To retrieve the name of one Excel workbook, you use the statement *myFile=Dir("*.xls")*. To get additional files that match the same pattern, you use *Dir* without any arguments. You must run *Dir* repeatedly because it returns only one file name at a time. When Visual Basic can't find any more matching files, the *Dir* function returns an empty string.

Suppose that you want to create a macro that retrieves the names of all the Excel files in the current folder. The list of files in the directory isn't a collection, so you can't use a *For Each* loop. You can't use a *For* loop either because you don't know how many files you'll get until you're finished. Fortunately, Visual Basic has one more way of controlling a loop: a *Do loop*.

The ListFiles macro in the Chapter7 workbook retrieves the first two Excel files from the current directory and puts their names into the first two cells in the first column of the active worksheet. Here's the original macro:

```
Sub ListFiles()
    Dim myRow As Integer
    Dim myFile As String

    myRow = 1
    myFile = Dir("*.xls")
    Cells(myRow, 1) = myFile

    myRow = myRow + 1
    myFile = Dir
    Cells(myRow, 1) = myFile
End Sub
```

Aside from the variable declaration statements, this macro consists of two groups of three statements. In each group, the macro assigns a row number to *myRow*, retrieves a file name using the *Dir* function, and then puts the file name into the appropriate cell. The first time the macro uses *Dir*, it specifies the pattern to match. The next time, the macro simply uses *Dir* without an argument to retrieve the next matching file.

Now see how you can convert this macro to loop until it has found all the files in the folder.

The names of the files your macro retrieves might differ from these.

1. In the Chapter7 workbook, activate the Files worksheet. From the File menu, click Open, change to the folder containing the practice files for the book, and then click Cancel. Doing this ensures that the current folder contains Excel workbooks.

2. In the Visual Basic Editor, click in the ListFiles macro and press F8 repeatedly to step through the macro. Make sure you understand the original macro.

The original macro retrieves two file names.

Tip As you step through the macro, move the mouse pointer over a variable name to see the current value stored in that variable.

---

3. Type **Do Until myFile = ""** on a new line after the first statement that contains a *Dir* function.

4. Type **Loop** on a new line after the second statement that contains a *Dir* function, and then delete the second *Cells(myRow, 1) = myFile* statement.

5. Indent the three statements between the *Do* and the *Loop* statements. The revised macro should look like this:

```
Sub ListFiles()
    Dim myRow As Integer
    Dim myFile As String

    myRow = 1
    myFile = Dir("*.xls")
    Do Until myFile = ""
        Cells(myRow, 1) = myFile

        myRow = myRow + 1
        myFile = Dir
    Loop
End Sub
```

The phrase after *Do Until* is a conditional expression, precisely like one you'd use with an *If* structure. The conditional expression must be something that Visual Basic can interpret as either True or False. Visual Basic simply repeats the loop over and over until the conditional expression is True.

If you want to increment a number during the loop, you must enter a statement to do so. You must always be careful to cause something to happen during the loop that will allow the loop to end. In this case, you retrieve a new file name from the *Dir* function.

6. Press F8 repeatedly to watch the macro work. Step through at least two or three loops, and then press F5 to finish the macro.

—— A *Do* loop allows you to loop as many times as necessary.

A *Do* loop is very flexible, but it's also a little bit dangerous because you have to be sure you provide a way for the loop to end. For example, if you forgot to add the statement to retrieve a new file name, or if you had included the argument to the *Dir* function inside the loop (so that *Dir* would keep returning the first file name over and over), you'd have what is called an *infinite loop*.

If you run a macro that contains an infinite loop, stop the macro by pressing Ctrl-Break. (The Break key often functions the same as the Pause key.)

Note *Do* loop structures have several useful variations. You can loop *until* the conditional expression is true or *while* the expression is true. You can put the conditional expression at the top of the loop or at the bottom of the loop. To find out more about *Do* loop structures, ask the Office Assistant for information using the words "do loop."

Managing Large Loops

A loop that executes only two or three times isn't much different from a program without a loop. It runs fast, and it's easy to step through to watch how each statement works. Once you start repeating a loop hundreds or thousands of times, however, you need some additional techniques to make sure the macro works the way you want it to.

Set a breakpoint

The Chapter7 workbook includes a macro named PrintOrders. You can think of this macro as one that your predecessor wrote just before leaving the company. Or you can think of it as one that you almost finished three months ago. In either event, you have a macro that you don't understand and that doesn't work quite right.

The PrintOrders macro is supposed to print a copy of the entire Orders database, but sorted by product Category. You give each Category manager the section of the report that shows only orders for that one category, so you need a new page every time the Category changes. Unfortunately, the macro doesn't do what it's supposed to. You need to find and fix the problem. Here's the macro as you first receive it:

```
Sub PrintOrders()
    Dim myRow As Long
    Dim myStop As Long
    Workbooks.Open FileName:="orders.dbf"
    Columns("E:E").Cut
    Columns("A:A").Insert Shift:=xlToRight
    Range("A1").CurrentRegion.Sort Key1:="Category", _
        Order1:=xlAscending, Header:=xlYes
    myStop = Range("A1").CurrentRegion.Rows.Count
    For myRow = 3 To myStop
        If Cells(myRow, 1) <> Cells(myRow + 1, 1) Then
            Cells(myRow, 1).Select
            ActiveCell.PageBreak = xlPageBreakManual
        End If
    Next myRow
    Cells(myRow, 1).Select
    ActiveSheet.PageSetup.PrintTitleRows = "$1:$1"
    ActiveSheet.PrintPreview
    ActiveWorkbook.Close SaveChanges:=False
End Sub
```

Probably the best approach is to start stepping through the macro.

Open button

1. Make sure the current folder is the one containing the practice files for this book. (From the File menu, click the Open button, change to the correct folder, and then click Cancel.)

2. In the Visual Basic Editor, click in the PrintOrders macro, and then press F8 three times to jump over the variable declarations and open the database. (The two variables are declared as *Long*, which means that they can hold whole numbers but aren't limited to the four-digit numbers of type Integer.)

	A	B	C	D	E	F	G	H
1	DATE	STATE	CHANNEL	PRICE	CATEGORY	UNITS	NET	
2	11/1/97	WA	Wholesale	High	Seattle	40	110.00	
3	11/1/97	WA	Wholesale	High	Art	25	68.75	
4	11/1/97	WA	Retail	High	Art	3	16.50	
5	11/1/97	WA	Retail	Low	Environment	50	175.00	

In the original database, the Category field is in Column E.

3. Press F8 three more times. These statements move the Category field over to column A and then sort the list by Category.

	A	B	C	D	E	F	G	H
1	CATEGORY	DATE	STATE	CHANNEL	PRICE	UNITS	NET	
2	Art	11/1/97	WA	Wholesale	High	25	68.75	
3	Art	11/1/97	WA	Retail	High	3	16.50	
4	Art	11/1/97	WA	Wholesale	Mid	30	67.50	
5	Art	11/1/97	WA	Retail	Mid	20	90.00	

The macro moves the Category field to column A and sorts the database by Category.

4. Press F8 twice to assign a number to *myStop* and to start the loop. Hold the mouse pointer over *myStop* and then over *myRow* to see the values that were assigned. The value of *myStop* is 3300, and the value of *myRow* is 3. Those values appear to be correct. The loop will execute from row 3 to row 3300.

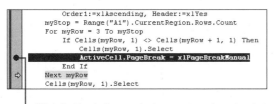

The Data Tip box shows the value of the variable.

5. Press F8 several times. Visual Basic keeps checking for whether the cell in the current row matches the cell below it. How many rows are in the Art category? Pressing F8 repeatedly until the macro finds the last row in the category could take a very long time. But if you just press F5 to run the rest of the macro, you can't watch what happens when the condition in the *If* statement is true. If only there were a way to skip over all the statements until the macro moves into the inside of the *If* structure…

6. Click in the gray area to the left of the statement starting with *ActiveCell*. A dark red circle appears in the margin, and the background of the statement changes to dark red. This is a *breakpoint*. When you set a breakpoint, the macro starts stepping just before it would execute the breakpoint statement.

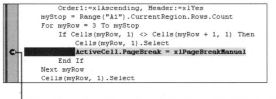

Click in the left margin to create a breakpoint.

7. Press F5 to continue the macro. The macro stops at the breakpoint. The active cell is the first one that the *If* statement determined is different from the cell below it.

Visual Basic stops when it reaches the breakpoint.

8. Press F8 to execute the statement that assigns a manual page break.

```
        Order1:=xlAscending, Header:=xlYes
    myStop = Range("A1").CurrentRegion.Rows.Count
    For myRow = 3 To myStop
        If Cells(myRow, 1) <> Cells(myRow - 1, 1) Then
            Cells(myRow, 1).Select
            ActiveCell.PageBreak = xlPageBreakManual
        End If
    Next myRow
    Cells(myRow, 1).Select
```

Press F8 to execute the statement containing the breakpoint.

The page break appears above the row, not below the row. This is a problem. The macro shouldn't set the page break on the *last* cell of a Category; rather, it should set the break on the *first* cell of a Category. The *If* statement should check to see whether the cell is different from the one *above* it.

9. Change the plus sign (+) in the *If* statement to a minus sign (–). The revised statement should look like this:

```
If Cells(myRow, 1) <> Cells(myRow - 1, 1) Then
```

10. Press F5 and F8 to watch the macro work—properly this time—as it assigns page breaks to the next couple of Categories.

Setting a breakpoint is an invaluable tool for finding a problem in the middle of a long loop. Read on to learn an exceptionally easy way to set a temporary breakpoint if you need to use it only once.

Set a temporary breakpoint

Suppose you're now stepping through the middle of the PrintOrders macro. The code to assign a page break seems to be working properly. There are still some statements at the end of the macro, however, that you'd like to step through.

1. Click the red circle in the margin to turn off the breakpoint.

2. Click anywhere in the *Cells(myRow,1).Select* statement after the end of the loop. You want a breakpoint on this statement, but one that you need to use only once.

```
    For myRow = 3 To myStop
        If Cells(myRow, 1) <> Cells(myRow - 1, 1) Then
            Cells(myRow, 1).Select
            ActiveCell.PageBreak = xlPageBreakManual
        End If
    Next myRow
    Cells(myRow, 1).Select
    ActiveSheet.PageSetup.PrintTitleRows = "$1:$1"
```

Click in the statement where you want a temporary breakpoint.

3. From the Debug menu, click the Run To Cursor command.

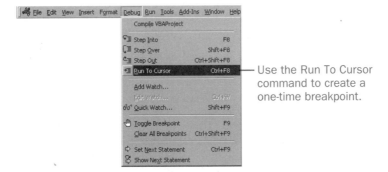

Use the Run To Cursor command to create a one-time breakpoint.

4. Press F8 three times to scroll to the bottom of the list, set the print titles, and preview the report.

5. Review the report. The end of the Art category should have come on page 11, but there's an extra page break because of the original error in the macro.

6. Close Print Preview, and press F8 twice more to finish the macro.

7. Save the Chapter7 workbook.

Turning off a breakpoint is just as easy as turning one on: just click in the left margin of the Visual Basic Editor window. But if turning a breakpoint on and off is still too much work, you can create a temporary one by running to the cursor.

Show progress in a loop

Even if the loop in a macro is working perfectly, you might get nervous about whether something has gone wrong if the macro takes a long time to execute. The best way to feel comfortable when a long loop is running (particularly if you're wondering whether you have time to go get a cup of coffee) is to show the progress in the loop.

You can show progress with any kind of loop. But a *For* loop lends itself particularly well to showing progress because at any point in the loop your macro can determine the current value of the loop counter and also what its final value will be.

1. In the PrintOrders macro, immediately following the *For* statement, insert this statement:

```
Application.StatusBar = "Processing row " & myRow & " of " &
myStop
```

The status bar is the gray strip at the bottom of the Excel window that usually says "Ready." The *StatusBar* property of the Application object allows you to make the status bar say whatever you want. The best message is one that shows progress and also gives you an idea of how long the task will take.

The statement above creates this message when it enters the loop the first time: "Processing row 3 of 4012." By using an ampersand (&) to join together message text with the numbers in the *myRow* and *myStop* variables, you can create a useful message. Just be careful to include an extra space before and after the numbers.

2. Press F5 to run the macro. Watch the status bar to see how the macro is progressing.

— The status bar shows progress.

3. Close the Print Preview screen to let the macro finish. The status bar indicates that the macro is still running. The status bar doesn't automatically reset when your macro ends. To return control of the status bar to Excel, you must assign the value *False* to it.

4. After the *Next* statement, insert the statement:

```
Application.StatusBar = False
```

5. Run the macro again, close the Print Preview screen at the appropriate time, and then look at the status bar. It's back to normal.

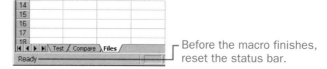
Before the macro finishes, reset the status bar.

6. Save the Chapter7 workbook.

Visual Basic provides extremely powerful tools for repeating statements in a loop. Coupled with the decisions that you can make using *If* structures, these tools let you create macros that are smart and very powerful.

Chapter Summary

To	Do this
Execute statements only if a condition is true	Insert the statements between an *If* statement and an *End If* statement.
Execute a first group of statements if a condition is true, and a second group of statements if a condition is false	Insert the first group of statements between an *If* statement and an *Else* statement, and the second group of statements between the *Else* statement and an *End If* statement.
Execute statements for each item in a collection	Insert the statements between a *For Each* statement and a *Next* statement.
Execute statements a specific number of times	Insert the statements between a *For* statement and a *Next* statement.
Execute statements until a condition becomes true	Insert statements between a *Do* statement and a *Loop* statement.
Stop a macro while it's running	Press Ctrl-Break.
Turn a breakpoint on or off	Click in the gray margin to the left of a statement in the Visual Basic Editor.
Display a message in the status bar	Assign a string to the *Application.StatusBar* property.
Restore the default message to the status bar	Assign *False* to the *Application.StatusBar* property.

For online information about	Ask the Office Assistant for help using the words
Using conditionals	"If Then"
Using *For Each* loops	"For Each"
Using *For* loops	"For Next"
Using *Do* loops	"Do Loop"
Conditional expressions	"Comparison operators"
Breakpoints and other debugging tools	"Breakpoints" or "Debugging"

Preview of the Next Chapter

So far, all the macros you've created in this book have been simple stand-alone procedures. In the next chapter, you'll learn how to create a whole new kind of macro: specialized ones that you can use in worksheet formulas or as extensions to Visual Basic's built-in capabilities.

Chapter 8

Extending Excel and Visual Basic

| Chapter Objectives | Estimated time: 30 minutes |

In this chapter, you'll learn how to:

- Create and use custom functions.

- Handle errors that occur while a macro is running.

Single-cell organisms are all small. Bacteria, amoebas, paramecia—none are even large enough to see with the naked eye. Still, they work fine. Large, sophisticated organisms, however, require multiple cells. Cells give structure and add specialization to living things.

Recorded macros are like single-cell organisms. The macro recorder puts everything you do into a single procedure. And, like single-cell organisms, single-procedure macros should be small. Large, sophisticated applications work best when you break them up into smaller procedures. And just as large, complex organisms need an immune system to deal with diseases, sophisticated applications need a mechanism for dealing with error conditions. In this chapter, you'll learn how to create custom functions, use arguments in procedures, and handle errors—tools you'll need to make more powerful applications.

| Start the lesson |

1. Start Microsoft Excel, and change to the folder containing the practice files for this book.

2. Open the Function workbook, and save a copy as **Chapter8.**

For more information about installing the practice files, see the Introduction to this book.

Creating Custom Functions

Once you assign a value to a variable, you can use that value in any expression. For example, after you assign the number 25 to the variable *myAge*, the value of the conditional expression *myAge > 20* would be *True*. You can use the variable as if it were the value that it contains.

A function is like a variable, except that a function is smarter. A function is a variable that figures out its own value whenever you use it. For example, Microsoft Visual Basic has a function named *Time*. When you use the conditional expression *Time > #8:00 PM#*, the *Time* function checks the time on your computer's clock at the time you use the expression.

Visual Basic has many built-in functions. Excel also has many built-in functions. Those functions are useful, but they aren't customizable. Even if you find a Visual Basic function that's "this close" to what you need, you can't worm your way into the innards of Visual Basic to change the way it works. You can, however, create a function of your own. Because your function can take advantage of any of the Excel or Visual Basic built-in functions, and because you can customize your function however you want, you get the same benefit you would get if you could tweak the built-in functions directly.

Use a custom function from a worksheet

Both Excel and Visual Basic have functions that return a random number between 0 and 1. Excel's function is named RAND(), and Visual Basic's function is named *Rnd*. You can use Excel's function in a worksheet cell, but you can use Visual Basic's function only in a macro.

You can't customize the Visual Basic *Rnd* function or the Excel RAND() function, but you *can* create a custom random-number function—let's call it *Random*—that you can use from Excel. Why would you want to create your own random-number function when you could use the built-in one for free? Because you want your *Random* function to behave just a little differently from the built-in one. Once you create your own function, you can make it do whatever you want.

1. Open the Function workbook, and save it with the name **Chapter8.**

2. Enter the formula =**Random()** into cell A12 on the TestFunction sheet. Excel displays the *#NAME?* error value because the *Random* function doesn't exist yet.

Using a function before it exists produces the *#NAME?* error.

3. Click the Run Macro button, type **Random** in the Macro Name box, and then click Create.

4. Double-click the word *Sub* at the beginning of the macro, and replace it with **Function**. The *End Sub* statement changes to *End Function*. You've now created a function. Next you need to tell Excel what to use as the value of the function.

To create a function, replace *Sub* with **Function** in a macro.

```
Function Random()

End Function
```

5. Type the statement **Random = Rnd** as the body of the function. The revised function should look like this:

```
Function Random()
    Random = Rnd
End Function
```

The way you tell a function what value to return is by assigning a value to the name of the function, as if the function name were a variable. This function simply takes the value of Visual Basic's *Rnd* function and assigns it to the *Random* function.

6. Switch back to Excel, select cell A12, and then click the Edit Formula button next to the formula bar. Excel displays the Formula Editor, which explains that the *Random* function doesn't take any arguments. Click OK to enter the random number into cell A12.

Edit Formula button

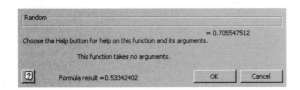

That's all there is to creating a simple worksheet function. In the Visual Basic Editor, you replace the word *Sub* with *Function*, and then somewhere in the function, you assign a value to the function name. In Excel, you put the function name into a formula, followed by parentheses.

Add arguments to a custom function

Suppose that you want random whole numbers equal to 100, plus or minus 25. Or that you want random whole numbers equal to 1000, plus or minus 100. Excel's RAND() function can't give you that kind of random number. Neither, for that matter, can yours, but because yours is a custom function, you can add additional capabilities to it by adding arguments.

To specify the random-number ranges mentioned above, you need three arguments: one to specify the midpoint, one to specify the plus or minus range, and one to specify whether or not to round the final number. You can add those arguments to your function.

1. In the Visual Basic Editor, type **Midpoint, Range, Round** between the parentheses after the name of the function. The statement that contains the function name and its arguments is called the *function declaration* statement. In this statement, you declare the name of the function and also the names of all the arguments. The revised function declaration statement should look like this:

```
Function Random(Midpoint, Range, Round)
```

These three words are arguments to the function. You can use them inside the function as variables that have been prefilled with values.

2. Change the statement that assigns a value to the function name to this:

```
Random = Rnd * (Range * 2) + (Midpoint - Range)
```

The *Rnd* function returns a random number between 0 and 1. If *Range* is equal to 25, that means that you want numbers from 25 below the midpoint to 25 above the midpoint, for a total range of 50. Multiplying *Rnd* by *Range* * 2 would then give you a random number between 0 and 50. If the target midpoint is 100, you need to add 75 (that is, 100 – 25), to the random number. That's what this statement does.

3. Insert these three statements to round the number if necessary:

```
If Round Then
    Random = CLng(Random)
End If
```

In Visual Basic, a *Long* is a whole number that can include large numbers. The Visual Basic function *CLng* converts a number to a *Long*, rounding it along the way. You round the random number only if the value of the *Round* argument is *True*. (Because the value of the *Round* argument already equals *True* or *False*, you don't need to compare it to anything to get a conditional expression.)

To see other functions that convert between data types, click CLng and press F1.

4. In Excel, enter **100** into cell B12, **25** into cell C12, and **TRUE** into cell D12. You'll use these values for the *Midpoint*, *Range*, and *Random* arguments of your function.

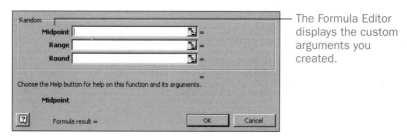

These cells control how the random number is calculated.

Edit Formula button

5. Select cell A12, and click the Edit Formula button next to the formula bar. The Formula Editor box appears, showing you the three new arguments of your function.

The Formula Editor displays the custom arguments you created.

6. Click in the Midpoint box, and then click in cell B12. Click in the Range box, and then click in cell C12. Click in the Random box, and then click in cell D12. Then click OK.

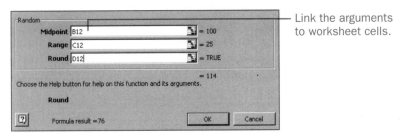

Link the arguments to worksheet cells.

Cell A12 contains a random number between 75 and 125. You use arguments to pass values to a function.

7. Change cell B12 to **1000** and cell C12 to **100**. The value of cell A12 changes to a random number between 900 and 1100. Whenever you change the value of a cell that the function refers to, the function calculates a new answer. Adding arguments is a way to make functions more flexible.

The function uses these values...

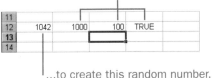

...to create this random number.

Make a function volatile

Most functions recalculate only when the value of a cell that feeds into the function changes. Other functions (such as Excel's RAND() function), called *volatile functions*, recalculate whenever any cell on the worksheet changes or whenever you press F9. You can make your function volatile; it then calculates a new random number whenever you press F9.

1. In Excel, press F9 repeatedly to see that the random number in cell A12 doesn't change.

2. In the Visual Basic Editor, insert this statement after the statement containing the name of the function:

```
Application.Volatile True
```

3. Switch back to Excel, and press F9. The random number in cell A12 changes. Press F9 several times to verify that the function generates random numbers in the appropriate range.

Most of the time, you don't want custom functions to be volatile. You want the function to recalculate only when a value that feeds into it changes. For those few cases in which you do want the formula to recalculate, just use the Application object's *Volatile* method with *True* as an argument.

Make arguments optional

The only problem with your new enhanced *Random* function is that it's now more complicated to use in those simple cases in which you don't need the new arguments. If you put *=Random()* into a cell, omitting the arguments, Excel displays the *#VALUE!* error message. To avoid this error message, you can tell Visual Basic that you want the arguments to be optional. Then you specify default values to use if the argument isn't supplied.

1. In the Visual Basic Editor, type the word **Optional** in front of each of the three argument names. The revised statement should look like this:

```
Function Random(Optional Midpoint, Optional Range,
    Optional Round)
```

You don't have to make all the arguments optional, but once you make one argument optional, all the arguments that follow it must be optional as well. In other words, you place optional arguments at the end of the argument list.

2. Type **= 0.5** after the word *Midpoint*, **= 0.5** after the word *Range*, and **= False** after the word *Round*. Break the statement into two lines after the first comma. The resulting statement should look like this:

```
Function Random(Optional Midpoint = 0.5, __
    Optional Range = 0.5, Optional Round = False)
```

You can specify a default value for any optional argument. You assign the default value to the argument name in the same way you would assign a value to a variable—by using a simple equal sign.

3. In Excel, enter **=Random()** into cell A13. A random number between 0 and 1 appears.

Optional arguments allow you to add powerful features to a function while keeping it easy to use in those cases in which you don't need the extra features. To make an argument optional, add *Optional* before the argument name. To add a default value for an optional argument, assign the value to the argument name the same way you would if it were a variable.

Use a custom function from a macro

You can use a custom function from a macro just as easily as you can use it from a worksheet cell.

1. In the Visual Basic Editor, at the bottom of the module, type **Sub TestRandom** and then press the Enter key to start creating a macro.

2. Type **MsgBox** and a space. Visual Basic shows the Quick Info box with the arguments for *MsgBox*.

3. Press Ctrl-Spacebar to show the list of global methods and properties, and then press R to scroll down to the words that begin with an R.

Your custom function appears as a method in the list of global methods and properties.

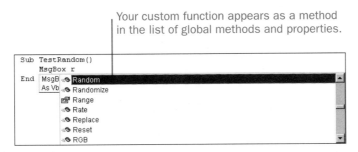

Your *Random* function is automatically included in the list. Your function has the icon for a method next to it. Excel methods are simply functions that are built into Excel. You create new global methods simply by writing new functions.

4. Press the Tab key to insert the function name into the statement, and then type an opening parenthesis to begin the argument list. Visual Basic displays the Quick Info box with the arguments for your custom function. The Quick Info box even shows the default values for the optional arguments.

The Quick Info box shows the custom arguments, along with their default values.

5. Type **200, 5, True** as the list of arguments, and then type a closing parenthesis.

6. Press F5 to run the macro. Click OK when your random number appears.

You can run a custom function from a macro.

A function is a procedure like a *Sub* procedure, except that it returns a value that you can use either in a cell in Excel or from a macro.

Note A function used in a worksheet cell can include only those actions that can be executed while Excel is recalculating a worksheet. (Remember that some cells might even recalculate more than once.) Actions such as opening files or displaying message boxes can be included in functions that are called from macros, but if you include them in a function that's called from a worksheet, the function simply returns the #VALUE! error value.

Handling Errors

Believe it or not, computer programs don't always work perfectly. Every now and then, you might actually write a macro that doesn't quite do what you want. These errors come in several different types:

- **Syntax errors** These are mistakes such as using an opening quotation mark and leaving off the closing quotation mark. When you type a statement into a procedure, the Visual Basic Editor checks the statement for syntax errors as soon as you leave the statement.

- **Compiler errors** Some mistakes can't be detected on a single-line basis. For example, you might start a *For Each* loop but forget to put a *Next* statement at the end. The first time you try to run a procedure, Visual Basic translates that procedure (along with all the other procedures in the module) into internal computer language. Translating to computer language is called *compiling*, and errors that Visual Basic detects while translating are called *compiler errors*. Syntax errors and compiler errors are usually easy to find and fix.

Tip   Visual Basic can check for spelling errors when you use variables. From Visual Basic's Tools menu, select the Options command and then select the Require Variable Declarations check box. After you do this, Visual Basic adds the statement *Option Explicit* to any new module that you create. When *Option Explicit* appears at the top of a module, Visual Basic displays a compiler error any time you use a variable that you didn't explicitly declare.

- **Logic errors** The computer can never detect some mistakes. For example, if you mean to change a workbook caption to "My Workbook," but you accidentally spell the caption "My Werkbook," the computer will never complain. Or if you compare the new values with the wrong copy of the old values, the computer won't find the error for you. You can toggle breakpoints, step through the procedures, and watch values, but you still have to find the problem on your own.

- **Run-time errors** Sometimes a statement in a procedure works under some conditions but fails under others. For example, you might have a statement that deletes a file on your hard disk. As long as the file exists and can be deleted, the statement works. If, however, the file doesn't exist, Visual Basic doesn't know what else to do but quit with an error message. These errors can't be detected until you run the procedure, so they're called *run-time* errors. Some run-time errors indicate problems. Other run-time errors are situations that you can anticipate and program Visual Basic to deal with automatically. Visual Basic has tools that can help you deal with any kind of run-time error.

Ignore an error

Suppose you want to create a macro that creates a temporary report worksheet. The macro gives the name Report to the report worksheet and replaces any existing Report worksheet in the active workbook. The Chapter8 workbook contains a macro named MakeReport that creates and names the Report worksheet. Here's the original macro:

```
Sub MakeReport()
    Dim mySheet As Worksheet
    Set mySheet = Worksheets.Add
    mySheet.Name = "Report"
End Sub
```

The macro adds a worksheet, assigning a reference to the new worksheet to the *mySheet* variable. It then changes the *Name* property of the sheet.

1. In the Visual Basic Editor, click in the white space at the bottom of the module, and press F5 to display the Macros dialog box. Select the MakeReport macro, and click Edit. Then press F5 to run it. You should see a new worksheet named Report in the active workbook. The macro works fine. Or at least it seems to work fine. What happens if you run the macro again?

 The macro creates a new worksheet.

2. Press F5 again to run the macro a second time. Visual Basic displays an error message informing you that you can't rename a sheet to the name of an existing sheet. The solution is simple: all you have to do is delete the old Report sheet before you rename the new one.

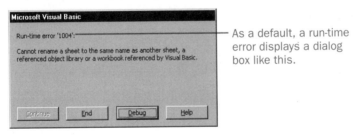 As a default, a run-time error displays a dialog box like this.

3. Click the End button to remove the error message, and then insert these two statements before the one that renames the worksheet:

```
Application.DisplayAlerts = False
Worksheets("Report").Delete
```

Turning off alert messages keeps Excel from asking if you really want to delete the sheet.

4. Press F8 repeatedly to step through the macro. You might see the macro step through the *Random* function because a volatile function often recalculates when you rename the worksheet. The macro creates a new worksheet, deletes the old Report worksheet, and then renames the new worksheet. Once again, the macro works fine. Or at least it seems to work fine. What happens if there's no Report worksheet in the workbook?

5. Switch to Excel, delete the Report worksheet, switch back to the Visual Basic Editor, and press F5 to run the macro. Once again, you get an error message, this time informing you that the subscript is out of range. In other words, there's no item named Report in the Worksheets collection.

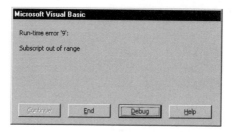

The interesting thing about this error is that you really don't care. You were just going to delete the worksheet anyway. If it already doesn't exist, so much the better.

6. Click the End button to clear the error message, and insert this statement above the one that deletes the worksheet:

```
On Error Resume Next
```

This statement tells Visual Basic to ignore any run-time errors and simply continue with the next statement.

7. Press F5 to test the macro. Test it again now that the Report worksheet exists.

Finally, the macro seems to work properly. Some errors deserve to be ignored.

Ignore an error safely

When you use an *On Error Resume Next* statement, Visual Basic ignores all run-time errors until you turn error checking back on or until Visual Basic gets to an *End Sub* or *End Function* statement. When you tell Visual Basic to ignore errors, you should be careful that you don't ignore errors you didn't mean to ignore.

If the statement Option Explicit appears at the top of the module, delete it.

1. In the MakeReport macro you created in the previous section, remove the quotation marks from around the word "*Report*" in the statement that gives the worksheet a new name. Removing these quotation marks creates a run-time error. The revised, erroneous statement should now look like this:

```
mySheet.Name = Report
```

2. Press F5 to test the macro.

The macro should have named the sheet *Report*.

The macro appeared to run just fine, but you don't have a Report worksheet when you're done. Visual Basic interpreted the word *Report*, without the quotation marks, as a new (empty) variable and was unable to assign that empty name to the worksheet. Unfortunately, because you told Visual Basic to ignore errors, it didn't even warn you of a problem. (Of course, if you had inserted *Option Explicit* at the top of the module, Visual Basic would have complained about using an undefined variable.)

The best way to ignore errors for just one or two statements is to put the statements into a *Sub* procedure of their own. When Visual Basic gets to an *End Sub* or *End Function* statement, it cancels the effect of the *On Error Resume Next* statement.

3. Create a new *Sub* procedure named DeleteSheet. This procedure quietly deletes the Report worksheet if it exists.

4. Move the three statements that delete the worksheet into the DeleteSheet macro. The new macro should look like this:

```
Sub DeleteSheet()
    Application.DisplayAlerts = False
    On Error Resume Next
    Worksheets("Report").Delete
End Sub
```

The *On Error Resume Next* statement loses its effect at the *End Sub* statement, so you just ignore a possible error in the single *Delete* statement. This is a much safer way to ignore a run-time error.

5. In the MakeReport macro, type **DeleteSheet** where the three statements had been. The revised MakeReport macro (still containing the error) should look like this:

```
Sub MakeReport()
    Dim mySheet As Worksheet
    Set mySheet = Worksheets.Add
    DeleteSheet
    mySheet.Name = Report
End Sub
```

The MakeReport macro no longer contains an *On Error Resume Next* statement, so Visual Basic should be able to alert you to the error.

6. Press F5 to run the macro, click the End button to close the error box, replace the quotation marks around the sheet name in the last line of the MakeReport macro, and test the macro when the report file exists as well as when it doesn't.

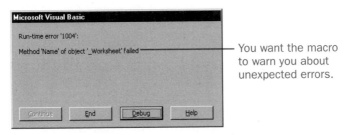

You want the macro to warn you about unexpected errors.

This time, the macro really does work well. It ignores the error you want to ignore and warns you of other, inadvertent errors.

Generalize the DeleteSheet routine

The DeleteSheet macro you created in the previous section quietly deletes the Report worksheet if it happens to exist. Unfortunately, it deletes only the Report worksheet. What if you sometimes need to delete a sheet named Report and other times need to delete a sheet named Analysis? This DeleteSheet procedure has too much potential to limit it to deleting only one specific sheet. You can add an argument to generalize the *DeleteSheet* routine, in much the same way that you added an argument to the *Random* function earlier in this chapter.

1. Type **SheetName** as an argument name between the parentheses after the DeleteSheet macro name.

2. Replace *"Report"* with **SheetName** in the body of the DeleteSheet macro. *SheetName* shouldn't have quotation marks around it.

3. Type **"Report"** after *DeleteSheet* in the MakeReport macro. Here's what the two revised macros should look like:

```
Sub MakeReport()
    Dim mySheet As Worksheet
    Set mySheet = Worksheets.Add
    DeleteSheet "Report"
    mySheet.Name = "Report"
End Sub

Sub DeleteSheet(SheetName)
    Application.DisplayAlerts = False
    On Error Resume Next
    Worksheets(SheetName).Delete
End Sub
```

The DeleteSheet macro now knows absolutely nothing about the name of the sheet it will delete. It will simply delete whatever sheet it's given, without asking any questions and without complaining if it discovers its services aren't really needed.

4. Press F5 to test the MakeReport macro.

5. Make a new macro named MakeAnalysis. Make it an exact copy of the MakeReport macro, except have it create a sheet named Analysis. The macro should look like this:

```
Sub MakeAnalysis()
    Dim mySheet As Worksheet
    Set mySheet = Worksheets.Add
    DeleteSheet "Analysis"
    mySheet.Name = "Analysis"
End Sub
```

6. Test the MakeAnalysis macro.

Generalize a sub procedure to work with any worksheet.

The DeleteSheet macro now not only avoids the inconveniences associated with deleting a worksheet but is also a generalized tool—an enhancement to Excel's built-in capabilities—that you can use from any macro you want.

Check for an error

When you use the *On Error Resume Next* statement in a macro, Visual Basic allows you to do more than merely ignore the error. Visual Basic contains a special debugging object named Err. The Err object has properties that you can check to see whether an error has occurred and, if so, what the error is.

Suppose that you want to create a Report worksheet, but without deleting any existing Report sheets. Rather, you want to put a suffix on the worksheet name, much as Excel does when you add a new worksheet. The Chapter8 workbook includes a macro named MakeNextReport. This macro creates a sheet named Report1 or, if that already exists, a sheet named Report2. Here's the original MakeNextReport macro:

```
Sub MakeNextReport()
    Dim mySheet As Worksheet
    Dim myBase As String
    Dim mySuffix As Integer

    Set mySheet = Worksheets.Add
    myBase = "Report"
    mySuffix = 1

    On Error Resume Next
    mySheet.Name = myBase & mySuffix
    If Err.Number <> 0 Then
        mySuffix = mySuffix + 1
        mySheet.Name = myBase & mySuffix
    End If
End Sub
```

This macro creates a new worksheet and then tries to name it using *Report* as the base name and *1* as the suffix. The *On Error Resume Next* statement tells Visual Basic not to stop if Excel is unable to rename the sheet. The *If* statement, however, checks to see whether the Err object's *Number* property is equal to 0. Zero as an error number means that there was no error. If an error occurred, the macro increases the suffix to *2* and tries again.

1. Go to the MakeNextReport macro, and then press F8 repeatedly to watch the macro work. Once again, Visual Basic might step through the *Random* function as the worksheet recalculates. The new worksheet should rename properly the first time, so the macro never has to increment the suffix.

The macro adds a suffix to the worksheet name.

2. Step through the macro a second time, and then run it a third time. The second time, the macro does have to increment the suffix number, and the third time it simply fails, leaving the new sheet with the wrong name. The *Number* property of the Err object is the key to knowing whether an error has occurred.

Sometimes you need to check for more than one error.

It would be nice if this macro were smart enough to keep incrementing the suffix until it finds one that works. That sounds like a job for a loop structure, and since you can't know when the loop begins or how many times you'll have to repeat the loop, you'll need to use a *Do* loop.

3. Replace the word *If* with **Do Until,** remove the word *Then* at the end of the statement, and change the not-equal sign (<>) to an equal sign (=). Then change *End If* to **Loop**. The last few lines of the macro should look like this:

```
On Error Resume Next
mySheet.Name = myBase & mySuffix
Do Until Err.Number = 0
    mySuffix = mySuffix + 1
    mySheet.Name = myBase & mySuffix
Loop
```

The loop should check to see whether the rename occurred successfully. If not, it increments the suffix, tries the rename again, and checks again until there's no error.

4. Press F8 repeatedly to step through the macro. The first time the macro tries to name the report sheet, it fails, because Report1 already exists, so the macro proceeds into the loop. At the end of the loop, the macro tries to rename the sheet again but fails again because Report2 already exists, so the macro reenters the loop a second time. At the end of the loop, the macro tries a third time to rename the sheet. This time the sheet renames properly.

5. Keep stepping through the macro. Something's wrong. The macro goes into the loop again, renaming the sheet as Report4 and then as Report5. This renaming could go on forever.

The macro didn't stop when
it created a valid name.

The macro doesn't realize that the error is over. The *Err.Number* value didn't automatically change back to 0 just because the macro successfully renamed the worksheet. You need to tell the macro that the error is no longer relevant.

6. Click the Reset button to stop the macro. Then, on the line immediately following the *Do* statement, type the statement **Err.Clear**. *Clear* is the name of a method for the Err object. It resets the error number to 0 and makes Visual Basic forget that an error ever occurred.

Important   Some macro statements change the *Err.Number* value back to 0 when they complete successfully. Others don't. To be safe, you should clear the Err object before a statement that you want to check and then inspect the value of *Err.Number* immediately after that statement executes.

---

7. Press F5 to test the macro. Test it again. And again. The macro is now able to create a new report sheet, incrementing as much as necessary—but no more!

Reset button

The macro works once
it clears the old error.

It's meaningful to check the value of *Err.Number* only after you use an *On Error Resume Next* statement; otherwise, Visual Basic would have halted with an error message box. Looking at the properties of the Err object is a good way to gain control over the way your macro handles errors.

Trap an error

So far, you've seen three ways to handle a run-time error: you can let Visual Basic display the error dialog box, you can ignore the error altogether, or you can check for a nonzero error number after each statement.

Having Visual Basic display an error message might not be a bad alternative if you're writing macros for yourself, but if you want to give a macro to someone else, you probably want more control over what the error message says. Checking for a nonzero error value after every statement, however, can make your macros hard to read. Fortunately, Visual Basic can monitor the error value for you in a process called *trapping* an error.

Suppose, for example, that you had a macro that opens, prints, and closes several workbooks. It's possible that one of the workbooks might be missing when the macro runs. The Chapter8 workbook contains a macro named CheckFiles that opens and closes several of the practice workbooks that came with the book. (In the interest of conserving trees, the macro doesn't actually print the workbooks.)

One of the workbook file names has been misspelled. Here's the original macro:

```
Sub CheckFiles()
    Workbooks.Open "Graphics"
    ActiveWorkbook.Close
    Workbooks.Open "Ranges"
    ActiveWorkbook.Close
    Workbooks.Open "Bad File Name"
    ActiveWorkbook.Close
    Workbooks.Open "Budget"
    ActiveWorkbook.Close
End Sub
```

Naturally, you can't tell which of the files won't be found until the macro actually runs. If you run this macro, you'll see Visual Basic's standard error message. If necessary, click the End button to close the dialog box.

Here are the steps you follow to add special code that Visual Basic will run whenever an error occurs.

1. At the end of the macro, type the statement **ErrorHandler:** just before the *End Sub* statement. The statement *ErrorHandler:* is called a *label*. A label consists of a single word followed by a colon. (You can indent the label if you want, but you might prefer to keep it lined up with the *Sub* and *End Sub* statements because it behaves like an appendix to the macro.) A label must always end with a colon.

Note   You can use any name you want for a label within the macro. You might want to always use the same name, such as ErrorHandler, as the error label in all your macros. That makes it easy to copy error handling code from one macro to another.

---

2. After the error label, type the statement **MsgBox Err.Number**. The statements below the label are the ones that the macro executes when it detects an error. These statements are called an *error handler*. The simplest error handler is a message box that displays the number of the error.

3. Immediately before the error label, type the statement **Exit Sub**. You don't want the statements in the error handler to execute if the macro completes normally. If the macro gets to the *Exit Sub* statement, no error was detected.

4. At the top of the macro, just under the *Sub* statement, type the statement **On Error GoTo ErrorHandler**. This statement tells Visual Basic that if it sees a run-time error, it should drop whatever it's doing and jump immediately to the label you specify. You don't put a colon after the label name here. You use a colon only when you create the actual label.

5. Press F5 to test the macro. Visual Basic should display a simple message box showing only the message number. You can make the message more elaborate. The Err object has a *Description* property that gives a longer text description of the error. That description is often a useful addition to an error message box.

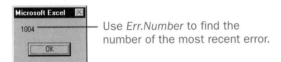 Use *Err.Number* to find the number of the most recent error.

6. Click OK. Delete the statement *MsgBox Err.Number,* and replace it with this statement:

```
MsgBox "Please notify Reed Jacobson with this error number: " & _
"Error Number: " & Err.Number & _
vbCrLf & vbCrLf & Err.Description
```

You can string many pieces together to form an error message. Just put an ampersand between each piece. The word *vbCrLf* is a built-in Visual Basic constant that means "Carriage Return Line Feed," which programmers often called a CRLF. A Carriage Return Line Feed is a computer term for a new line. You can put vbCrLf into a string anytime you want to force the message to go to a new line. (When you create your own macros, I'd be most grateful if you'd substitute your own name for mine in the error message. Thanks.)

7. Press F5 to run the macro and see the more elaborate error message.

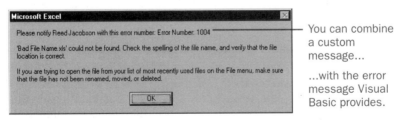 You can combine a custom message...

...with the error message Visual Basic provides.

The finished macro should look like this:

```
Sub CheckFiles()
    On Error GoTo ErrorHandler
    Workbooks.Open "Graphics"
    ActiveWorkbook.Close
    Workbooks.Open "Ranges"
    ActiveWorkbook.Close
    Workbooks.Open "Bad File Name"
    ActiveWorkbook.Close
    Workbooks.Open "Budget"
    ActiveWorkbook.Close
    Exit Sub
ErrorHandler:
    MsgBox "Please notify Reed Jacobson with this error
        number: " & _
    "Error Number: " & Err.Number & _
    vbCrLf & vbCrLf & Err.Description
End Sub
```

If you're creating an application for someone else to use and you don't want that person ever to see Visual Basic's default error dialog box, you should always include an error handler in every macro that the user launches directly. If you have some statements where the error should be handled differently—either ignored or checked on a statement-by-statement basis—put those statements into a separate procedure and use an *On Error Resume Next* statement within that procedure. Visual Basic automatically restores the error handler when the procedure ends.

Errors are a frustrating, but inevitable, part of life when working with computers—that's especially the case when the human error factor compounds the likelihood of other types of errors Of course, not all errors are equal. Some are serious, some are trivial, and some are even useful. It's fortunate that Visual Basic provides flexible tools for dealing with all kinds of errors.

Chapter Summary

To	Do this
Create a custom function	Replace the word *Sub* at the beginning of a macro with the word *Function*.
Determine the return value for a function	Create a statement inside the function that assigns a value to the function name.
Add arguments to a function	Put names for the arguments inside the parentheses following the function name, and then use the arguments as if they were prefilled variables.

To	Do this
Make a custom function recalculate each time the worksheet recalculates	Use *Application.Volatile True* at the beginning of the function.
Make an argument optional	Use *Optional* in front of the argument name in the function declaration statement.
Create a default value for an optional argument	Assign a value to the argument name in the function declaration statement.
Ignore a run-time error	Use *On Error Resume Next* before the statement that might have an error.
Ignore an error for only certain statements	Create a separate *Sub* procedure or function that contains the statements with the error you want to ignore, and put an *On Error Resume Next* statement in that procedure.
Check to see if an error has occurred in a macro that uses an *On Error Resume Next* statement	Look for a nonzero value in the *Number* property of the Err object.
Reset the Err object when an error has occurred	Use the statement *Err.Clear* after the statement with the error.
Make the macro jump to the label *ErrorHandler:* when a run-time error occurs	Use the statement *On Error GoTo ErrorHandler* at the top of the macro.

For online information about	Ask the Assistant for help using the words
Creating a function procedure	"Writing a function procedure"
Using arguments	"Arguments"
Handling errors	"Handling errors"

Preview of the Next Chapter

So far, you've launched macros by clicking the Run Macro button on the Visual Basic toolbar, pressing a shortcut key, or pressing F5 in the Visual Basic Editor. In the next chapter, you'll learn how to launch macros using events—the key to creating macros that are easy to use.

Part 3

Review and Practice

Review and Practice Objectives   Estimated time: 30 minutes

You'll review and practice how to:

- Create a function and use it from both a worksheet and a macro.

- Simplify recorded macros.

- Use various loops.

- Use conditional tests.

- Input a value when a macro runs.

In Part 3, you learned how to control a macro using Microsoft Visual Basic tools.

A completed Part3 workbook is in the Finished folder. Your macros don't need to match the sample exactly.

Display the Full File Name

Your company has a standard requirement that all printed documents display the full path name of the document file. Since you store documents in a variety of folders—both on your hard drive and on the network—you wish that Microsoft Excel had a way to display the full file name on a worksheet. Now that you know how to create custom functions, you can fulfill that wish.

Step 1: Create a Function That Returns the Full File Name

First, create a function that you can use from a worksheet.

1. Open the List workbook in the folder where you installed the practice files for this book.

2. Save a copy of the List workbook as Part3, and in it create a new function named **FullName**.

3. Assign the full name of the active workbook to the *FullName* function.

4. In cell H1 of the List worksheet, create a formula that displays and tests the *FullName* function.

For more information about	See
Creating a function	Chapter 8, "Creating Custom Functions"
Using a custom function from a worksheet	Chapter 8, "Use a custom function from a worksheet"

Step 2: Put the Full File Name in the Page Footer

After using your *FullName* function for a while, you decide that you need the file name on every page of a document, but you don't want it cluttering up the worksheet—you need it only when the worksheet prints. You can't put a custom function into a page footer, but you can create a macro that adds the full file name to the page footer.

1. Record a macro named **FooterPath**. While the recorder is running, enter **Hello** as the left page footer for the active sheet. Then turn off the recorder.

2. Edit the FooterPath macro. Delete everything that doesn't directly involve assigning a value to the left footer. Remove any unnecessary *With* structures.

3. Make the FooterPath macro assign the value of the *FullName* function as the left footer in place of the word "Hello."

4. Run the macro, and display the page in page preview mode to see whether the footer is correct.

For more information about	See
Using a function from a macro	Chapter 8, "Use a custom function from a macro"
Simplify a recorded macro	Chapter 1, "Eliminate unnecessary lines from the macro"

Create Selective Totals from a List

You have a worksheet that shows the orders by state and month for the current year. You want to do some analysis to see how much of the total comes from peak months. You want to be able to see quickly the total of all states that sold more than 4000 units in one month. You want to see a running total just of the rows that match your criteria, and then a grand total at the top of the worksheet where it's easy to see.

	A	B	C	D	E
1	DATE	STATE	Units	201,976	
2	1/1/00	AZ	1,385		
3	1/1/00	CA	4,252	4,252	
4	1/1/00	NV	3,792		
5	1/1/00	OR	4,950	9,202	
6	1/1/00	WA	5,321	14,523	

Step 1: Create a Macro to Count Units

First, create a macro that adds a running total to rows with more than 4000 units worth of sales.

1. Activate the List worksheet, and then create a macro named **TotalRows**. Declare the variables **myUnits** and **myCell** as Range objects, and declare the variable **mySum** as a Double.

2. Assign *myUnits* to be the third column of the current region that surrounds cell A1.

3. Create a loop that assigns each cell in turn from the myUnits range to the *myCell* variable. (Use the Cells collection of the myUnits range to loop through each cell of the range.)

4. Inside the loop, test to see whether the value of *myCell* can be interpreted as a number. (Use the *IsNumeric* function.)

5. For those cells that are numeric, test to see whether the value of *myCell* is greater than 4000.

6. For those cells that contain values greater than 4000, add the value from the cell to the existing value of the *mySum* variable, and put the current cumulative total into the next cell to the right.

7. After the loop checks each cell in the list, assign the total to the cell to the right of the Units label. (Your macro might complete this task differently than does the one in the Finished workbook.)

8. Test the macro. Manually clear column D of the worksheet, step through the macro, and assign breakpoints as necessary until the macro works correctly.

For more information about	See
Referring to a column from a range	Chapter 4, "Explore calculated ranges"
Looping through each item in a collection	Chapter 7, "Loop through a collection using a For Each loop"
Executing statements only if a condition is true	Chapter 7, "Using Conditionals"
Referring to a cell adjacent to a range	Chapter 4, "Explore calculated ranges"

Step 2: Generalize the Macro to Use Any Limit

After using the TotalRows macro for a while, you like it so much that you decide to make it work for any arbitrary limit. Make these changes to the TotalRows macro.

1. Declare two new variables: **myInput** as a String, and **myLimit** as a Double.

2. Before the loop begins, clear the range one column to the right so that you can run the macro multiple times.

3. Prompt for a lower limit value, assigning the input value to the *myInput* variable.

4. Test the *myInput* variable to see whether the user canceled, and exit the macro if so.

5. Test the *myInput* variable to see whether it can be interpreted as a number, and exit the macro if it can't. (Use the keyword *Not* to change a value from False to True.)

6. Assign the value of *myInput* to *myLimit* to convert it from a string to a number.

7. Replace the constant 4000 in the loop with the variable *myLimit*.

8. Test the macro with various limit values (including canceling and entering text).

For more information about	See
Prompting for a value	Chapter 7, "Ask yourself a question"
Exiting a macro based on user input	Chapter 7, "Ask with a message"
Converting a value from False to True	Chapter 1, "Toggle the value of a property with a macro"

Step 3: Prompt Until a Valid Value Is Entered

As you use the enhanced TotalRows macro, you find that you often inadvertently type text into the box. Rather than have the macro simply end when you do so, you'd like to have it keep prompting you for a limit until you either enter a valid number or click Cancel (or leave the input box blank).

1. Put a *Do* loop around the statements that request input, and test for whether the user canceled.

2. Test for whether the value of *myInput* is numeric at the end of the *Do* loop. (You can choose to make the loop repeat either *until* the value is numeric, or *while* it isn't numeric.)

3. Delete the (now redundant) test that terminates the macro if *myInput* isn't numeric.

For more information about	See
Using indefinite loops	Chapter 7, "Loop indefinitely using a *Do* loop"

Part 4

Making Macros Easy to Use

Chapter 9

Launching Macros with Events

Chapter Objectives   Estimated time: 30 minutes

In this chapter, you'll learn how to:

- Create custom toolbar buttons.

- Create custom menu commands.

- Create custom command buttons.

- Create worksheet and workbook event handlers.

My grandmother used to use her sewing machine to embroider names on out-fits for us. She had a powerful old sewing machine, with lots of pulleys and levers and loops. When she changed the thread, she had to poke the new thread up and over and through countless turns and spools and guides, before even getting to the needle. I still don't know how she managed embroidering the names. She'd move levers and twist the fabric, and the names somehow appeared. She was very good, and the results were beautiful. Few people could create embroidered names the way she did.

Now, even I can embroider names onto clothes. I flip the thread around a couple of guides and the machine is threaded. I type in the name, select the lettering style, and push another button to embroider the name. The machine sews in all directions so I don't even have to turn the fabric. Anyone can use a sewing machine these days.

One purpose of macros is to make your own life simpler. An even more important purpose might be to enable others to accomplish tasks that they wouldn't be able to do without your help. In this chapter and the chapters that follow, you'll learn how to make macros easy for others to use.

Start the lesson

1. Start Microsoft Excel, and change to the folder that contains the practice files for this book.

2. Open the Events workbook, and save a copy as **Chapter9**.

For more information on installing the practice files, see the Introduction to this book.

209

Creating Custom Toolbars and Menus

You might feel perfectly comfortable running a macro by pressing a shortcut key combination or even pressing F5 in the Microsoft Visual Basic Editor. But if you're going to give a macro to somebody else, you want to make it as easy to run as possible. One way to make a macro easy to run is to integrate it into the Excel environment. You can initiate most built-in commands by choosing a menu command or clicking a toolbar button. By adding your macros to menus and toolbars, you can make them seem as if they're integral parts of Excel.

Try out the ZoomIn and ZoomOut macros

The Chapter9 workbook already contains two simple macros, ZoomIn and ZoomOut, that change the size of your display. These are macros that you'll assign to custom toolbar buttons and menu commands. Here are the macros:

```
Sub ZoomIn()
    Dim myZoom As Integer
    myZoom = ActiveWindow.Zoom + 10
    If myZoom <= 400 Then
        ActiveWindow.Zoom = myZoom
    End If
End Sub

Sub ZoomOut()
    Dim myZoom As Integer
    myZoom = ActiveWindow.Zoom - 10
    If myZoom >= 10 Then
        ActiveWindow.Zoom = myZoom
    End If
End Sub
```

Each macro considers a new value for the *Zoom* property of the active window. If the new value is within the acceptable limits (between 10% and 400%, the range of zoom factors in Excel), it changes the property; otherwise it does nothing.

1. Go to the ZoomIn macro. Press F5 a few times to see how the worksheet zooms in. Step through the macro if you want, to feel comfortable with how it works.

The ZoomIn macro enlarges the worksheet.

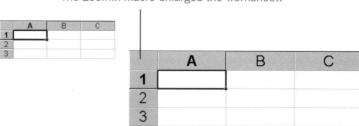

2. Go to the ZoomOut macro. Press F5 as necessary to redisplay the window at a normal size.

These are typical macros. In this chapter, you'll learn new ways to run them.

Create a custom toolbar

A toolbar button is a convenient way to launch a macro. A toolbar is small and easy to show or hide. An icon can make a tool easy to find, and a ToolTip can make it easy to remember.

1. Activate the Excel window, right-click any toolbar, and click the Customize command.

Use the Customize command to create a new toolbar.

2. In the Customize dialog box, click the Toolbars tab.

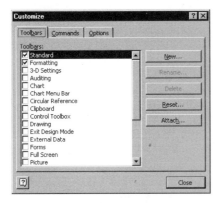

3. Click the New button, type **Zoom** as the name for the toolbar, and then click OK. A new, empty toolbar appears. The Customize dialog box is still open and available to help you fill the toolbar.

The name you assign to the toolbar appears beneath the toolbar in the interface.

4. Click the Commands tab in the Customize dialog box, and select Macros from the Categories list.

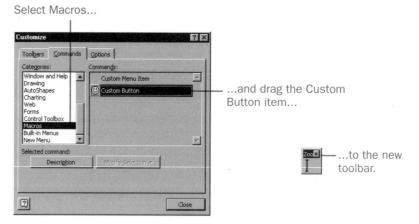

Select Macros...

...and drag the Custom
Button item...

...to the new
toolbar.

5. Drag the Custom Button item (complete with its happy face) from the Commands list onto the Zoom toolbar. When you drag the item onto the toolbar, the Modify Selection button becomes available.

6. Click the Modify Selection button, press N to select the Name box, and type **Zoom &In** as the new name. Don't press the Enter key.

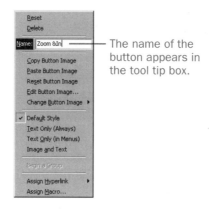

The name of the
button appears in
the tool tip box.

The value in the Name box determines what the ToolTip for the button will be. The ampersand (&) precedes the letter that will be underlined if you use this command on a menu. The ampersand has no effect on the toolbar button, but put it there anyway.

*If the menu
disappeared,
click the Modify
Selection button
again to
redisplay it.*

7. Click the Change Button Image command, and click the Up Arrow icon. The icon on the button changes, and the menu disappears.

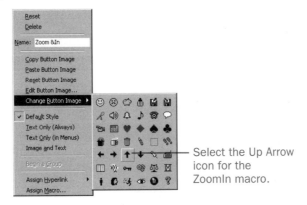

Select the Up Arrow icon for the ZoomIn macro.

8. Click the Modify Selection button, and click the Assign Macro command. Select the ZoomIn macro, and then click OK.

9. Repeat steps 4 through 8, but this time give the button the name **Zoom &Out**, select the Down Arrow icon, and assign the ZoomOut macro to the button.

10. Click the Close button, and then try out the toolbar buttons. Hold the mouse over the button to see the ToolTip appear. Hide and redisplay the toolbar.

The custom button displays a ToolTip, just as a built-in button does.

Once you have a macro, it's easy to assign it to a toolbar button. Use the Customize dialog box to create and add buttons to the toolbar. Use the Modify Selection button to change the name, icon, and macro for a button.

Create a custom menu

A menu command is another convenient way to launch a macro. A menu command stays out of the way, reducing clutter on the desktop, but the menu it belongs to is always available, whereas a toolbar can be temporarily hidden. In

Microsoft Office 2000, a menu is really just a specialized toolbar, which means that adding a command to a menu is just as easy as adding it to a toolbar.

1. Right-click any toolbar, and click the Customize command to display the Customize dialog box.

2. If you don't see the Zoom toolbar, try moving the Customize dialog box out of the way. Click the Commands tab, and select New Menu from the Categories list.

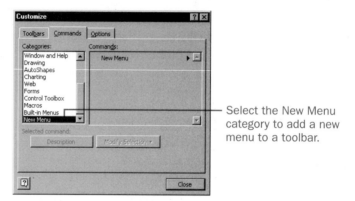

Select the New Menu category to add a new menu to a toolbar.

The New Menu category has only a single item: New Menu. You can use this item to create a new menu on a menu bar or a new submenu on an existing menu.

3. Drag the New Menu item up to Excel's menu bar, dropping it between the Window and Help menus.

The new menu appears in Excel's menu bar.

4. Click the Modify Selection button, change the value in the Name box to **&Zoom**, and press the Enter key.

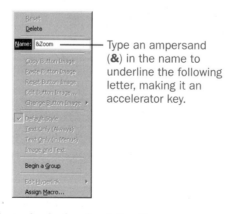

Type an ampersand (**&**) in the name to underline the following letter, making it an accelerator key.

If you look closely at the Zoom menu, you can see that the letter *Z* is underlined. That's because there's an ampersand (&) in front of the *Z* in the menu item name. The underlined letter, which lets you execute the

command by pressing the Alt key followed by that letter, is called an
access key or an *accelerator key*.

You could add brand new commands to the Zoom menu, but since
you already have the toolbar buttons on the Zoom toolbar, you can copy
them to the Zoom menu. (It's often a good idea to put commands on
both a toolbar and a menu bar, giving a user the choice of which to use.)

5. Drag the Zoom In toolbar button (the one with the Up Arrow icon) up
to the Zoom menu. A small, blank menu appears. Drag the button onto
the menu, and then press and hold the Ctrl key as you release the
mouse button.

In this step, be careful not to release the mouse button too soon.

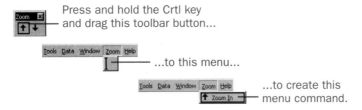

Press and hold the Crtl key
and drag this toolbar button...

...to this menu...

...to create this
menu command.

If you don't press and hold the Ctrl key when you release the mouse
button, you'll move the toolbar button rather than make a copy. If you
do accidentally move the button, simply press and hold the Ctrl key as
you drag it back from the menu to the toolbar.

The command name for the new menu item is the same as the
ToolTip for the toolbar button. The command name has the letter *I*
underlined because you had the foresight to add the ampersand when
you created the button in the "Create a custom toolbar" section,
earlier in this chapter. When you add a name to a toolbar button,
think about what letter you want underlined if you move the button
to a menu, and insert an ampersand in front of the letter when you
first name the button.

6. Drag the Zoom Out toolbar button up to the Zoom menu, and press and
hold the Ctrl key as you release the mouse.

7. Close the Customize dialog box, and try out the menu commands. Test
them using the keyboard shortcuts. Press Alt, Z, I, and Alt, Z, O to make
sure the accelerator keys work properly.

When you add a command to a toolbar, you can easily copy it to a menu.
Or if you add a command to a menu, you can easily copy it to a toolbar. The
general term that includes both toolbars and menus is *command bar*. The new
Customize dialog box for command bars makes moving between toolbars and
menus delightfully simple.

Run macros from a closed workbook

Normally, you can run a macro only when the workbook that contains the macro is open. Toolbar buttons and menu commands, however, have a unique capability: they remember where to find a macro, even when that macro's workbook is closed.

New button

1. Save and close the Chapter9 workbook. Click the New button to create a new workbook.

2. Click the Zoom In toolbar button on the Zoom toolbar. The Chapter9 workbook automatically opens and hides behind the active workbook, and the macro runs.

3. Close the temporary workbook that you created, revealing the Chapter9 workbook.

Remove menus and toolbars

Toolbar buttons and menu commands customize a user's workspace. Once you create a custom menu or toolbar, it remains a part of Excel on that computer until you remove it. Since you probably won't be using the Zoom toolbar or menu on an ongoing basis, you should remove them now. Here's how:

1. Right-click any toolbar, and click Customize to show the Customize dialog box.

2. Click the Toolbars tab, select the Zoom toolbar in the list, click the Delete button, and then click OK.

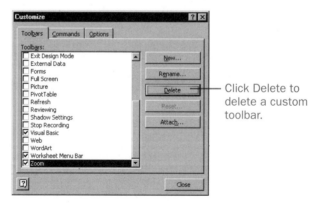

Click Delete to delete a custom toolbar.

3. Click the Zoom menu, press and hold the mouse button, and drag the menu off onto the Excel worksheet. The menu permanently disappears.

While the Customize dialog box is visible, drag the menu off the menu bar to delete the menu.

4. Click the Close button in the Customize dialog box.

Toolbar buttons and menu commands are effective tools for customizing a user's copy of Excel. They remain available and active even when you close the workbook containing the macros they're attached to. Sometimes, however, you might want to give someone a button that's available only when a specific workbook is open. A command button is such a tool.

Creating Custom Command Buttons

Toolbar buttons and menu commands respond to a single event: a click. You tell the button or command which macro to run by using the Assign Macro command. Command buttons, on the other hand, not only can trigger an event when you click them, but also can respond to additional events, such as the simple movement of the mouse above the button. Because command buttons can respond to a complex set of events, they require a whole new way of linking a macro to the button. This new approach uses what are called *event handler procedures*. Event handler procedures are special macros that are linked to an object such as a command button. First create a command button, and then you can see how to add event handler procedures to make it work.

Create a custom command button

A command button is useful for running macros that relate to a specific worksheet. Command buttons are usually large and easy to click, with a label describing what the button does.

1. With the Chapter9 workbook open, click the Control Toolbox button on the Visual Basic toolbar to display the Control Toolbox toolbar.

— The Control Toolbox toolbar.

Control Toolbox button

The Control Toolbox is a toolbar that contains a number of controls that you can use on a worksheet or on a form. These controls are called *ActiveX controls*. An ActiveX control is a special kind of drawing object that carries out an action when you click it. The ActiveX control we'll work with in this chapter is the command button control.

You'll put controls on a worksheet in Chapter 10 and controls on a form in Chapter 11.

2. Click the Command Button button, and drag a rectangle on the worksheet from the top-left corner of cell A1 to the bottom-right corner of cell B2. A command button appears on the worksheet. It has white handles on the edges, showing that it is currently selected.

Command Button button

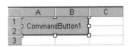

218 Part 4 **Making Macros Easy to Use**

> **Tip** You can easily "snap" any drawing object to align with the corners of a cell by pressing the Alt key as you drag a rectangle for the object. You can also press and hold the Alt key to snap to cell gridlines as you move or resize an existing drawing object.

While the command button is selected, you can change its properties. Up to now, you've changed properties using Visual Basic commands. ActiveX controls, however, have a special Properties window that allows you to change properties directly.

*Properties
button*

3. On the Control Toolbox toolbar, click the Properties button. The Properties window appears. The box at the top shows you which object's properties are being displayed. In this case, it's CommandButton1, which is a CommandButton object.

This window shows various properties of the command button. One important property of the command button is its name. This property appears as *(Name)* in the Properties window. The parentheses make the *Name* property sort to the top of the list. The *Name* property affects how you use the button in your macros.

4. Replace the default value of the *Name* property with **btnZoomIn**. You can't put spaces into the name. Many people use three-letter prefixes when naming controls. The three-letter prefix helps identify what kind of control it is; in this case, *btn* stands for "button."

Type a new name for the control here.

Changing the name of the button doesn't change the label displayed on it, however. That's the function of the *Caption* property.

5. Replace the default value of the *Caption* property with **Zoom In**. The caption on the button changes as soon as you change the *Caption* property. With ActiveX controls, you don't use an ampersand to

specify the accelerator; instead, there's a separate *Accelerator* property for that purpose.

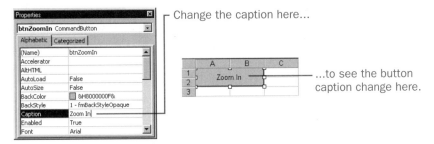

Change the caption here...

...to see the button caption change here.

6. We want the letter *I* to be the accelerator key. Type **I** as the value of the *Accelerator* property. As soon as you assign *I* to the *Accelerator* property, the letter *I* in the caption becomes underlined.

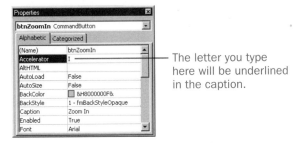

The letter you type here will be underlined in the caption.

There's one more property that you should set when you create a custom command button. It affects the active cell in Excel. Suppose cell B4 is the active cell when you click the command button. You'd normally expect cell B4 to be the active cell even after clicking the button (unless the button runs a macro that changes the active cell). But the default behavior of a command button is to remove the dark border around the active cell, making it impossible to see which cell is active.

7. Scroll down to the *TakeFocusOnClick* property, and change it to *False* in the resulting drop-down list. (*TakeFocusOnClick* is a complicated name for a simple property. Setting it to *False* simply means, "Leave the active cell alone when you click this button.")

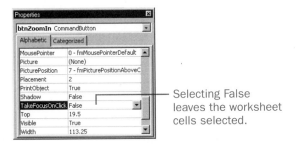

Selecting False leaves the worksheet cells selected.

You've now created and customized the command button. All that's left is to link it to a macro and make it run.

You don't assign a macro to a command button. Instead, you create a macro with a special name, in a special place, and the macro automatically links to the button. Fortunately, the Control Toolbox has a button that will do all the work for you.

View Code button

1. With the command button still selected, click the View Code button.

The first part of the name
matches the object name.

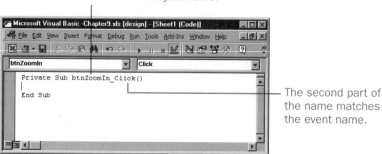

The second part of the name matches the event name.

The Visual Basic Editor window appears with a new macro. The word *Private* before the macro name means that this macro won't appear in the Run Macro dialog box. The macro name is btnZoomIn_Click. The name is important. The part of the name that precedes the underscore matches the command button. The part of the name that follows the underscore matches the name of the event that this macro will handle. In this example, the macro runs whenever you click the button. A macro linked to an event like this is called an *event handler*.

Note The word *procedure* is a more technical synonym for a macro. Excel uses the word *macro* because "macro recorder" is less intimidating than "procedure recorder." In general, this book uses *macro* to refer to those procedures that you can run from the Macro dialog box and *procedure* to refer to functions and event handlers.

You could copy the code from the ZoomIn macro into the btnZoomIn_Click procedure, but it's easier simply to run that macro (since it already exists) from this one.

2. Type **ZoomIn** as the body of the procedure. You're now ready to try clicking the button.

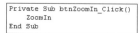

3. Switch back to Excel, click in any cell in the worksheet to deselect the button, and then click the button. The procedure doesn't run. You simply reselected the button.

   You need some way of letting Excel know whether clicking an ActiveX control should run the event handler or simply select the control. You do that by controlling *design mode*. When Excel is in design mode, clicking a control selects it. When Excel isn't in design mode (a condition called *run mode*), clicking a control runs the event handler procedure. Whenever you put an ActiveX control on a worksheet, Excel automatically switches to design mode.

4. Click the Exit Design Mode button. The selection handles disappear from the command button.

Exit Design Mode button

5. Try out the button: click it. Press Alt-I to try out the accelerator key.

6. Click the Design Mode button to turn design mode back on, and click the command button. It becomes selected.

Design Mode button

Attaching an event handler procedure to a control is different from attaching a macro to a toolbar button:

- With a toolbar button, you can name the macro whatever you want and then use the Assign Macro dialog box to link the macro to the button. With an event handler, the combination of the name and the location of the procedure is what creates the link to the control.

- With a toolbar button, you make Excel ignore events by opening the Customize dialog box. With a control, you do this by clicking the Design Mode button.

Create an event handler on your own

You can create an event handler for a control by clicking the View Code button. You might find it enlightening to see how you can also create an event handler directly in the Visual Basic Editor.

1. Repeat steps 2 through 7 of the section "Create a custom command button" to create a Zoom Out command button. Drag a rectangle on the worksheet from the top-left corner of cell A3 to the bottom-right corner of cell B4. In the Properties window, give it the name **btnZoomOut,** the caption **Zoom Out**, and the letter **O** as its accelerator. Also, set the *TakeFocusOnClick* property to *False*. Don't create an event handler procedure.

2. Switch to the Visual Basic Editor, and click anywhere in the btnZoomIn_Click procedure.

The Object box

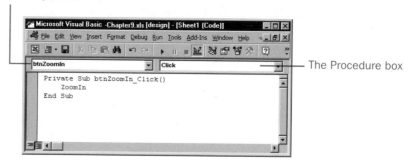

The Procedure box

Above the code portion of the window are two boxes. The box on the left contains the first half of the procedure name (*btnZoomIn*), and the box on the right contains the second half of the procedure name (*Click*). These two boxes are named Object and Procedure, respectively.

3. Click the arrow next to the Object list. The list shows all the objects related to the current worksheet that can have event handlers: here, btnZoomIn, btnZoomOut, and Worksheet.

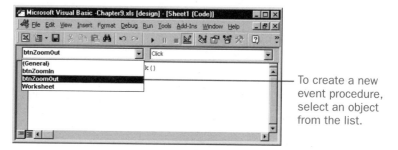

To create a new event procedure, select an object from the list.

4. Select btnZoomOut from the list. A new procedure appears. Click is the default event for a button, so the new procedure is named btnZoomOut_Click, which is precisely what you need.

5. Type **ZoomOut** as the body of the procedure.

6. Switch to Excel, turn off design mode, and try out both buttons.

The lists at the top of the code window can help you build event handlers by combining an object with an event.

Make a button respond to mouse movements

The command button can recognize several different events. Three of the most useful events are a click (the *Click* event), a double-click (the *DblClick* event), and a mouse movement (the *MouseMove* event). The *MouseMove* event is especially useful because it provides information to the procedure in the form of arguments.

1. In the Visual Basic Editor, select btnZoomOut from the Object list, and then select MouseMove from the Procedure list.

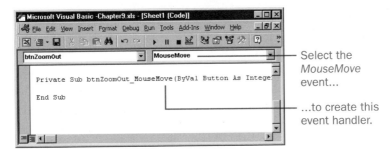

Select the *MouseMove* event...

...to create this event handler.

The declaration for the new procedure is relatively long. This is what it looks like when divided into shorter lines:

```
Private Sub btnZoomOut_MouseMove( _
    ByVal Button As Integer, _
    ByVal Shift As Integer, _
    ByVal X As Single, _
    ByVal Y As Single)
```

This event handler procedure has four arguments: *Button, Shift, X,* and *Y.* (The word *byVal* means that Excel will ignore any changes the procedure makes to an argument.) The arguments communicate information to you that you can take advantage of as you write the macro. The *Button* argument indicates whether a mouse button is down as the mouse moves. The *Shift* argument indicates whether the Shift, Ctrl, or Alt keys are pressed. The *X* and *Y* arguments indicate the horizontal and vertical position of the mouse.

2. Insert **ZoomOut** as the body of the new procedure, switch to Excel, and move the mouse over the Zoom Out button. (You don't even have to click. Just moving the mouse over the button causes the procedure to run. Events can happen fast.)

Just move the mouse over the button to zoom out.

You can use the arguments that the *MouseMove* event provides you to control the procedure. Specifically, if the value of the *Shift* argument is equal to 1, the Shift key is down. If the value of the *Shift* argument is equal to 2, the Ctrl key is down. You can change the procedure so that it zooms in when the Shift key is down and zooms out when the Ctrl key is down.

3. Replace the body of the btnZoomOut_MouseMove procedure with these statements:

```
If Shift = 1 Then
    ZoomIn
ElseIf Shift = 2 Then
    ZoomOut
End If
```

Note   The *ElseIf* keyword allows you to combine *Else* and *If* statements into a single statement.

---

4. Switch to Excel, and try out the event handler. Try moving the mouse by itself. Then try pressing and holding the Shift key as you move it. Then try pressing and holding the Ctrl key as you move it.

As you move the mouse over the button, you can practically see the procedure running over and over. Each time the button detects the mouse moving, it triggers another event and the event handler procedure runs again. Event handler procedures can be a powerful way to make things happen.

Explore the Visual Basic project

You might wonder where all these event handlers are stored and how they relate to the macros that you create with the macro recorder. When you use the macro recorder to create a macro, the macro is stored in a module. You can have multiple macros in a single module, and you can have multiple modules in a workbook. (Each time you close and reopen a workbook, the macro recorder creates a new module for any new macros you record.) Event handler procedures for a command button are attached to the worksheet that contains that button. Visual Basic refers to all the code in a single workbook—whether the code is in a module or attached to a worksheet—as a *project*. The Visual Basic Editor has a special window that allows you to explore the project.

Project Explorer button

1. In the Visual Basic Editor, click the Project Explorer button. The Project window appears. The name of the project is VBAProject, and the name of the workbook (Chapter9.xls) appears in parentheses. Procedures can be stored either on module sheets (grouped under Modules in the Project window) or attached to workbooks and worksheets (grouped under Microsoft Excel Objects in the Project window).

Behind each worksheet is a hidden page that contains any code for that worksheet or for objects on that worksheet. When you create a new worksheet, a new code page appears in the Project window. When you delete a worksheet, the worksheet's code page disappears.

2. Double-click the entry labeled Module1. The main Visual Basic Editor window displays the macros stored in Module1.

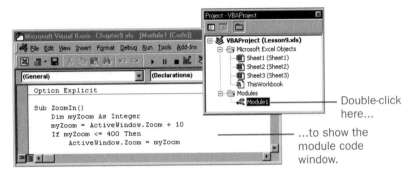

Double-click here...

...to show the module code window.

3. Double-click the entry labeled Sheet1. The main Visual Basic Editor window displays the event handlers for the objects on Sheet1.

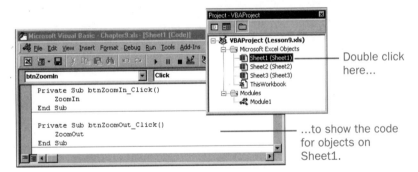

Double click here...

...to show the code for objects on Sheet1.

4. In Excel, drag the sheet tab for Sheet1 to the right, and then press and hold the Ctrl key as you release the mouse. Excel creates a copy of the sheet. The copy's name is Sheet1 (2), and it has its own copy of the command buttons.

Create a new worksheet in Excel.

5. Switch to the Visual Basic Editor, and look at the Project window. There's a new sheet in the list under Microsoft Excel Objects. The name in parentheses, Sheet1 (2), matches the name on the worksheet tab. The name in front of the parentheses, Sheet4, is a unique name that Visual

Basic generates. If you use Insert Worksheet to create a new Sheet4, Visual Basic will give it Sheet5 as its new unique name!

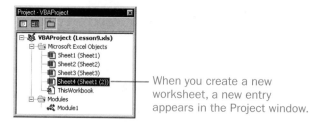

When you create a new worksheet, a new entry appears in the Project window.

6. Double-click the Sheet4 worksheet item in the Project window. The main Visual Basic Editor window now shows the event handler procedures for the copies of the command buttons. These procedures look just like the procedures that are linked to the command buttons on Sheet1, but they're now separate entities. Even if you change the btnZoomIn_Click procedure on Sheet4, the btnZoomIn_Click procedure on Sheet1 remains unchanged.

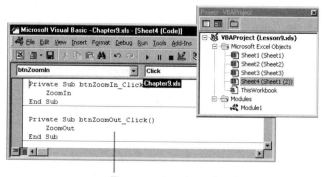

The new sheet's code window contains copies of the event handler procedures.

7. In Excel, delete the Sheet1 (2) worksheet. Then switch back to the Visual Basic Editor and look at the Project window. As you probably anticipated, the entry for Sheet11 has disappeared, along with the procedures that were associated with it.

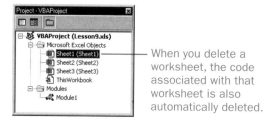

When you delete a worksheet, the code associated with that worksheet is also automatically deleted.

> **Important** When you delete a worksheet that has event handler procedures associated with it, all the procedures are destroyed with the worksheet. Save your work frequently when you write event handlers for worksheets so that you can recover your work if you accidentally delete a worksheet.

Handling Worksheet and Workbook Events

ActiveX controls aren't the only objects in Excel that can have events. Worksheets and workbooks have events, too. Each of these objects has different events that it can respond to.

Run a procedure when the selection changes

1. In the Visual Basic Editor, activate the Sheet1 code window. (Activate the Project window and double-click Sheet1(1).)

2. From the Objects list, at the top left of the code window, select Worksheet. A new procedure appears with the name Worksheet_Selection-Change. This event happens whenever you change the selection on the worksheet. It doesn't matter whether you click in a cell or use the arrow keys to move around; the event happens either way.

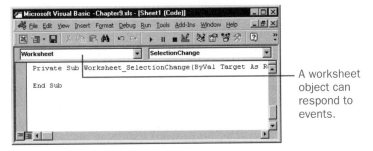

A worksheet object can respond to events.

Just to see what events are available for a worksheet, click the arrow next to the Procedure list, at the top right of the code window. The list shows the seven events that a worksheet can respond to. *SelectionChange* is the default event for a worksheet, just as *Click* is the default event for a command button.

This list shows the available events for the Worksheet object.

3. Press the Esc key to close the list of events, and enter these statements as the body of the Worksheet_SelectionChange procedure:

```
If ActiveCell.Interior.Color = vbCyan Then
    Selection.Interior.Color = vbYellow
Else
    Selection.Interior.Color = vbCyan
End If
```

Cyan is the Visual Basic name for the color labeled Turquoise in the Excel color palette. The procedure now changes all the selected cells to turquoise unless the active cell already happens to be turquoise.

4. Activate Sheet1 in Excel, and click in several different cells. Press arrow keys to move between cells. Drag a selection rectangle through several cells. The cell colors change every time you change which cells are selected.

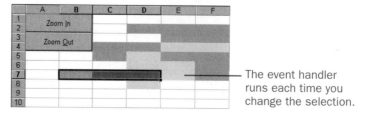

The event handler runs each time you change the selection.

5. Now activate Sheet2 and select a cell. Nothing happens. The Worksheet_SelectionChange event handler is active only for the original worksheet.

Handle an event on any worksheet

When you create an event handler for Sheet1's *SelectionChange* event, that handler applies only to that worksheet. If you activate Sheet2 and change the selection, nothing happens. Worksheet event handlers respond to events only on their own worksheet. To handle an event on any worksheet, you must use a workbook-level event handler.

1. In the Visual Basic Editor, activate the Project window and double-click the ThisWorkbook item.

2. From the Object list, select Workbook. A new procedure appears with the name Workbook_Open. *Open* is the default event for a workbook. This is the event you'd use if you wanted to run a procedure every time you opened the workbook.

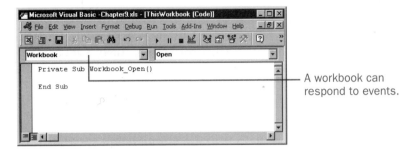

A workbook can respond to events.

3. Click the Procedures list to see the events available for a workbook.

This list shows the events available for a workbook object.

A workbook can respond to any of 19 different events. It just so happens that seven of the events begin with *Sheet*. These seven workbook *Sheet* events correspond to the seven events for a worksheet, except that they apply to any worksheet in the workbook, even worksheets that don't exist yet.

4. Select the *SheetSelectionChange* event. This creates a new Workbook_SheetSelectionChange procedure.

5. Delete the Workbook_Open procedure. You won't need this one.

6. Type **Selection.Interior.Color = vbRed** as the body of the procedure.

```
Private Sub Workbook_SheetSelectionChange(ByVal
    Selection.Interior.Color = vbRed
End Sub
```

7. Switch to Excel, activate Sheet2, and click in various cells. The cells change to red.

8. Activate Sheet1, and click in various cells. The cells change to red. What happened to the SelectionChange event handler procedure for this sheet? It might seem that the event handler for the workbook replaces the one for an individual sheet, but that's not quite true. In fact, they both ran. The workbook one just ran last. The property for the interior color of the cell changed to blue (or yellow) and then quickly changed to red. You didn't see the intermediate color because Windows doesn't refresh the screen until the macro finishes. So all you ever see is the final color.

You can create event handler procedures for events that take place on a worksheet. Worksheet event handler procedures can exist either at the worksheet level or at the workbook level. If the procedure is at the workbook level, it handles events for all worksheets, regardless of whether a worksheet has an event handler of its own.

Suppress a workbook event

It might seem strange that a worksheet event handler wouldn't override a workbook event handler for the same event. In fact, having the worksheet event occur first gives you a great deal of control over how to take advantage of events.

If you want both event handlers to run, you don't have to do anything. If you want the worksheet event handler to suppress the workbook event handler, you can make the worksheet event handler tell the workbook event handler to do nothing. The way you do that is by creating a custom property at the workbook level.

1. Double-click ThisWorkbook in the Project window. At the top of the code window, enter this statement above the event handler procedure:

    ```
    Public ProcessingEvent As Boolean
    ```

    This declares *ProcessingEvent* as a *public* variable in ThisWorkbook. When you declare a variable above all the procedures in a module, the variable becomes visible to all the procedures in that one module and is called a *module-level* variable. If you use the word *Public* to declare a module-level variable, that variable is then visible to any procedure in the entire workbook. A public variable is essentially a simple property. Declaring the variable as Boolean means that it can be only *True* or *False*. If you don't assign something to it, it will be *False*.

2. Change the body of the event handler to this:

    ```
    If ProcessingEvent = True Then
        ProcessingEvent = False
    Else
        Selection.Interior.Color = vbRed
    End If
    ```

    The event handler will now change the color of the selection only if the *ProcessingEvent* variable is not *True*. If *ProcessingEvent* is *True*, the event handler changes the variable back to *False*. (Otherwise, suppressing the event handler once would disable this event handler until you close the workbook.)

3. Double-click Sheet1 in the Project window. At the bottom of the SelectionChange event handler, type **ThisWorkbook.ProcessingEvent = True** just before the *End Sub* statement.

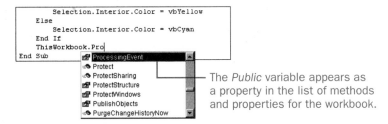

The *Public* variable appears as a property in the list of methods and properties for the workbook.

The new *ProcessingEvent* property is in the list of members. It even has a standard Property icon next to it. With this statement, the worksheet event handler tells the workbook event handler not to do anything.

4. Activate Sheet1 in Excel, and change the selection. The selection should change to yellow or blue. The worksheet event handler is suppressing the workbook event handler.

5. Activate Sheet3, and change the selection. The selection should change to red. The workbook event handler still functions properly as long as it's not overridden by the worksheet.

Creating a simple custom property inside ThisWorkbook in the form of a public variable allows you to suppress the workbook event handler. You now have total control over which event handlers function at which time. You can have an event handler run only at the worksheet level, only at the workbook level, at both levels, or as a mixture.

Cancel an event

Some events are made to be canceled. For example, Excel displays a shortcut menu when you right-click on a worksheet. What if you want to prevent the shortcut menu from appearing? You can create an event handler procedure that cancels that event.

Events that can be canceled all have the word *Before* in front of the event name. A worksheet has a *BeforeDoubleClick* event and a *BeforeRightClick* event. A workbook has corresponding *SheetBeforeDoubleClick* and *SheetBeforeRightClick* events, and also *BeforeClose*, *BeforeSave*, and *BeforePrint* events. Each event procedure that can be canceled has a *Cancel* argument. To cancel the corresponding event, assign *True* to the *Cancel* argument.

1. In the Sheet1 code window, select Worksheet from the Object list and BeforeRightClick from the Procedures list.

2. In the event handler procedure that appears, type **Cancel = True** as the body.

```
Private Sub Worksheet_BeforeRightClick(ByVal Target As
    Cancel = True
End Sub
```

3. Activate Excel, and select Sheet1. Try right-clicking in a cell. The color changes, but the shortcut menu doesn't appear. The event handler executed before the actual event occurred, and you prevented the event from happening.

Toolbars and menus can be linked to macros. Command buttons, worksheets, and workbooks can be linked to event handlers. All these tools allow you to create applications that are easy for anyone to use.

Chapter Summary

To	Do this	Button
Customize toolbars or menu bars	Display the Customize dialog box by right-clicking any toolbar and clicking Customize.	
Add a command to a toolbar or a menu	In the Customize dialog box, click the Commands tab, select the Macros category, and then drag one of the commands to the menu or toolbar.	
Assign a macro to a custom toolbar button or menu	With the Customize dialog box open, click the button or command, click the Modify Selection button, click the Assign Macro command, and then select the macro.	
Copy a toolbar button or menu command	Press and hold the Ctrl key as you drag the item to a new location.	
Add a custom command button to a worksheet	Click the Control Toolbox button on the Visual Basic toolbar, click the Command Button button, and then drag a rectangle on the worksheet.	
Make a command button snap to cell gridlines as you move or resize it	Hold down the Alt key as you drag or resize the button.	
Create an event handler that will run when you click a command button	First give the command button a name you like, and then click the View Code button on the Control Toolbox toolbar.	
Enable a command button	Click the Exit Design Mode button.	
Select a command button without running its event handler	Click the Design Mode button.	

To	Do this	Button
Create an event handler that will run whenever you change the selection on a specific worksheet	In the Project window, double-click the worksheet name, and then select Worksheet from the Object list and SelectionChange from the Procedure list.	
Create an event handler that will run whenever you change the selection on any worksheet in a workbook	In the Project window, double-click ThisWorkbook, and then select Workbook from the Object list and SheetSelectionChange from the Procedure list.	
Prevent an event from occurring	Look for an event that has the word *Before* as part of the name. In the event handler, assign *True* to the *Cancel* argument.	

For online information about	Ask the Assistant for help using the words
Creating custom toolbars and menus	"Overview of command bars"
Creating command buttons	"Command buttons"
Using events	"Events"

Preview of the Next Chapter

You typically think of list boxes, scroll bars, and other graphical controls in connection with dialog boxes. Excel allows you to add these active controls directly to worksheets, however. In the next chapter, you'll learn how to make a worksheet easy to use by adding active controls, the same controls you'll later use in custom dialog boxes.

Chapter 10

Using Dialog Box Controls on a Worksheet

Estimated time: 30 minutes

In this chapter, you'll learn how to:

- Add ActiveX controls to a worksheet.

- Link the value of a control to a worksheet cell.

- Link a list box to a worksheet range.

- Create a list box with multiple columns.

- Protect a worksheet that uses ActiveX controls.

Microsoft Excel is a great program. Many people purchase it to use at work. At least, people *say* they're going to use it at work. Of course we all know the real reason most of us buy it: to calculate car payments. (The rest of us buy it for figuring out mortgage payments.) It's *after* buying it that we discover that it's also good for one or two other projects as well.

Anyway, say you have a friend who just bought Excel to calculate loan payments, but who doesn't know how to use it very well yet. You want to help out by building a model your friend can use for calculating the payments. You want your friend to be able to try out several possible prices, interest rates, and repayment periods, but you want to eliminate the chance for mistakes. Happily for both of you, Excel has some powerful tools to help you do just that.

Start the lesson

1. Start Excel, and change to the folder containing the practice files for this book.

2. Open the Loan workbook, and save a copy as **Chapter10**.

For more information about installing the practice files, see the Introduction to this book.

Using a Loan Payment Calculator

When you interact with Excel, you do so through Excel's graphical user interface. A graphical user interface includes menus, dialog boxes, list boxes, scroll bars, buttons, and other graphical images. A graphical user interface makes a program easier to learn and also helps reduce errors by restricting choices to valid options.

Historically, creating a graphical user interface was the domain of professional computer scientists. More recently, users of advanced applications have been able to add graphical controls to custom dialog boxes. Now, with Excel, you can take advantage of dialog box–style controls directly on the worksheet, without doing any programming at all. These controls are called ActiveX controls. For example, the command button you created in Chapter 9 was an ActiveX control.

In this chapter, you'll create a worksheet model to calculate a car loan payment. You'll add ActiveX controls to the worksheet to make it easy to use for a friend who's unfamiliar with worksheets. In the process, you'll become familiar with how ActiveX controls work, which will be useful when you create custom forms—as you'll do in Chapter 11.

Create a loan payment model

The Loan sheet of the practice workbook contains labels that will help you create a model that uses an Excel worksheet function to calculate the monthly payments for a car loan.

These are the labels for the loan payment calculator.

Cells B2 through B7 contain the labels Price, Down, Loan, Interest, Years, and Payment. Go through the following steps to create a fully functional loan payment calculator.

There are no named ranges on this worksheet.

1. Type **$5000** in cell C2 (to the right of Price), type **20%** in cell C3 (to the right of Down), type **8%** in cell C5 (to the right of Interest), and type **3** in cell C6 (to the right of Years).

These are the constant values for a sample loan payment.

2. In cell C4 (to the right of Loan), type **=Price*(1-Down)** and press the Enter key. The value $4,000 appears in the cell. Excel interprets which cells contain the price and down payment by looking at the labels next to the cells.

	A	B	C	D
1				
2		Price	$ 5,000	
3		Down	20%	
4		Loan	$ 4,000	
5		Interest	8.00%	
6		Years	3	
7		Payment		
8				

The formula =Price*(1-Down) calculates the loan amount.

Tip If you want to make sure that Excel is using the correct cells in the formula, select cell C4, and then click in the formula bar. The word *Price* in the formula changes to blue, and a blue border appears around cell C2, the price value. The word *Down* also changes to green, and a green border appears around cell C3, the down payment value. You can now feel confident that Excel is using the correct cell references. Press the Esc key to return Excel to its normal mode.

---

3. In cell C7 (to the right of Payment), type **=PMT(Interest/ 12,Years*12,Loan)** and press the Enter key. The payment amount, $125.35, appears in the cell. Once again, Excel uses the labels next to the cells to determine which cells you meant to use.

	A	B	C	D
1				
2		Price	$ 5,000	
3		Down	20%	
4		Loan	$ 4,000	
5		Interest	8.00%	
6		Years	3	
7		Payment	($125.35)	
8				
9				

The formula =PMT(Interest/12,Years*12,Loan) calculates the loan payment.

This is the monthly payment amount for the hypothetical car. The red text and the parentheses around the number in the worksheet indicate a negative number. Unfortunately, you don't receive this amount; you pay it. (If you want to change the monthly payment to a positive number, put a minus sign in front of *Loan* in the formula.)

Use the loan payment model

1. Enter **$12000** in cell C2. The loan amount should change to $9,600, and the payment should change to $300.83. This simple model calculates monthly loan payments for a given set of input variables. You change the input variables to anything you like, and the payment changes accordingly. You can even enter outlandish values.

	A	B	C	D
1				
2		Price	$12,000	
3		Down	20%	
4		Loan	$ 9,600	
5		Interest	8.00%	
6		Years	3	
7		Payment	($300.83)	
8				

A new price...

...results in a new payment amount.

2. Enter **$1500000** as the price of the car. This is a very expensive car. The payment formula bravely calculates the monthly payment, but you can't read it because it's too big.

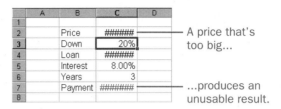

A price that's too big...

...produces an unusable result.

3. Press Ctrl-Z to change the price back to $12,000. (The monthly payment for the expensive car, in case you're interested, would be $37,603.64.)

One of the problems with this model is that it's *too* flexible. You can enter ridiculously large prices, even ridiculously high interest rates. (Try **500%**.) You can even enter something totally useless as the number of years, such as "Dog." The wide spectrum of choices available, only a few of which are meaningful, might be confusing when your friend is using the model. You can add controls to the worksheet that will eliminate any possible confusion.

Creating an Error-Resistant Loan Payment Calculator

Excel has tools that enable you to make an error-resistant loan payment calculator. By restricting options to valid items, you can make your model less likely to produce erroneous results and also much easier to use. The Control Toolbox, the same toolbar you used to create a command button in Chapter 9, contains all kinds of useful ActiveX controls that you can put on a worksheet: list boxes, spin buttons, combo boxes, and so on.

Restrict the years to a valid range

Start by making it difficult to enter an invalid number of years. Typically, for car loans you can borrow for up to five years in units of a year. Just to be safe, allow values from 1 to 6 for the number of years. A spin button is an effective way to specify such integer values.

Control Toolbox button

1. Activate the Control Toolbox. (Click the Control Toolbox button on the Microsoft Visual Basic toolbar.)

2. Click the Spin Button button on the Control Toolbox.

Spin Button button

3. Press and hold the Alt key, and click close to the top-left corner of cell E6. (Pressing the Alt key as you drag makes the control snap to the cell grid line.)

4. Release the Alt key, and drag the bottom-right corner of the new spin button to the center of the bottom of cell E6. This makes the spin button rotate sideways and fit on the row.

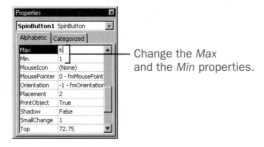

— Add a spin button control to change the number of years.

5. Click the Properties button to display the Properties window.

Properties button

6. Type **1** as the value of the *Min* property, and type **6** as the value of the *Max* property. You want the spin button to control the value in cell C6.

— Change the *Max* and the *Min* properties.

7. For the *LinkedCell* property, type **C6** and press the Enter key.

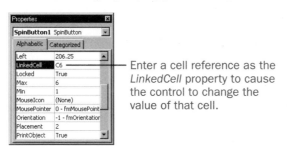

— Enter a cell reference as the *LinkedCell* property to cause the control to change the value of that cell.

An ActiveX control has many properties. For most of the properties, you can simply accept the default values. Only change the properties for which you need a custom value.

8. Click the Exit Design Mode button, and try clicking the spin button. The number in cell C6 changes as you click the spin button, and the payment amount changes accordingly. Now your friend will find it easy to select only valid loan duration values.

Exit Design Mode button

Restrict the down payment to valid values

Unfortunately, your friend can still enter an invalid value for the down payment percentage: –50%, for example, or "Dog." You need to help out. A reasonable range of values for the down payment would be anywhere from 0% to 100%, counting in 5% increments. You specify the down payment as a percentage (which is a fraction, not an integer). The minimum change for a spin button is an integer, but you can still use a spin button as long as you utilize an extra cell to hold the intermediate value.

Design Mode button

Copying the control makes both controls exactly the same size.

1. Click the Design Mode button to switch back to design mode.

2. Press and hold both the Alt key and the Ctrl key, and drag the spin button from cell E6 to cell E3. When you release the mouse button, a copy snaps to the top-left corner of cell E3.

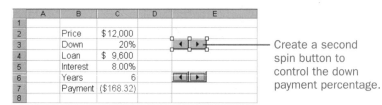

Create a second spin button to control the down payment percentage.

3. In the Properties window, type **100** as the value of the *Max* property, **0** (zero) as the value of the *Min* property, and **H3** as the value of the *LinkedCell* property. Cell H3 holds an intermediate—integer—value, because the spin button can increment only in integers. Dividing the value in cell H3 by 100 converts the integer created by the spin button into a percentage suitable for use as a down payment.

4. As the value of the *SmallChange* property, type **5** and press the Enter key. This property controls how much the number will change each time you click the control.

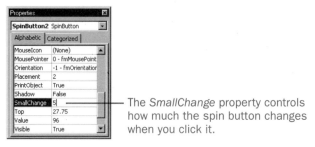

The *SmallChange* property controls how much the spin button changes when you click it.

Exit Design Mode button

5. Click the Exit Design Mode button, and then click the control. A percentage value appears in the cell.

6. Select cell C3, type **=H3/100**, and press the Enter key. The value in cell H3 changes between 0 and 100. Now you need a value in cell C3 that changes between 0% and 100%.

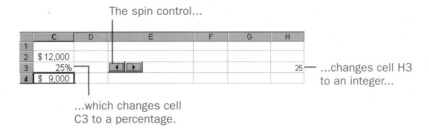

The spin control...

...which changes cell
C3 to a percentage.

...changes cell H3
to an integer...

7. Click the spin button to see both the integer in cell H3 and the derived value in cell C3 change in tandem.

Restrict the interest rate to valid values

The interest rate is another input value your friend might make a mistake entering. The interest rate is similar to the down payment rate; both are percentages. You probably want to allow interest rates to vary by as little as 0.25%, and within a range from 0% through about 20%. Because you're allowing so many possible values, you'll have many more steps than with the down payment rate, so you'll use a scroll bar control instead of a spin button. Like a spin button, the scroll bar returns only integers, so you'll still need to link the control to an intermediate cell.

1. Click the Scroll Bar button on the Control Toolbox, and then press and hold the Alt key as you click the top-left corner of cell E5.

Scroll Bar button

2. Continue to press the Alt key as you drag the bottom-right corner of the new scroll bar to the bottom-right corner of cell E5.

	B	C	D	E	F
1					
2	Price	$ 12,000			
3	Down	25%			
4	Loan	$ 9,000			
5	Interest	8.00%			
6	Years	6			

Create a scroll bar to
set the interest rate.

3. In the Properties window, type **2000** as the value of the *Max* property, **25** as the value of the *SmallChange* property, **100** as the value of the *LargeChange* property, and **H5** as the value of the *LinkedCell* property. Press the Enter key.

4. Click the Exit Design Mode button, and try out the scroll bar control by clicking the arrows as well as the area in between them. If you click one of the arrows on either end, the number in cell H5 changes by 25 (the *SmallChange* value). If you click between the box and the end, the number changes by 100 (the *LargeChange* value).

Exit Design Mode button

5. Select cell C5, type **=H5/10000**, and press the Enter key. You divide by 100 to turn the number from H5 into a percentage and by another 100 (100 * 100 = 10000 total) to allow for hundredths of a percent.

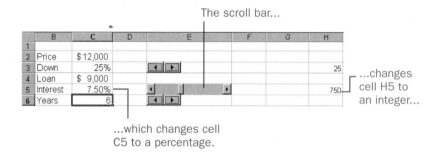

The scroll bar...

...changes cell H5 to an integer...

...which changes cell C5 to a percentage.

Now your friend can easily modify the number of years for the loan (using one spin button), the down payment percentage (using the other spin button), or the interest rate (using the scroll bar control). All these controls were easy to create. Creating a control to automatically fill in the price of the car requires a little more work.

Retrieving a Value from a List

You could specify the price of the car by creating another scroll bar, but the price of a car is actually determined by which car you want to buy. You know that your friend has been looking through the want ads and has come up with a list of used cars to consider. You can make the model friendly to use by allowing your friend to select the description of the car and have the price appear automatically in the Price cell.

Prepare a list of cars

The Chapter10 practice file contains a hypothetical list of your friend's cars and their prices. The list starts in cell K2. You can create a list box that displays this list of cars.

	J	K	L	M
1				
2		91 Mercury Sable	$10,500	
3		88 Nissan Pulsar NX	$6,350	
4		90 Toyota Camry	$8,950	
5		88 Dodge Lancer ES	$6,299	
6		87 BMW 325	$7,959	
7		91 Chev Camaro	$6,796	
8		88 Mazda MX6	$8,500	
9				

1. Select cell K2, and press Ctrl-Shift-* to select the entire block of cells.

2. From the Insert menu's Name submenu, click Define. Type **CarList** as the name of the list, and click OK. The defined name contains both the list of car names and the corresponding list of prices.

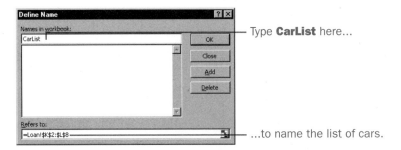

Type **CarList** here...

...to name the list of cars.

3. In the Control Toolbox, click Combo Box, press and hold the Alt key, and drag a rectangle from the top-left corner to the bottom-right corner of cell E2.

Combo Box button

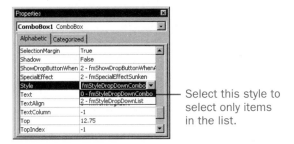

Create a Combo Box control to select the desired car.

A combo box can have either of two styles. It can be a drop-down list box, allowing you to select only items from the list, or it can be a list box combined with an edit box, allowing you to enter new values as well as select from the list. Because you want to confine your friend to the existing list of cars, you want the combo box to be a drop-down list box.

4. In the Properties window, for the value of the *Style* property, select *2 – fmStyleDropDownList*.

Select this style to select only items in the list.

5. Type **C2** as the value of the *LinkedCell* property, and press the Enter key. The price from cell C2 appears as the value of the combo box. But because the combo box has a sunken appearance, the text in the box is too large to read. You can reduce the size of the font to make it visible.

6. Click the three-dot ellipsis button at the right of the *Font* property, change the font size to 8 points, and click OK. Now you can change the combo box to retrieve the list of cars.

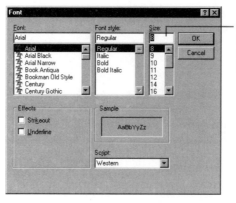

Reduce the size of the font to make the text in the combo box readable.

7. Type **CarList** as the value of the *ListFillRange* property, and press the Enter key. Nothing seems to happen, but the combo box now knows to get its list of values from the CarList range. You can also watch the value of cell C2 change when you select a new car from the combo box.

Exit Design Mode button

8. Click the Exit Design Mode button, click the arrow on the combo box, and select *90 Toyota Camry* from the list. The name for the Toyota appears in the drop-down control, but also unfortunately in cell C2. The loan payment calculator doesn't seem to like having a car name entered as the price.

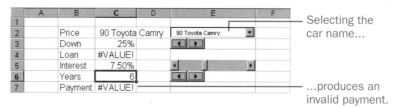

Selecting the car name...

...produces an invalid payment.

You can now select a car name from the combo box, but you want the combo box to put the price of the car—not the name of the car—into cell C2. Because the ListFillRange, CarList, contains an extra column with the car prices, you can tell the combo box to get the value from that second column.

Retrieve the price from the list

1. Click the Design Mode button, and click the combo box.

Design Mode button

2. In the Properties window, type **2** as the value of the *ColumnCount* property. The *ColumnCount* property informs the combo box that there are really two columns of values in the *ListFillRange*.

3. Type **2** as the value of the *BoundColumn* property, and press the Enter key. The *BoundColumn* property tells the combo box which column's value to

put into the linked cell. And sure enough, the price of the Toyota, $8,950, appears in the cell.

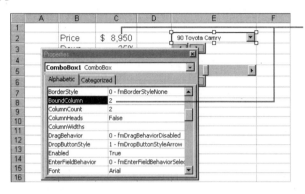

The *BoundColumn* property controls which column's value goes into the cell.

4. Turn off design mode, and click the arrow on the combo box.

Select the car from the list to put the price into cell C2.

5. Select *87 BMW* from the drop-down list of cars. The price changes to $7,959.

Now your friend won't accidentally calculate the payment for a $1,000,000 car. Your friend can just select various cars from the list, and Excel will automatically insert the correct price in the Price cell.

Set the column widths

The combo box works fine, but while the list was dropped down, there was a horizontal scroll bar across the bottom. Even though there's plenty of room for the price, the combo box makes the price column just as wide as the car name column. As the default, a combo box uses the same width for each column. If, as in this example, you want the columns to have different widths, you can manually control the column widths.

1. Turn on design mode, and select the combo box.

2. In the Properties window, type **1 in; .5 in** as the value of the *ColumnWidths* property (to specify 1 inch for the first column and 0.5 inch for the second), and press the Enter key. The displayed value of the

A point is equal to 1/72 inch.

property changes to *72 pt; 36 pt.* This is the equivalent value in points. You can type the value of the property using inches (in), centimeters (cm), or points (pt), but the value is always displayed in points.

3. Turn off design mode, and click the combo box arrow. The combo box, complete with multiple columns, looks great!

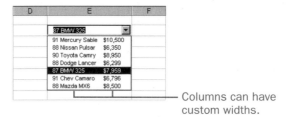

Columns can have custom widths.

Protecting the Worksheet

The model works fine now. It doesn't require any typing into cells. And you were able to create it without using any macros! The model still isn't bullet-proof, however. There's nothing in the model to prevent your friend from accidentally typing, say, "Dog" in cell C2 as the price of the car, thereby destroying the formula.

You might protect the worksheet. That would keep your friend from typing invalid values into the model; but unfortunately it would also keep the ActiveX controls from changing the values of the linked cells. You can, however, set the worksheet protection in such a way that Visual Basic for Applications procedures can still change the cells. All you need are five simple event handler procedures to protect the model effectively.

Create an event handler for the combo box

Right now, each of the four ActiveX controls links directly to a cell. Before you can protect the worksheet, you must create four event handler procedures to put the new values into the cells.

1. Turn on design mode, and select the combo box.

View Code button

2. In the Properties window, change the *Name* property to **cboPrice**. (The prefix *cbo* stands for "combo box.") Clear the *LinkedCell* property box, and then click the View Code button on the Control Toolbox. A new event handler procedure named cboPrice_Change appears. *Change* is the default event for a combo box.

3. As the body of the macro, insert this statement:

```
Range("C2").Value = cboPrice.Value
```

An event handler can replace the *LinkedCell* property.

This event handler procedure changes cell C2 to match the new value of the combo box whenever that value changes.

4. Activate Excel, turn off design mode, and try out the combo box. The value in cell C2 should change to the correct price each time you select a new car.

5. Repeat steps 1 through 4 for the spin button that sets the down payment percentage. Give it the name **spnDown**, clear the *LinkedCell* property box, and in its event procedure enter the statement:

```
Range("C3").Value = spnDown.Value / 100
```

```
Private Sub spnDown_Change()
    Range("C3").Value = spnDown.Value / 100
End Sub
```

6. Repeat steps 1 through 4 for the scroll bar. Give it the name **scrRate**, clear the *LinkedCell* property box, and in its event procedure enter the statement:

```
Range("C5").Value = scrRate.Value / 10000
```

```
Private Sub scrRate_Change()
    Range("C5").Value = scrRate.Value / 10000
End Sub
```

7. Repeat steps 1 through 4 for the spin button that sets the number of years. Give it the name **spnYears**, clear the *LinkedCell* property box, and in its event procedure enter the statement:

```
Range("C6").Value = spnYears.Value
```

```
Private Sub spnYears_Change()
    Range("C6").Value = spnYears.Value
End Sub
```

8. Clear cells H3 and H5 since you no longer need the values in them.

You now have an event handler procedure for each control, and none of the controls is linked to a cell. You're finally ready to protect the worksheet.

Protect the worksheet

You typically protect a worksheet by clicking the Protection command from the Tools menu and then clicking the Protect Sheet command. When you protect a worksheet this way, you can't subsequently change the value of any locked cells. On a worksheet that you protect with a menu command, nothing can change locked cells—not the user, ActiveX controls, or macros.

For more information about locking cells, activate Excel and ask the Assistant for help using the keywords "locked cells."

A macro, however, can protect a worksheet in such a way that a macro can still change locked cells. This special kind of protection doesn't last when you close and reopen the workbook, so you must protect the worksheet each time you open the workbook. Isn't there an event that runs each time you open a workbook? Yes, indeed, there is.

*Project Explorer
button*

1. Activate the Visual Basic Editor, click the Project Explorer button, and then double-click the ThisWorkbook object.

2. From the Object list (above the code window), select Workbook.

3. Insert this statement as the body of the Workbook_Open procedure:

```
Sheets("Loan").Protect UserInterfaceOnly:=True
```

```
Private Sub Workbook_Open()
    Sheets("Loan").Protect UserInterfaceOnly:=True
End Sub
```

*See Chapter 1
for information
on creating a
Digital Signature.*

The *UserInterfaceOnly* argument to the *Protect* method is what allows a macro to make changes even if a user or control can't. If you have a digital signature, you can sign the Visual Basic for Applications project to avoid the warning message when you open the workbook.

4. On the Tools menu, click Digital Signatures. Verify the Sign As information, and then click OK.

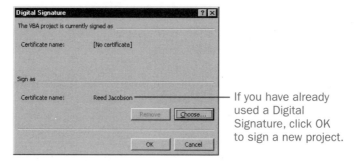

If you have already used a Digital Signature, click OK to sign a new project.

5. Save and close the Chapter10 workbook. Then reopen it.

6. Try typing numbers into the model. Excel politely explains that the worksheet is protected.

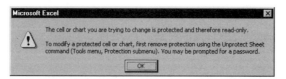

7. Try changing the model using the ActiveX controls. Everything works fine.

The loan payment calculator model is now robust and ready to give to your friend. Your friend can now experiment with various scenarios without having to worry about typing invalid inputs into the model. In fact, your friend can't type anything into the model—because the worksheet is protected. Besides, there's nothing to type. Your friend can control everything on the worksheet just by clicking controls with the mouse. One of the greatest benefits of a graphical user interface is the ability to restrict choices to valid values, thereby reducing or eliminating user error while also making a model easier to use.

Chapter Summary

To	Do this
Add ActiveX controls to a worksheet	Activate the Control Toolbox, click a control button, and drag a rectangle on the worksheet.
Link the value of a control to a cell	Assign the cell address to the *LinkedCell* property of the control.
Set limits for scroll bar and spin button controls	Assign minimum and maximum values to the *Min* and *Max* properties of the controls.
Link the list for a list box or combo box to a range on a worksheet	Assign the range address or its name to the *ListFillRange* property of the control.
Show multiple columns in a list box or combo box	Assign the number of columns to the *ColumnCount* property of the list box or combo box.
Protect the worksheet while still allowing ActiveX controls to change to the value of cells	Use event handler procedures to assign the values of the controls to cells, and then run the worksheet's *Protect* method with the *UserInterfaceOnly* argument set to *True*.

For online information about	Ask the Assistant for help using the words
Using ActiveX controls on a worksheet	"ActiveX controls"
Protecting a worksheet	"Protect worksheet"

Preview of the Next Chapter

In this chapter, you learned how to use ActiveX controls on a worksheet. You can use the same controls, plus others that are unavailable on a worksheet, in a dialog box. In the next chapter, you'll learn how to create an effective dialog box for a custom Excel application.

Chapter 11

Creating a Custom Form

Chapter Objectives   Estimated time: 55 minutes

In this chapter, you'll learn how to:

- Create a custom form.

- Initialize a form.

- Check for invalid input values in a text box.

- Run macros from a form.

Take a 3-foot by 4-foot piece of plywood and cans of blue, yellow, and orange paint. Drip, dribble, splash, and spread the paint on the plywood. You now have— a mess. But put a $500 frame around the painted plywood, and you now have—a work of art! Seriously, even serious art doesn't look earnest without a good frame, and the best diamond brooch doesn't seem to be a precious gift if given in a paper bag.

Similarly, you can write macros that are practical, convenient, and useful, but until you put a frame around them—until you tighten up the edges and make them easy to use, until you package them—you don't have a truly valuable application. Creating a custom form is an excellent way to make functionality easy to use and valuable. In this chapter, you'll learn how to create a custom form, create the functionality for the form, and link the two together into an integrated tool.

Start the lesson

1. Start Microsoft Excel, and change to the folder containing the practice files for this book.

2. Open the Budget workbook (the same one you used for Chapter 1), and save a copy as **Chapter11**.

Creating a Form's User Interface

The Budget worksheet shows detailed budget information for the year 2000. It includes both detail and summary rows.

For more information about how to install the practice files from the companion CD, see the Introduction to this book and the readme.txt file on the CD.

251

	A	B	C	D	E	F
1	Summary		Rates	Jan-2000	Feb-2000	Mar-2000
2	Projected Units			29000	30000	31000
3	Projected Revenues			71000	73000	75000
4	**Projected Pre-tax Profit**			26819.9	27057.9	30295.9
5						
6	Variable					
7	Ink		0.095	2755	2850	2945
8	Emulsion		0.012	348	360	372
9	Reducers		0.002	58	60	62
10	Rags		0.002	58	60	62

Suppose that you need to print different versions of the budget. The managers want a version that shows only the summary rows. The data entry person wants a version that shows only the detail rows, without the totals. The budget analyst wants both the detail and the summary rows but doesn't want to see months that are completed.

To make it easy to print the various versions of the report, you can create a custom dialog box, or *user form*. Here's the strategy for creating the form:

1. Design what the form will look like. The way the form looks and acts, called the *user interface,* is the first thing that the user sees, and it suggests how to use the form. The easiest way to design a form in Microsoft Visual Basic for Applications is to just jump in and create it.

2. Create the macros you need to make the form work. These are the procedures that interact with Excel objects. The tasks that the form executes are called its *functionality.* Adding functionality might involve making changes to the worksheet that enable the macros to work.

3. Make the form run the macros, and provide a way to show the form. Integrating the user interface with the functionality of the form is the final *implementation.*

The process of designing the form's user interface can help you figure out what functionality you need to develop.

Create the form

1. With the Chapter11 workbook open, click the Visual Basic Editor button. The second button from the left on the Standard toolbar in the Visual Basic Editor is the Insert UserForm button.

2. Click the arrow next to the Insert UserForm button to display a list of objects that you can insert.

Visual Basic Editor button

Insert UserForm button

The button might have a different picture depending ing on whether you've previously used it.

Click the UserForm option to create a new form.

3. Click the UserForm option to create a new, empty user form. The form is stored in your project just as a module is. You can "run" the form from Visual Basic for Applications in the same way that you run a macro.

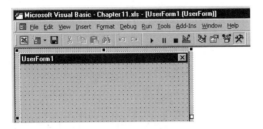

4. Double-click UserForm1 to display the form, and then click the Close Window button to close it. By default, the caption of the form is UserForm1. The caption is a property; you can change the caption using the Properties window.

Close Window button

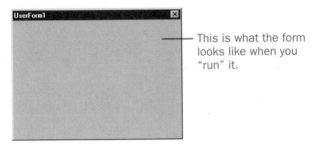

This is what the form looks like when you "run" it.

5. Click the Properties Window button, and change the value of the *Caption* property to **Print Options**. The caption changes in the form as you change the value in the Properties window.

Properties Window button

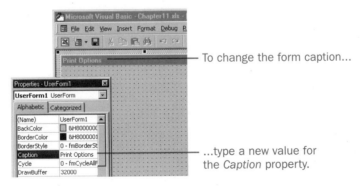

To change the form caption...

...type a new value for the *Caption* property.

6. Change the value of the *(Name)* property to **frmPrint**. (The Name property has parentheses around it, which cause it to appear at the top of the list.) The prefix *frm-* is short for "form." The *Print* part of the name tells you the intended purpose of the form. If you ever need to refer to the form inside a procedure, you can use this meaningful name.

That's all there is to creating a user form! Of course, you might want to put something a little fancier inside it.

Add option buttons

You want the user to be able to choose one of three layouts when printing the report: all the rows, only the summary rows, or only the detail rows. Option buttons provide a way to select a single item from a short, predefined list. Generally, option buttons go inside a frame.

When Visual Basic for Applications displayed the user form, it automatically displayed the Control toolbox for forms. This Control toolbox is similar to the Control toolbox you use to add ActiveX controls to a worksheet.

1. Click the Form window.

Frame button

If you don't see the Control toolbox, click the Toolbox button on the Standard toolbar to display it.

Toolbox button

2. In the Control toolbox, click the Frame button, and then click near the top-left corner of the form. A large frame control appears on the form. You can move or resize the frame later.

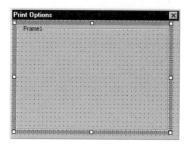

Your next task is to add the option buttons. You can avoid clicking the control button on the toolbox each time you add a button by double-clicking the control button. Double-clicking activates the button until you click it again.

OptionButton button

3. Double-click the OptionButton button, click in three places on the form to create three buttons, and then click the OptionButton button again to turn it off.

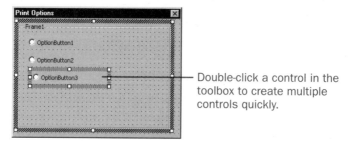

Double-click a control in the toolbox to create multiple controls quickly.

4. Activate the Properties window, and select Frame1 from the drop-down list at the top.

5. Type **Rows** as the value of the *Caption* property, and type **grpRows** as the value of the *Name* property. (The prefix *grp-* is short for "group," which is an old name for a frame. The prefix *frm-* is already reserved for a form.)

6. Select the first option button. Type **All** as the value of the *Caption* property, **optAll** as the value of the *Name* property, and **A** as the value of the *Accelerator* property. (You've probably guessed what the prefix *opt-* is short for.) With the optAll control still selected, type **True** as the value of the *Value* property. Setting the *Value* property to *True* makes this the default option.

7. Give the second option button the caption **Summary**, the name **optSummary**, and the accelerator key **S**.

8. Give the third option button the caption **Detail**, the name **optDetail**, and the accelerator key **D**.

9. Select all three option buttons by clicking between the bottom option button and the bottom of the frame and dragging a rectangle that touches each of the option button captions.

10. On the Format menu in the Visual Basic Editor, click Vertical Spacing, and then click Remove. From the Format menu, click Align and then click Left. Again, from the Format menu, click Size To Fit. Finally, drag the group of controls up close to the top-left corner of the frame, and resize the frame just to fit around the option buttons.

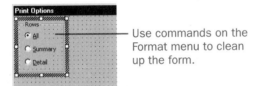

Use commands on the Format menu to clean up the form.

The Format menu provides powerful tools for getting the controls on a form to line up properly.

11. Save the workbook, press F5 to see how the option buttons will look (try clicking the option buttons), and then close the Print Options window.

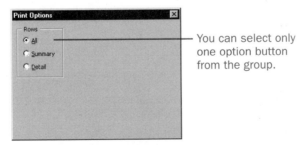

You can select only one option button from the group.

A frame with a set of option buttons is a good user interface for selecting a single option from a predefined list.

Add a check box with a related text box

Your form needs some way for you to specify whether to print all the months or only the remaining months. This is basically a "yes or no" choice. The best control for a "yes or no" choice is a check box. When the check box is selected, the macro will print starting with the current month.

Still, even though the budget analyst says that the report should start with the current month, you know that exceptions inevitably will arise. You should therefore add a text box that lets you specify a different start month, just to be prepared.

CheckBox button

1. With the form window visible, click the CheckBox button in the Control toolbox, and then click below the frame on the form where you want the check box to appear.

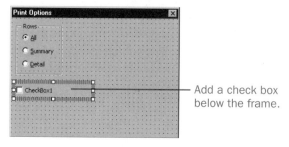

Add a check box below the frame.

2. In the Properties window, change the caption for the check box to **Start with month**, change the name to **chkMonth**, and change the Accelerator to **m**. You must use a lowercase letter, because the letter in the caption is lowercase. The accelerator character must match the character in the caption exactly.

3. Double-click the right size handle of the check box selection rectangle to shrink the rectangle to fit the caption.

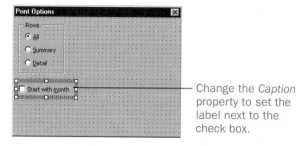

Change the *Caption* property to set the label next to the check box.

You'll now add the text box for the month right after the caption for the check box so that the contents appear to complete the "Start with month" caption.

4. Click the TextBox button in the toolbox, and then click to the right of the check box caption.

TextBox button

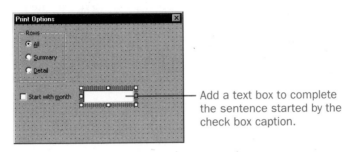

Add a text box to complete the sentence started by the check box caption.

5. Change the text box name to **txtMonth**, set the *Value* property to **7/1/ 2000**, and then change the *Enabled* property to **False**. You won't need to change the value of the month if the check box is cleared. Setting the *Enabled* property to *False* makes the contents of the box appear gray. You want the text box to become enabled whenever the user selects the check box. This is a job for an event.

6. Double-click the chkMonth check box control. A new window captioned frmPrint (Code) appears. It contains a new event handler procedure, chkMonth_Click. The *Click* event is the default event for a check box.

Double-click the check box to create an event handler for the default event.

7. Insert the following statement as the body of the new chkMonth_Click procedure:

```
txtMonth.Enabled = chkMonth.Value
```

This statement enables the text box whenever the check box is selected and disables the text box whenever the check box is cleared.

8. Save the workbook, press F5 to run the form, and click the check box a couple of times. Then close the form.

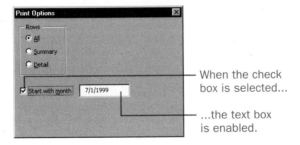

When the check box is selected...

...the text box is enabled.

When the check box is cleared, you can't change the date. When it's selected, you can.

Adding an event to the check box control makes the user interface work better, but it doesn't change anything in Excel. Even though the event is Visual Basic for Applications code, it doesn't really contribute to the functionality of the application.

Initialize the text box

When you created the month text box, you assigned 7/1/2000 as a default date. Since most of the time you'll want the current month in that box, you can make the form easier to use by initializing the text box with the current month. That means that you must calculate the appropriate date for the text box at the time you display the form.

1. Double-click the background of the form. A new procedure named UserForm_Click appears.

Double-click the form to create an event handler for the default event.

The name of the object for a form is always UserForm. No matter what name you give the form, the event handler procedures always use the name UserForm. The default event for a form is *Click,* but you don't want to wait until the user clicks the form to initialize the month. You therefore need a different event.

2. From the Procedures list, select the *Initialize* event. After the UserForm_Initialize procedure appears, delete the UserForm_Click procedure.

3. Enter the following statement as the body of the procedure:

```
txtMonth.Value = Date
```

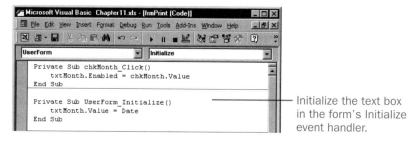

Initialize the text box in the form's Initialize event handler.

Date is a built-in Visual Basic function that returns the current date, based on your computer's internal clock.

4. Press F5 to run the form.

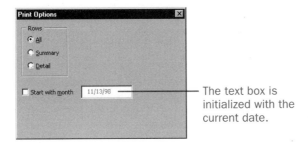

The text box is initialized with the current date.

The purpose of the date is to identify the month you want the report to start with. You'll create a macro that searches the top row of the worksheet to find a date that matches the one in the text box. The dates in the top row of the worksheet are all for the first day of the month. To find a match, therefore, the date in the text box must be for the first day of the month as well. The date that the macro puts into the text box, however, is the current date. Because it's highly unlikely that the current date is the first day of the month, you need a way to convert the current date to the first day of the current month.

5. Close the form, and then double-click the background to get back to the UserForm_Initialize procedure. You're now going to create a custom function that will convert any date into the first day of the month.

6. Below the UserForm Initialize procedure, add this custom function:

```
Function StartOfMonth(InputDate)
    If IsDate(InputDate) Then
        StartOfMonth = DateSerial(Year(InputDate), _
            Month(InputDate), 1)
    Else
        StartOfMonth = Empty
    End If
End Function
```

This function accepts an input date as an argument. It first checks to see whether the input date is a date or can be turned into one. If it can, the function extracts the year and the month from the input date and uses the *DateSerial* function to create a new date. You give the *DateSerial* function a year, a month, and a day, and it gives you back the appropriate date. The *StartOfMonth* function ignores the day portion of the input date and always uses 1 as the day instead. If the input date can't be interpreted as a date for some reason, the function returns the special value *Empty*. The *Empty* value is the same as when a variable has never been initialized. The Visual Basic *Date* function in the UserForm_Initialize procedure always returns a valid date, so if you call only the *StartOfMonth* function from the UserForm_Initialize procedure, it doesn't have to handle an invalid date. But whenever you write a custom function, you should write it to work in a variety of situations that might arise. Returning an *Empty* value when the argument is an invalid date is one way to make your function more flexible.

Tip If you want to test the function, you can do so from the Immediate window. Because this function is part of the code for a form object, however, you must include the form name before the function name. For example, you could test the function in the Immediate window by entering the following statement: **?frmPrint.StartOfMonth("May 23, 2000")**.

---

7. Change the statement in the UserForm_Initialize procedure to **txtmonth.Value = StartOfMonth(Date)**.

8. Press F5 to run the dialog box, check the date in the month box, and close the form. The date should be the first day of the current month.

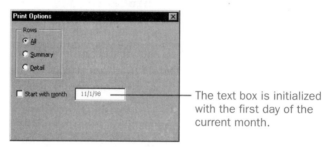

The text box is initialized with the first day of the current month.

Many controls need to be initialized. Some controls, such as the option buttons, can be initialized when you create the form. Other controls, such as the month text box, need to be initialized when you run the form, and the Initialize event handler is the place to accomplish that task.

Add command buttons

Your form now allows you to specify what both the rows and columns of the report should look like. You still need a way to start printing. To do that, you add a command button. In theory, you don't need a cancel button, because you can always just click the Close Window button to close the form. But a cancel button is easier to understand and use, and the whole purpose of a good user interface is to make the form easy to understand and use.

1. Activate the Form window.

2. Click the CommandButton button in the Control toolbox, and then click on the form, to the right of the Rows frame.

3. Press and hold the Ctrl key, and drag the new button down to make a copy of it. The top button prints the report, and the bottom one will be a Cancel button.

CommandButton button

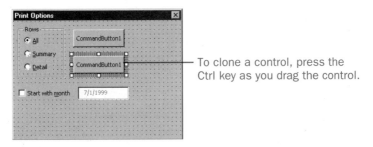

To clone a control, press the
Ctrl key as you drag the control.

4. Change the caption on the top button to **Print**, assign **P** as the
accelerator key, change the name to **btnPrint**, and change the *Default*
property to **True**. Only one command button on a form can be the
default. A default button is the one that gets "clicked" when you press
the Enter key.

5. Change the caption on the bottom button to **Cancel**, don't assign an
accelerator key, change the name to **btnCancel**, and change the *Cancel*
property to **True**.

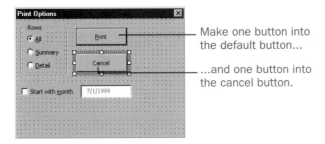

Make one button into
the default button...

...and one button into
the cancel button.

Only one command button on a form can be a cancel button. A cancel
button is the one that gets "clicked" when you press the Esc key.
Normally, when you click a cancel button, you expect the form to close.
A cancel button by itself, however, doesn't close the form. First, you have
to add an event handler to it.

6. Double-click the cancel button to create an event handler named
btnCancel_Click, and enter the statement **Unload Me** as the body of the
procedure.

The cancel button
unloads the form without
doing anything else.

The *Unload* command removes a form from memory. The *Me* keyword
refers to the current form. The macro statement *Unload Me* therefore
removes from memory the form that contains the control whose event
handler is currently running.

7. Select btnPrint from the Objects list at the top of the code window to create a new procedure called btnPrint_Click, and enter these two statements as the body of the procedure:

```
Unload Me
MsgBox "Printing"
```

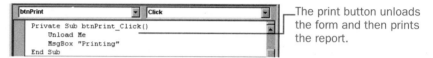

The print button unloads the form and then prints the report.

The first statement removes the form, and the second statement is a placeholder until you add the functionality to print the report.

8. Save the workbook, and run the form several times. Try clicking the Cancel and the Print buttons. Try pressing the Esc or Enter keys.

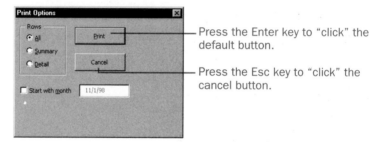

Press the Enter key to "click" the default button.

Press the Esc key to "click" the cancel button.

Either pressing the Enter key or clicking the Print button should display the *Printing* message. Either pressing the Esc key or clicking the Cancel button should make the form disappear quietly.

Set the tab order for controls

1. Run the form one more time. Select the Start With Month check box to enable the month text box. Press the Tab key repeatedly. Watch the small gray box move from control to control.

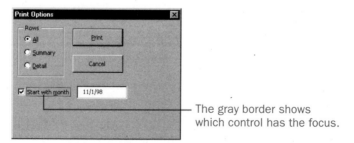

The gray border shows which control has the focus.

The gray box identifies the control that has the *focus*. When you use the keyboard, you can press the Tab key to move the focus from control to control.

2. Click Cancel to close the form. Some people prefer to use the keyboard rather than a mouse. For them, you should make sure that accelerator keys are properly defined and that the tab order is logical. For this form, the tab order should be optAll, optSummary, optDetail, chkMonth, txtMonth, btnPrint, and btnCancel. If that's not the tab order for your controls, the Visual Basic Editor provides a simple way to change it.

3. Click the background of the form. From the View menu, click the Tab Order command. The Tab Order dialog box shows five controls: grpRows, chkMonth, txtMonth, btnPrint, and btnCancel. It treats the grpRows frame control (along with the controls it contains) as a single item. If a control is out of place in the sequence, you simply select the control and click the Move Up or Move Down button to put it in the right place.

If you don't see a Tab Order command, move the mouse over the arrow at the bottom of the View menu.

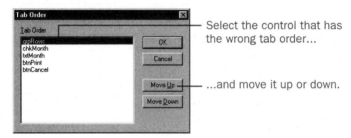

Select the control that has the wrong tab order...

...and move it up or down.

4. After making any necessary adjustments, click OK to close the dialog box. Select the frame box (or any of the option buttons), and from the View menu, click the Tab Order command again. This time, the Tab Order dialog box shows only the controls inside the frame.

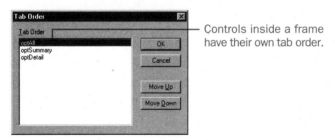

Controls inside a frame have their own tab order.

5. After making any necessary adjustments, click OK to close the dialog box. Save the workbook.

The tab order is easy to set, but remember that you need to set the order for the controls in each frame separately.

Preparing a Form's Functionality

The form now looks good. The next step is to build the functionality for printing the report. You need a way to change between the different row views, and you need a way to hide any unwanted columns. Excel can store different views of a worksheet that you specify, which you can then show later as needed. If you build some views into the worksheet, creating a macro to change between views will be easy.

Create custom views on a worksheet

A custom view allows you to hide rows or columns on a worksheet and then give that view a name so that you can retrieve it easily. You need to create three views. The first view shows all the rows and columns. That one is easy to create. The second view shows only the total rows. The third view shows only the detail rows. Hiding the rows can be a tedious process. Fortunately, you need to hide them only once. You can also use Excel's Go To Special command to help select the rows faster.

1. Activate Excel. From the View menu, click the Custom Views command.

2. In the Custom Views dialog box, click the Add button, type **All** as the name for the new view, clear the Print Settings check box, leave the Hidden Rows, Columns And Filter Settings check box selected, and then click OK.

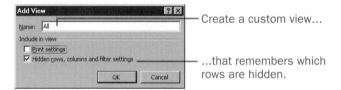

Create a custom view...

...that remembers which rows are hidden.

You just created the first view, the one with all rows and columns displayed. You now need to create the Summary view, showing only the total rows. That means that you need to hide the detail rows. You notice that only the detail rows have labels in column B.

3. Select column B. From the Edit menu, click Go To and then click Special. Select the Constants option, and click OK. Only the cells in the detail rows are still selected.

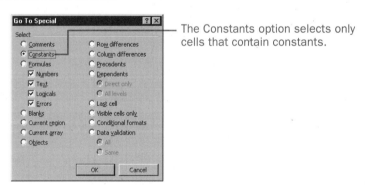

The Constants option selects only cells that contain constants.

4. Hide the selected rows. (From the Format menu, click Row, and then click Hide.)

	A	B	C	D	E
1	Summary		Rates	Jan-2000	Feb-2000
2	Projected Units			29000	30000
3	Projected Revenues			71000	73000
4	**Projected Pre-tax Profit**			26819.9	27057.9
5					
6	Variable				
13	Total Variable			7598	7860

The rows with constants in Column B are hidden.

The only remaining rows that you want to hide all have blank cells in column D. Does that give you any ideas?

5. Select column D. Click Edit, Go To, and Special. Select Blanks, and then click OK. Hide the selected rows as you did in step 4. This is the view for the managers.

	A	B	C	D	E
1	Summary		Rates	Jan-2000	Feb-2000
2	Projected Units			29000	30000
3	Projected Revenues			71000	73000
4	**Projected Pre-tax Profit**			26819.9	27057.9
13	Total Variable			7598	7860
21	Total Salaries			16546	16546

The rows with constants in Column B or blanks in Column D are hidden.

6. With only these total rows visible, create another view named **Summary**. (From the View menu, click Custom Views, click Add, type **Summary**, clear Print Settings, and then click OK.) Now you need to create the detail view. For the detail view, you want to hide all the summary rows. The rows you want to hide have labels in the range A4:A68.

7. Show the All custom view to unhide all the rows. Select the range A4:A68, use Go To Special to select the cells with constants, and then hide the rows. Select column D, and hide all the rows with blank cells.

	A	B	C	D	E
1	Summary		Rates	Jan-2000	Feb-2000
2	Projected Units			29000	30000
3	Projected Revenues			71000	73000
7	Ink		0.095	2755	2850
8	Emulsion		0.012	348	360
9	Reducers		0.002	58	60
10	Rags		0.002	58	60

The summary rows are hidden.

8. With these detail rows visible, create a new view named **Detail**, again clearing the Print Settings option.

9. Save the workbook, and try showing each of the three views. Finish with the All view.

Creating the views is bothersome, but you have to do it only once. Once the views are created, making a macro to switch between views is easy.

Create a macro to switch views

1. Start recording a macro named **ShowView**. Show the Summary view, turn off the recorder, and look at the macro. It should look like this:

```
Sub ShowView()
    ActiveWorkbook.CustomViews("Summary").Show
End Sub
```

A workbook has a collection named CustomViews. You use the name of the view to retrieve an item from the collection. The item has a *Show* method. To switch between views, all you need to do is substitute the name of the view in parentheses. And rather than create three separate macros, you can pass the name of the view as an argument.

2. Type **ViewName** between the parentheses after *ShowView*, and then replace *"Summary"* (quotation marks and all), with **ViewName**. The revised macro should look like this:

```
Sub ShowView(ViewName)
    ActiveWorkbook.CustomViews(ViewName).Show
End Sub
```

Next, you'll test the macro and its argument using the Immediate window.

3. Press Ctrl-G to display the Immediate window.

4. Type **ShowView "Detail"** and press the Enter key. The worksheet should change to show the detailed view.

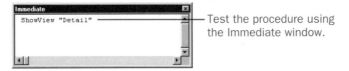
Test the procedure using the Immediate window.

5. Type **ShowView "All"** and press the Enter key. Then type **ShowView "Summary"** and press the Enter key again. The macro works with all three arguments.

6. Close the Immediate window, and save the workbook.

You now have the functionality to show different views. Creating the views might not have been fun, but it certainly made writing the macro a lot easier. Also, if you decide to adjust a view (say, to include blank lines), you don't need to change the macro. You still need to create the functionality to hide columns containing dates earlier than the desired starting month.

Dynamically hide columns

You don't want to create custom views to change the columns, because you'd need to create 36 different custom views: one for each month times the three different row settings. You need to change the columns dynamically, based on the choices in the dialog box. If you're going to hide columns, you'll start with column C and end with an arbitrary month specified. One good way to find the month is to use Excel's *Find* method.

1. In Excel, select all of row 1, and then start recording a macro named **HideMonths**.

2. From the Edit menu, click the Find command, type **5/1/2000** in the Find What box, select the Find Entire Cells Only check box, and make sure the Look In drop-down list box says Formulas.

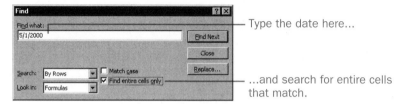

— Type the date here...

...and search for entire cells that match.

By searching for the formula, you look for the underlying date in the cell. The underlying date uses the system date format, regardless of how the cell happens to be formatted. By searching only entire cells, you make sure that 1/1/2000, for example, will find only January (1/1/2000), and not November (11/1/2000), which differs only by having an extra digit at the beginning.

If your system uses a date format other than mm/dd/yyyy (the default United States date format), you'll need to experiment to find the date format that works for you.

3. Click Find Next, close the Find dialog box, stop the recorder, and then edit the HideMonths macro. Put a line continuation (a space, an underscore, and a new line) after every comma to make the statement readable. The macro should now look like this:

```
Sub HideMonths()
    Selection.Find(What:="5/1/2000", _
        After:=ActiveCell, _
        LookIn:=xlFormulas, _
        LookAt:=xlWhole, _
        SearchOrder:=xlByRows, _
        SearchDirection:=xlNext, _
        MatchCase:=False).Activate
End Sub
```

The macro searches the selection (in this case, row 1), starting with the active cell (in this case, cell A1), searches for the specified date, and activates the matching cell. You don't want the macro to change the selection, and you don't want the macro to activate the cell it finds. Rather, you want the macro to assign the found range to a variable so that you can refer to it.

4. Make these changes to the macro: Declare the variable *myFind* as a Range. Change *Selection* to **Rows(1)** and *ActiveCell* to **Range("A1")**. Delete *.Activate* from the end of the second statement, and add **Set myFind =** to the beginning.

Be sure to type "2000" rather than "00" for the year. The revised macro looks like this:

```
Sub HideMonths()
    Dim myFind as Range
    Set myFind = Rows(1).Find(What:="5/1/2000", _
        After:=Range("A1"), _
        LookIn:=xlFormulas, _
        LookAt:=xlWhole, _
        SearchOrder:=xlByRows, _
        SearchDirection:=xlNext, _
        MatchCase:=False)
End Sub
```

If the *Find* method is successful, then *myFind* will contain a reference to the cell that contains the month. You want to hide all the columns from column C (the Rates column) to one column to the left of *myFind*.

5. Before the *End Sub* statement, insert this statement:

```
Range("C1",myFind.Offset(0,-1)).EntireColumn.Hidden = True
```

This selects a range starting with cell C1 and ending one cell to the left of the cell with the month name. It then hides the columns containing that range.

6. Save the workbook, and press F8 repeatedly to step through the macro. Watch as columns C through H disappear.

You'll be changing this subroutine to hide columns up to any date. You need some way of knowing whether or not the *Find* method finds a match. If the *Find* method does find a match, it assigns a reference to the variable. If it doesn't find a match, it assigns a special object reference, *Nothing*, to the variable. You can check to see whether the object is the same as *Nothing*. Because you're comparing object references and not values, you don't use an equal sign to do the comparison. Instead, you use a special object comparison word, *Is*.

Note A variable that's declared as a variant contains the value *Empty* when nothing else is assigned to it. A variable that's declared as an object contains the reference *Nothing* when no other object reference is assigned to it. *Empty* means "no value," and *Nothing* means "no object reference." To see whether the variable *myValue* contains the *Empty* value, use the expression *IsEmpty(myValue)*. To see whether the variable *myObject* contains a reference to *Nothing*, use the expression *myObject Is Nothing*.

---

7. Replace the statement that hides the columns with this *If* structure:

```
If Not myFind Is Nothing Then
    Range("C1", myFind.Offset(0, -1)).EntireColumn.Hidden = True
End If
```

The statement that hides the columns is unchanged. If the *Find* method fails, it assigns *Nothing* to *myFind*, so the conditional expression is *False* and no columns are hidden.

8. Test the macro's ability to handle an error by changing the value for which the *Find* method searches, from *5/1/2000* to **Dog**. Then step through the macro and watch what happens when you get to the *If* structure. Hold the mouse pointer over the *myFind* variable and see that its value is *Nothing*.

```
        After:=Range("A1"), _
        LookIn:=xlFormulas, _
        LookAt:=xlWhole, _
        SearchOrder:=xlByRows, _
        SearchDirection:=xlNext, _
        MatchCase:=False)
   If Not myFind Is Nothing Then
      ⌐myFind = Nothing┐ myFind.Offset(0, -1)).EntireColumn.
   End If
End Sub
```

The *Find* method returns *Nothing* if it doesn't find a match.

If you search for a date that's in row 1, *myFind* will hold a reference to the cell containing that date and the macro will hide the months that precede it. If you search for anything else, *myFind* will hold a reference to *Nothing*, and the macro won't hide any columns.

9. Press F5 to end the macro.

10. The final step is to convert the date to an argument. Type **StartMonth** between the parentheses after *HideMonths*, and replace "5/1/2000" or "Dog" (including the quotation marks) with **StartMonth**. The revised (and finished) procedure should look like this:

```
Sub HideMonths(StartMonth)
    Dim myFind As Range
    Set myFind = Rows(1).Find(What:=StartMonth, _
        After:=Range("A1"), _
        LookIn:=xlFormulas, _
        LookAt:=xlWhole, _
        SearchOrder:=xlByRows, _
        SearchDirection:=xlNext, _
        MatchCase:=False)
    If Not myFind Is Nothing Then
        Range("C1", myFind.Offset(0, -1)).EntireColumn.Hidden _
        = True
    End If
End Sub
```

11. Now test the macro. Press Ctrl-G to display the Immediate window. Enter **ShowView "All"** and then enter **HideMonths "8/1/2000"**.

Be sure to type "2000," not "00," for the year.

⌐ The months before August are hidden.

	A	B	M	N	O
1	Summary		Aug-2000	Sep-2000	Qtr3
2	Projected Units		35000	36000	106000
3	Projected Revenues		85000	87000	255000
4	Projected Pre-tax Profit		39247.9	40985.9	117481.7

12. Close the Immediate window, and save the workbook.

You now have macros that can handle the functionality of the form by hiding appropriate rows and columns. It's now time to put the form and the functionality together.

Implementing a Form

You've created a user interface for the form. The user interface allows you to specify which rows and columns to print. You've also created the functionality for the form. The ShowView and HideMonths macros show the appropriate rows and columns. You now need to make the user interface drive the functionality. You need to implement the form.

For this form, the Print button is what formats and prints the report. You'll put all the code that links the form to the functionality into the btnPrint_Click procedure.

Project Explorer button

Implement option buttons

To implement the option buttons, you need a way to determine which option button value is *True*. The frame control has a *Controls* property that returns a collection of all the controls in the frame. You can loop through those controls and determine which option button value is *True*.

1. In the Visual Basic Editor, click the Project Explorer toolbar button, double-click the frmPrint form, and then close the Project window.

Use the Project window to get back to the form.

When you have a project with several components, the Project window is often the easiest way to get to the right place.

2. Double-click the Print button to show the btnPrint_Click event handler procedure.

3. Insert these statements at the beginning of the procedure, before the *Unload Me* statement:

```
Dim myOption As Control
Dim myView

For Each myOption In grpRows.Controls
    If myOption.Value = True Then
        myView = myOption.Caption
    End If
```

```
Next myOption
ShowView myView
```

This *For Each* loop inspects each control in the frame, looking for a value of *True*. You declare the loop variable as a *Control* (not as an OptionButton) because it's possible for a frame to contain other types of controls besides option buttons.

Note If you loop through the controls of a frame that contains controls other than option buttons, you should check to see whether the control is an option button. If you prefix each option button name with *opt-*, you can use the conditional expression *Left(myOption.Name,3) = "opt"* to determine whether the control is an option button.

The loop stores the caption of the selected option in a variable, and the macro later uses that variable as the argument when it runs the ShowView macro. What a fortuitous coincidence that we used the same names for the custom views and the captions of the option buttons!

4. Save the workbook, and press F8 to run the form. (Press F8 repeatedly to step through the initialization procedures.) You can run the form by pressing F5 while either the form design window or the form code window is active, but the form code window must be active to use F8. If you press F8 to run the form, you can step through any event handler procedures triggered by controls on the form.

5. Click the Summary option, and then click Print. Press F8 repeatedly to step through the btnPrint_Click procedure. Close the message box as necessary.

An option button can be easy to implement if you plan ahead. In this example, giving the custom views in the worksheet the same names as the captions of the option buttons made the option buttons easy to implement. Also, if you had to add a fourth view option, all you'd have to do is define a new view on the worksheet and add an option button with the appropriate caption to the form. You wouldn't need to make any changes to any of the procedures.

Implement a check box

If the check box is selected, the Print button event handler should run the HideMonths macro. Actually, the HideMonths macro will do nothing if you give it a date that it doesn't find. You can take advantage of that by assigning to a variable either the date from the month box or an invalid value.

1. Double-click the Print button to show the btnPrint_Click procedure, and add the following statements after *Dim myView*:

```
Dim myMonth

If chkMonth.Value = True Then
    myMonth = txtMonth.Value
Else
    myMonth = "no date"
End If
```

These statements assign to the *myMonth* variable either the value from the month text box or an obviously invalid value.

2. Insert the statement **HideMonths myMonth** after the statement *ShowView myView*. You place this statement after the *ShowView* statement because you want to change the view before hiding the months; showing the custom view redisplays all the hidden columns.

3. Save the workbook, and press F5 to run the form. Select the check box, type **9/1/2000** in the month box, and click Print. The worksheet now shows only the months starting from September.

	A	B	N	O	P
1	Summary		Sep-2000	Qtr3	Oct-2000
2	Projected Units		36000	106000	37000
3	Projected Revenues		87000	255000	89000
4	Projected Pre-tax Profit		40985.9	117481.7	43223.9

The date in the text box of the form determines the first visible month.

4. Click OK to close the message box.

Check for errors in an edit box

What if you run the form and type "Dog" as the date? The macro shouldn't hide any columns, but it should point out the error. What if you type "4/15/2000" as the date? Ideally, the macro should automatically convert *4/15/2000* to the appropriate *4/1/2000*. Look in your library of useful macro routines and see if you can find a function to convert a date to the start of the month.

1. Double-click the Print button. In the btnPrint_Click procedure, replace *myMonth = txtMonth.Value* with **myMonth = StartOfMonth(txtMonth.Value)**. The *StartOfMonth* function converts a date to the first of the month. If the input date isn't a valid date, the function returns the *Empty* value. (That was remarkably prescient of you to write the *StartOfMonth* function to handle invalid dates.) If the *myMonth* variable contains the *Empty* value, you'll want to show a message and make the value easy to fix.

2. Insert these statements before the *Else* statement:

```
If myMonth = Empty Then
    MsgBox "Invalid Month"
    txtMonth.SetFocus
    txtMonth.SelStart = 0
    txtMonth.SelLength = 1000
    Exit Sub
End If
```

When you run the form, if you type an invalid date, the macro appropriately displays a message box explaining the problem. After you close the message box, you should be able to just start typing a corrected value. For that to happen, however, the macro must move to the text box and preselect the current, invalid contents.

The *SetFocus* method moves the focus to the text box. Setting the *SelStart* property to 0 (zero) starts text selection from the very beginning of the text box. Setting the *SelLength* property to 1000 extends text selection to however much text there is in the box. Using an arbitrarily large value like 1000 simply avoids having to calculate the actual length of the contents of the box.

3. Save the workbook, and then press F5 to run the form. Try enabling the month, typing **Dog**, and clicking Print. Try typing **Jun 23, 00** and clicking Print. (Close the message box.)

When you put an edit box onto a form, you must think about what the macro should do if the user enters an invalid value. In many cases, displaying an error message and preselecting the invalid entry is the best strategy. The *SetFocus* method and the *SelStart* and *SelLength* properties are the tools that allow you to implement that strategy.

Print the report

The Print form now does everything it needs to do—everything, that is, except print. If you make the report display the report in print preview mode, you can then decide whether to print it or just admire it.

1. Double-click the Print button. In the btnPrint_Click procedure, replace *MsgBox "Printing"* with **ActiveSheet.PrintPreview**. After the report prints, you should restore the rows and columns in the worksheet.

2. After the statement *ActiveSheet.PrintPreview*, type the statement **ShowView "All"**.

3. Save the workbook, press F5 to run the form, select the Summary option, limit the months to August and later, click the Print button, and then click Zoom to see the beautiful report.

Use Print Preview to see what the report will look like.

4. Close the Print Preview window.

The user interface of the form is now linked to its full functionality. All that's left is to provide a way for the user to run the form from Excel instead of from the Visual Basic Editor.

Launch the form

To launch the form, you create a standard macro that displays the form. Once you've done that, you can make event procedures that automatically add a menu command when the workbook opens and remove it when the workbook closes.

Project Explorer button

1. Click the Project Explorer button to show the Project window, double-click the Module1 module (that is, the module that contains the ShowView and HideMonths macros), activate the code window, and scroll to the bottom of the module.

2. Insert this macro:

```
Sub ShowForm()
    frmPrint.Show
End Sub
```

The *Show* method of a form displays the form. To refer to the form, simply use the name that you gave it when you created it.

Tip   Ordinarily, you can't activate a worksheet while a form is displayed. When a form prevents you from selecting the worksheet, it's called a *modal* form. If you want the user to be able to use the worksheet while the form is displayed, add the argument **False** after the *Show* method. This creates what is called a *nonmodal* form. Nonmodal forms are a new feature in Excel 2000. All of Excel's built-in dialog boxes are modal, but Microsoft Word uses several nonmodal dialog boxes. If you use Microsoft Word, the Find And Replace dialog box is an example of a nonmodal form.

---

3. In the Project window, double-click the ThisWorkbook object. Select Workbook from the Objects list, and insert these statements as the body of the Workbook_Open procedure:

```
Dim myButton As CommandBarButton
Set myButton = _
    Application.CommandBars("Worksheet Menu Bar").Controls.Add
myButton.Caption = "&Print Report"
myButton.Style = msoButtonCaption
myButton.BeginGroup = True
myButton.OnAction = "ShowForm"
```

The CommandBars collection works like any other collection; you specify an item using the name of the item. The Controls collection also works like other collections; you add an item—in this case, a command bar button—using the *Add* method. The *Add* method returns a reference to the new object, which you can assign to an object variable. Unless you specify otherwise, the *Add* method adds the control to the end of the collection.

Assigning a value to the *Caption* property sets the text for the command. Assigning *msoButtonCaption* to the *Style* property makes the control display the caption, rather than an icon. The *BeginGroup* property adds a line before the command, separating it from the built-in commands. The *OnAction* property is the name of the macro you want to have run. This menu item will appear on the main Excel menu bar whenever you open the workbook.

4. From the Procedures list at the top of the code window, select BeforeClose. Insert these statements as the body of the Workbook_BeforeClose procedure:

```
ActiveWorkbook.Save
On Error Resume Next
Application.CommandBars("Worksheet Menu Bar") _
    .Controls("Print Report").Delete
```

The first statement saves the workbook. This prevents Excel from asking whether or not to save the workbook. The second statement keeps the macro from displaying an error if the Print Report command doesn't exist for some reason. The third statement deletes the new Print Report menu command. These statements will execute whenever the workbook closes, removing any trace of the Print Report command.

5. If you have a digital signature, sign the Visual Basic for Applications project.

6. Switch to Excel; save the workbook, and close it.

See Chapter 1 for details about creating and using a digital signature.

7. Open the Chapter11 workbook. The new command appears on the main worksheet menu as soon as you open the workbook.

8. Click the new Print Report menu command, and then click Cancel.

9. Close the workbook. The new command disappears. Your custom form is completely integrated with Excel.

Creating a fully usable form entails three major steps: creating the user interface, creating the functionality, and joining them together into a working tool. Now that you've created one form, go andcreate dozens more for your own projects.

To	Do this
Add a form	Click the Insert UserForm button.
Test run an active form	Press F5 (or press F8 to step through the form's procedures).
Arrange controls on a form	Select multiple controls, and then choose commands from the Visual Basic Editor's Format menu.
Initialize a control when you design the form	Set the value of a property for the control in the Properties window.
Initialize a control when you run the form	Assign a value to a property for the control in the UserForm_Initialize event handler procedure for the form.
Make an event handler procedure close the form	Use the *Unload Me* statement.
Set the tab order for controls on a form or in a frame	Select the form or the frame, and click the Tab Order command from the View menu.
Check to see whether the *Find* method found a matching cell	Assign the result of the *Find* method to an object variable, and use *Is Nothing* to examine the variable.
Determine which option button in a frame is selected	Use a *For Each* loop to search the Controls collection of the frame, looking for a *True* value.
Select the contents of a text box that contains an error	Use the *SetFocus* method to activate the text box, and then assign 0 to the *SelStart* property and 1000 to the *SelLength* property.
Show a form named *frmPrint* from a macro	Use the statement *frmPrint.Show*.
Show a form named *frmPrint* in such a way that you can still select cells in the worksheet (that is, as a nonmodal form)	Use the statement *frmPrint.Show False*.
Add a command to the worksheet menu bar	Use the statement *Application.CommandBars ("WorksheetMenuBar"). Commands.Add*.
Create procedures that run when the workbook opens or closes	Add procedures named Workbook_Open and Workbook_BeforeClose to the ThisWorkbook object in a workbook.

For online information about	Ask the Assistant for help using the words
Creating a custom form	"User form"
Using option buttons	"Option buttons"
Using menus and toolbars	"Command bars"

Preview of the Next Chapter

In the next chapter, you'll create a management reporting tool. You'll create an effective user interface, use a PivotTable and a chart, and retrieve information dynamically from an external database.

Chapter 12

Creating an Enterprise Information System

In this chapter, you'll learn how to:

- Retrieve data from an external database.

- Create a graphical front end to an application.

- Create an animated logo.

- Change and restore workbook settings.

While I was in college, I spent two years in Japan. Before departing, I spent two months in an intensive language training program. At the end of the two months, I was reasonably satisfied with my ability to speak Japanese. Then I arrived in Tokyo. For the first two weeks, I was unable to detect *any* similarity between the language I had studied and the language the local inhabitants were speaking. It was, shall we say, a humbling experience.

Within a few weeks, however, I was able to pick out words, and within a few months I could communicate reasonably well. By the end of the two years, I once again felt reasonably satisfied with my ability to speak Japanese. And I learned along the way that classroom practice isn't the same as real-world experience.

Learning to write macros is in some ways similar to learning a new foreign language. Once again, classroom practice isn't the same as real-world experience. In this chapter, you'll build a simple but complete Enterprise Information System (EIS) that will allow people in all parts of a hypothetical enterprise to look at orders for the past two years. Creating a packaged application turns up numerous new real-world challenges that you don't encounter when building macros for yourself. This chapter will show you how to solve many such challenges.

Most of the concepts in this chapter have been introduced earlier in the book. This chapter shows how to put those concepts to work in packaging an application, and also introduces a few new tricks that you may need.

Start Microsoft Excel.

Examining an Existing Enterprise Information System

In this chapter, you'll create an Enterprise Information System (EIS) that displays order information for each state in the Miller Textiles territory. It will be easier for you to understand the pieces that you have to build if you have a vision of what you'll end up with. So let's take a look at the finished product before you start building it yourself.

Look at the application

Open button

Up One Level button

For more information on installing the practice files, see the Introduction to this book.

1. Click the Open button, change to the Finished subfolder under the folder containing the practice files for this book, select Chapter12, and press Ctrl-C to copy it.

2. Click the Up One Level button in the Open dialog box, and press Ctrl-V to paste a copy of the Chapter12 workbook into the folder where you installed the practice files. Then open the workbook. When the workbook opens, it displays an introductory animation and shows you a colored, shaded map of the western United States.

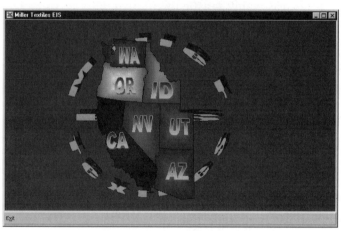

3. Click the map for California. The screen switches to display quarterly orders for the past two years, complete with a graph.

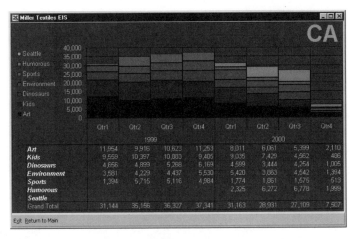

	Qtr1	Qtr2	Qtr3	Qtr4	Qtr1	Qtr2	Qtr3	Qtr4
		1999				2000		
Art	11,954	9,916	10,623	11,253	8,011	6,061	5,399	2,110
Kids	9,559	10,397	10,883	9,405	9,035	7,429	4,562	486
Dinosaurs	4,656	4,899	5,268	6,169	4,599	3,444	4,254	1,005
Environment	3,581	4,229	4,437	5,530	5,420	3,863	4,542	1,394
Sports	1,394	5,715	5,116	4,984	1,774	1,861	1,575	513
Humorous					2,325	6,272	6,778	1,999
Seattle								
Grand Total	31,144	35,156	36,327	37,341	31,163	28,931	27,109	7,507

Exit Return to Main

4. Click the Return To Main command at the lower-left corner of the Workbook window to return to the map.

5. Click the Exit command at the bottom of the window to close the workbook.

This is a simple EIS. It displays information from one of the company's databases in an easy-to-use, visually powerful way.

Take a closer look at the application

Many small details make the difference between an application that's intuitive and easy to use and one that's frustrating. Take another look at the Miller Textiles EIS, and notice some details worth including in yours.

1. Before reopening the EIS workbook, open and position several toolbars. Make the Excel window short and wide so you can tell if the application puts it back to the original size when it finishes.

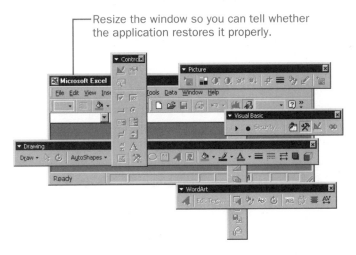

Resize the window so you can tell whether the application restores it properly.

2. Open the finished Chapter12 workbook again. Wait for the animation to begin, but before it ends, press Ctrl-Break. The animation stops, and the procedure that controls it jumps directly to its end and then displays the map. Animations are good for attracting attention, but they can be annoying to an impatient user. It's often a good idea to provide a mechanism for bypassing a lengthy animation.

3. Move the mouse over the notch where Nevada interlocks with Arizona. Click once when the mouse is over Nevada, return to the main sheet, and click again when the mouse is over Arizona. You can click anywhere within the exact border of the state to show the data for that state.

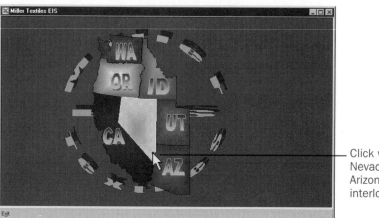

Click where Nevada and Arizona interlock.

This new screen with the table and the map is really a worksheet. Sometimes you want to use the features of an Excel worksheet but disguise that fact from the user.

4. Try selecting a cell on the worksheet. This is a "look but don't touch" screen. The application makes use of a worksheet, but from the user's perspective it could be a completely custom application. Not only is the worksheet protected, but you can't even see an active cell anywhere on it. Although the data grid looks somewhat like a PivotTable, it also has some differences.

5. Look at the caption at the top of the application. The caption says Miller Textiles EIS, rather than Excel. The caption contributes to the custom appearance of the application.

6. Look at the button at the bottom of the screen. It appears to be a toolbar or a menu bar, but unlike most toolbars, it doesn't have a double bar at the left, so you can't move it. Many times in an EIS application, you want to limit the ways that the user can modify the environment.

7. Click the Exit button. The Excel window returns to the way it was before: the same size and shape, with the same configuration of toolbars.

This EIS has many subtle features—features that you'll build into your EIS as you go through this chapter.

Charting Data from a Database

Your first task is to build the core functionality of the application: the data sheet. This sheet will use a PivotTable to retrieve the data from an external database. You'll link a chart to the PivotTable, and then format the chart and the PivotTable to make a dramatic presentation.

Retrieve external data into a PivotTable

When you retrieve data from an external database into a PivotTable, Excel uses a separate program, Microsoft Query, to assist you in specifying what data you want. Microsoft Query doesn't actually retrieve the data from the database; rather, it returns the definition of the data you want and its location. The PivotTable then uses that information to retrieve the data.

1. Save a new, blank workbook as **Chapter12** in the folder containing the practice files for this book, replacing the copy of the Finished workbook that you created earlier. Then rename Sheet1 to **Data**.

2. From the Data menu, click PivotTable And PivotChart Report. In Step 1 of the Wizard, select the External Data Source option and the PivotTable option, and then click Next.

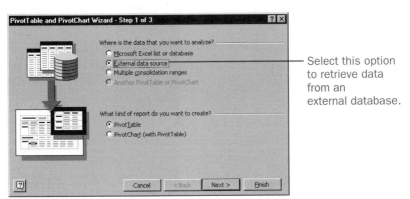

Select this option to retrieve data from an external database.

3. In step 2 of the Wizard, click the Get Data button. The Choose Data Source dialog box appears. You use a data source to tell Microsoft Query where the data is and what kind of driver to use to retrieve it.

If you don't already have the Query tool installed, you'll need access to the CD or network drive containing the Excel installation files.

4. Select the <New Data Source> option, and then click OK.

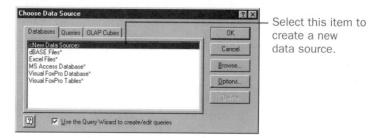

Select this item to create a new data source.

5. Type **Miller Textiles** as the name for the new data source, select the Microsoft dBase Driver as the driver, and then click Connect.

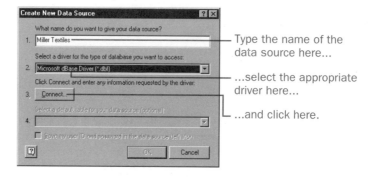

Type the name of the data source here...

...select the appropriate driver here...

...and click here.

Note ODBC is the abbreviation for "Open DataBase Connectivity," an industry-standard mechanism for letting applications communicate with any database. All major database vendors distribute ODBC drivers with their databases. If you install the ODBC drivers for another type of database, such as Oracle or SQL Server, that driver will appear in the list.

---

6. Clear the Use Current Directory check box and click the Select Directory button.

If the OK button isn't available, select the folder name in the Folder list.

7. Select the folder containing the practice files for this book. The file name orders.dbf appears in the File Name box, even though you can't select it. Click OK four times, moving through four dialog boxes. This closes all the data source dialog boxes, selects the new data source, and moves on to the Query Wizard.

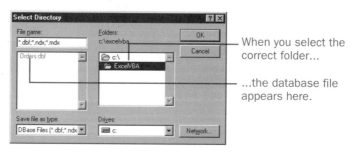

When you select the correct folder...

...the database file appears here.

8. In the Query Wizard - Choose Columns dialog box, click the plus sign next to the ORDERS table, and then double-click the DATE, STATE, CATEGORY, and NET columns. These are the only fields you'll need for the EIS.

A "column" in the Query Wizard is equivalent to a field in a PivotTable.

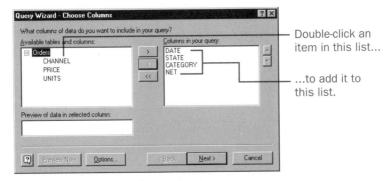

Double-click an item in this list...

...to add it to this list.

9. Click Next to go to the Query Wizard - Filter Data dialog box. Select Date as the Column To Filter, select Is Greater Than Or Equal To from the first drop-down list box, and select 1999-01-01 from the second list box. The EIS displays data for the current and previous years only.

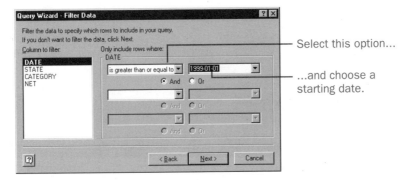

Select this option...

...and choose a starting date.

10. Click Next twice, and then click Finish to return the definition of the data to the PivotTable Wizard. At this point, you have returned to the PivotTable Wizard the names of the columns and the instructions for retrieving the data.

Query returns field names and instructions for retrieving the data.

Define the PivotTable

Once Microsoft Query has returned the information to the PivotTable Wizard, you can specify how you want the PivotTable to appear.

1. Click Next to go to step 3 of the PivotTable Wizard, and click the Options button. Turn off Grand Totals For Rows and AutoFormat Table, and then click OK. You'll format the PivotTable the way you want it to look, and you certainly don't want it to change.

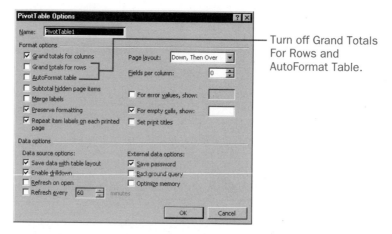

Turn off Grand Totals For Rows and AutoFormat Table.

2. Still in step 3 of the PivotTable Wizard, click the Layout button.

3. Drag STATE to the page area, DATE to the column area, CATEGORY to the row area, and NET to the data area.

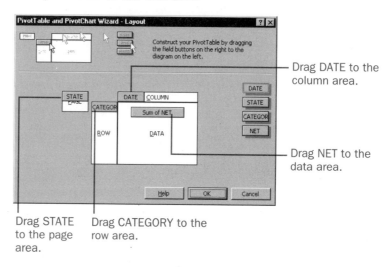

Drag DATE to the column area.

Drag NET to the data area.

Drag STATE to the page area.

Drag CATEGORY to the row area.

4. Double-click the DATE tile (in the column area), select the Show Items With No Data check box, and then click OK.

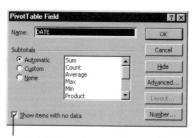

Select this option to always show all the items.

You want to show all the months for all the states, so by always showing items without data, the grid will always be the same size, and it will be easy to see which states have orders for only some of the months.

5. Double-click the CATEGORY tile (in the row area), again select the Show Items With No Data check box, and then click the Advanced button. Select Descending as the AutoSort option, and select Sum Of NET from the Using Field list box at the bottom of the AutoSort group. Then click OK twice.

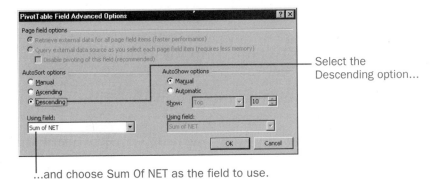

Select the Descending option...

...and choose Sum Of NET as the field to use.

Once again, you don't want the grid to change size just because not all states sell products from all categories. The Sort option will automatically sort the categories for each state, based on which category produced the most revenue.

6. Double-click the Sum Of NET tile, and click the Number button. Select the Number category, specify no decimal places, and select the 1000 Separator check box. Then click OK twice. This formats the revenue values with commas, which makes the numbers easier to read.

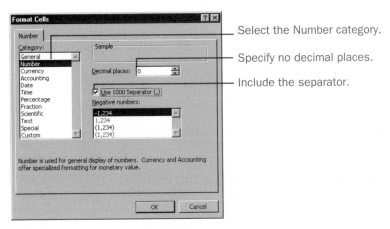

Select the Number category.

Specify no decimal places.

Include the separator.

7. Click OK to return to step 3 of the PivotTable Wizard, type **B5** as the location for the table, and then click OK to create the table.

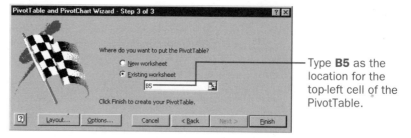

Type **B5** as the location for the top-left cell of the PivotTable.

8. Save the Chapter12 workbook.

Note Even though you create a data source (Miller Textiles) in Microsoft Query in order to retrieve the data, the PivotTable doesn't use the data source. Microsoft Query uses the data source to determine the connection information, and the PivotTable stores only that connection information. If you don't need the data source for a different application, you can remove it once the PivotTable is created.

To remove a data source, use the ODBC data source administrator tool. Activate the Control Panel and open the 32-bit ODBC item. Click the File DSN tab, select the data source name (here, Miller Textiles), and click Remove. You don't need the data source to refresh the PivotTable, only to create it.

Format the PivotTable

The table looks good, except that you want to display quarters instead of months. You also want to add a slightly more dramatic look to the sheet, and you want the columns to stay the same size, instead of adjusting as the data changes.

Group button

1. Right-click the DATE tile, and on the Group and Outline submenu, click Group. In the By list box in the Grouping dialog box, deselect Months, select Quarters and Years, and then click OK.

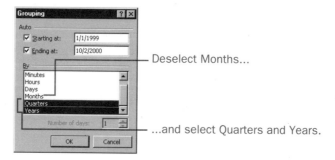

Deselect Months...

...and select Quarters and Years.

When you group dates, you end up with two rows of labels. The chart can use one or more rows as labels. Because you specified Show Items With No Data for the Date field, the table shows extra "catch-all" dates at the beginning and the end. You don't want those in the table.

2. Click the arrow next to the Year tile, deselect the top and bottom items, and then click OK. The unnecessary first and last items disappear.

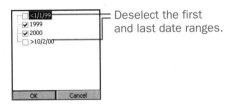

Deselect the first
and last date ranges.

3. Set the width of column A to 3.5, the width of column B to 18, the width of columns C through J to 9, and the width of column K to 1.3.

Note If you want a chart based on a PivotTable to have a different orientation than the PivotTable, you need to make a second copy of the PivotTable to use as the basis for the chart. Because both PivotTables share the same data cache, creating a copy of the PivotTable doesn't require significant additional system resources.

---

4. Before continuing to format the PivotTable, make the copy of the Data sheet. Press and hold the Ctrl key as you drag the Data sheet tab to the right. Rename the new sheet **ChartData**, and reselect the Data sheet.

5. You want the background to be dark gray (so that the black outlines in the PivotTable are distinguishable) and the font for most of the cells to be light gray. Press Ctrl-A to select the entire Data worksheet. On the Formatting toolbar, click the Fill Color button and select Gray-80% (the top color in the rightmost column). Click the Font Color button and select Gray-25% (the fourth color down in the rightmost column). Then select cell A1 to deselect the worksheet.

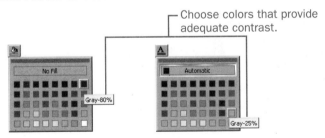

Choose colors that provide
adequate contrast.

6. Move the mouse pointer over the top of cell B7 until it turns into a black downward-pointing arrow, and then click. (If the mouse pointer never turns into a black arrow, click in the PivotTable, and on the PivotTable toolbar, click the PivotTable menu, the Select submenu, and the Enable Selection command.)

7. Change the Category labels to bold and italic. Change the font color to White (the bottom right color in the Font Color palette).

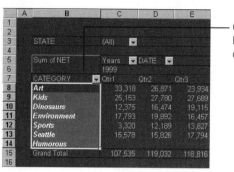

Click above the Category button to select all the category labels.

You won't need the column headings from the PivotTable, because the chart will have labels for the years and quarters. You can hide the top part of the PivotTable to get ready to add the chart, but first put a formula at the top of the sheet to show which state is currently displayed.

8. In cell J1, enter the formula **=C3**. Format the cell as right-aligned, bold, and italic, with 36 as the font size, and Turquoise (fourth row, fifth from the left) as the font color.

9. Hide rows 3 through 7. Then save the Chapter12 workbook.

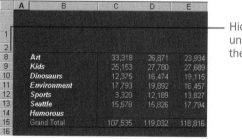

Hide rows that contain unwanted labels for the PivotTable.

The PivotTable is ready. Next, you'll create a chart to display the PivotTable data.

Create a PivotChart

A chart can make the numbers in the table easier to interpret. In order to show both the total orders for a state, and also show what portion of those orders came from each category, a *stepped area chart* is a good choice. A stepped area chart is a stacked column chart with no gaps between the columns.

When you associate a chart with a PivotTable, the chart becomes a PivotChart. The row headings in the PivotTable always correspond to the horizontal axis of the PivotChart. You, however, want the dates as row headings in the PivotTable and as horizontal labels in the PivotChart, so you need to base the chart on the copy of the PivotTable.

1. Activate the ChartData sheet, click in the PivotTable, and then click the Chart Wizard button to create a new PivotChart.

Chart Wizard button

2. Drag the Category tile to the legend area, and drag the Year and Date tiles down to the horizontal axis.

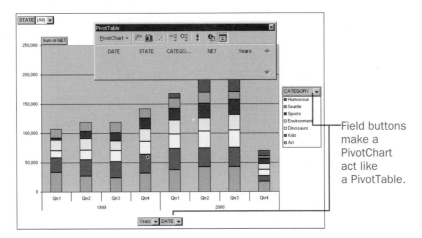

Field buttons make a PivotChart act like a PivotTable.

Rearranging the chart also rearranges the PivotTable it's based on. You won't be manipulating the chart any more, so you won't need the field buttons on the chart.

3. On the PivotTable toolbar, select the PivotChart menu, and click Hide PivotChart Field Buttons.

4. Make a few more changes to the general chart layout. On the Chart menu, click Chart Options. On the Gridlines tab, select Category Major Gridlines. On the Legend tab, select Left as the placement option. Then click OK.

5. Double-click any of the columns, and select the Options tab. Change the Gap Width setting to 0, and click OK.

6. Before you move the chart to the sheet with the table, you need to ensure that the font won't change size. Double-click in the white space above the chart to format the Chart Area. On the Font tab, deselect the Auto Scale check box, and then click OK.

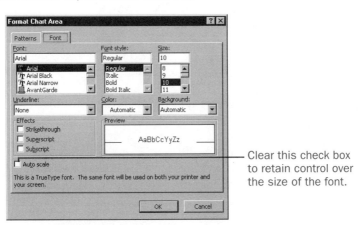

Clear this check box to retain control over the size of the font.

7. Now you can move the chart to the Data sheet. On the Chart menu, click Location, select As Object In Data, and then click OK.

You want the chart tips to display the value for any item, but you don't want the name of the item to show. You set a global charting option to make that change.

8. On the Tools menu, select Options. Select the Chart tab, clear the Show Names check box, and then click OK.

9. If you change the chart so that it doesn't automatically resize, you can temporarily change row heights to precisely position the chart. On the Format menu, click Selected Chart Area, and select the Properties tab. Select the Don't Move Or Size With Cells option, and then click OK.

10. Change the height of row 1 to 20, the height of row 2 to 183. Then press and hold the Alt key as you drag the top-left corner of the chart to the top left corner of cell A2, and as you drag the lower-right corner of the chart to the lower-right corner of cell K2.

11. Change the height of row 1 to 40, and the height of row 2 to 150. The chart overlaps the state identifier and part of the table, but that ensures that the pieces will all flow together when you make the chart transparent.

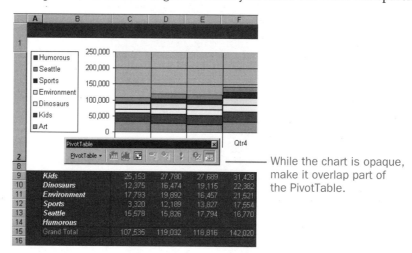

While the chart is opaque, make it overlap part of the PivotTable.

You can now turn off the row and column headings, because you won't need them again.

12. On the Tools menu, select Options. Click the View tab, clear the Row And Column Headers check box, and then click OK.

Format a PivotChart

You need to make the chart transparent so that it will integrate smoothly with the table. To make the chart completely transparent, you need to change the chart area, the plot area, and the legend. Rather than select and change each object interactively, you can make the changes using Microsoft Visual Basic for Applications from the Immediate window. While you're at it, you can change the color of the fonts in the chart to a light shade of gray.

1. Activate the Visual Basic Editor, and in the Immediate window type the following statements:

```
set x = Activesheet.ChartObjects(1).Chart
x.ChartArea.Font.ColorIndex = 54
x.ChartArea.Fill.ForeColor.SchemeColor=xlNone
x.ChartArea.Border.LineStyle = xlNone
x.Legend.Fill.ForeColor.SchemeColor = xlNone
x.Legend.Border.LineStyle = 0
x.PlotArea.Fill.ForeColor.SchemeColor=xlNone
x.PlotArea.Border.Color = vbBlack
```

Tip To make Visual Basic show you lists of methods and properties, create a macro containing the statement *Dim x as Chart* and step through the declaration before entering statements in the Immediate window.

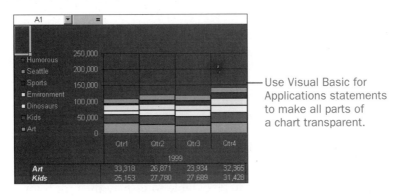

Use Visual Basic for Applications statements to make all parts of a chart transparent.

The name of the state should be just over the top of the plot area, and the lines around the horizontal labels should just barely touch the PivotTable lines. The grids don't match perfectly on the left, but because the alignment changes whenever the value scale changes, you'll create a macro later to fix the vertical alignment.

You can also change the colors of the chart to be evenly spaced shades from black to turquoise. Excel uses the eight colors from 17 through 24 as fill colors in a chart. You have seven series in the chart. By changing the colors in the palette, you can change the colors on the chart. The color turquoise contains the maximum possible amount (255) of green and blue, but no red. By dividing 255 by 6, you can obtain seven evenly spaced shades of turquoise.

2. In the Immediate window, enter the following two lines:

```
set x = ActiveWorkbook
For i=0 To 6:x.Colors(17+i)=RGB(0,i*(255/6),i*(255/6)):Next
```

The colors change to shades of turquoise.

3. Switch back to Excel, and save the Chapter12 workbook.

The chart now blends in almost perfectly with the background. Next you can add some simple macros to control both the PivotTable and the PivotChart.

Controlling the Report with Macros

The users of your PivotTable and PivotChart will use the map to change states. You'll need to create a macro that both changes the state and adjusts the width of the chart to make it match the PivotTable grid. In addition, you'll need to create a macro that refreshes the PivotTable, so that new data appears as changes are made to the database.

Make a macro change the PivotTable

If you create a macro that takes an argument giving the state code, you can use that one macro for any state. First create a macro that changes the PivotTable to display orders for an arbitrary state, and then add the argument to generalize the macro.

*Run Macro
button*

1. On the Visual Basic toolbar, click the Run Macro button. Type **SetPivot** as the macro name, and click Create. The Visual Basic Editor opens with a new macro named SetPivot.

2. Enter these statements as the body of the SetPivot macro:

```
Worksheets("Data").Select
ActiveSheet.PivotTables(1).PageFields(1).CurrentPage = "OR"
Worksheets("ChartData").PivotTables(1).PageFields(1).CurrentPage
= "OR"
```

This macro changes the PivotTable to display the orders for Oregon. The first statement selects the Data sheet, just in case it wasn't already the active sheet. The second statement changes the value of the *CurrentPage* property for the one page field of the one PivotTable on the sheet. The third statement makes the same change to the one PivotTable on the Chart sheet. For now, the new state (OR for "Oregon") is a constant.

3. Press F5 to run the macro, which now changes the state to Oregon. Change the state code in the macro (in both places) to **NV** (for "Nevada"), and try it again.

4. Next you can change the macro to accept an argument for the state code. Insert **NewState** between the parentheses after the name of the macro. Then replace both occurrences of *NV* with **NewState**.

5. Press Ctrl-G to display the Immediate window, and in that window type **SetPivot "ID"** and then press the Enter key. The state changes to Idaho. The SetPivot macro is ready to change both the PivotTable and the chart to any state.

6. Save the Chapter12 workbook.

A state with few orders, such as Idaho, has narrower labels than some of the larger states. The macro needs to adjust the horizontal position of the chart whenever you or another user changes the state.

Make a macro adjust a chart

A stepped area chart looks best if it doesn't have borders around each area. Unfortunately, even if you remove the borders, each time you change the PivotTable, the borders reappear. Fortunately, you can write a simple macro to remove the borders each time the PivotTable changes. Also, the size of the value labels affects how the chart label gridlines align with the PivotTable gridlines. That's also something you can fix with a macro whenever the state changes.

1. Activate the Visual Basic Editor, and click below the SetPivot macro. From the Insert menu, click File, change to the folder containing the practice files for this book, and double-click the Code12a file. This AdjustChart macro appears in the module:

```
Sub AdjustChart()
    Dim myObject As ChartObject
    Dim myChart As Chart
    Dim myWidth As(?)
    Dim myLeft As(?)
    Dim mySeries As Series
    Set myObject = ActiveSheet.ChartObjects(1)
    Set myChart = myObject.Chart

    myWidth = myChart.PlotArea.Width _
      - myChart.PlotArea.InsideWidth
    myWidth = myChart.ChartArea.Left _
      + myChart.PlotArea.Left + myWidth
    myWidth = myWidth - 0.5

    myLeft = Range("C1").Left - myWidth
    myObject.Left = myLeft
    myObject.Width = Range("L1").Left - myLeft

    On Error Resume Next
    For Each mySeries In myChart.SeriesCollection
        mySeries.Border.LineStyle = xlNone
    Next mySeries
End Sub
```

This macro consists of four parts, separated by blank lines. The first part declares some variables and assigns references to both the chart's container object and the chart itself.

The second part of the macro calculates the width of the area from the left edge of the chart to the left edge of the plot area rectangle. A plot area on a chart has two definitions. The plot area you select on the chart is actually the "inside" plot area. The outer plot area includes the area with the axis labels. By subtracting the inside width of the plot area from the width, you get the size of the labels. Adding that to the starting position of the chart area and the outer plot area gives you the total width from the edge of the chart container to the edge of the inner plot area. Subtracting a half point from the width makes the grid line up better. This is what needs to match the left edge of column C.

On a PivotChart, you can't adjust the positions of any of the objects within the chart. You can adjust only the location of the container. The third part of the macro calculates how much the chart needs to be shifted to the right, and then subtracts that same amount from the width to keep the right side aligned.

The fourth and final part of the macro removes the border lines from each of the series in the chart. The *On Error Resume Next* statement is there because some of the charts contain "empty" series—series that are technically in the SeriesCollection collection but don't appear on the screen—and can't be modified.

2. Add the statement **AdjustChart** to the end of the SetPivot macro, and in the Immediate window, execute the statement that changes the report to Idaho.

3. Insert the statement **Application.ScreenUpdating = False** at the top of the SetPivot macro, and change the PivotTable to Washington.

4. Save the Chapter12 workbook.

The SetPivot macro is ready to use. Later, you'll create a graphical interface that calls the SetPivot macro, passing the appropriate state code as an argument.

Make a macro refresh the PivotTable

A PivotTable has an option named Refresh On Open. The purpose of this option is to automatically refresh the data in the PivotTable whenever you open the workbook. Unfortunately, when you protect a worksheet that contains a PivotTable (as you'll do to this worksheet before you're through with it), the Refresh On Open option stops working. That means that you'll need to create a macro to refresh the PivotTable.

That's the bad news. The good news is that while you create a macro to refresh the PivotTable, you can also make the connection to the data source more flexible. When you create the PivotTable, Microsoft Query tells the PivotTable where the database is located. The PivotTable stores the entire location of the database. If you move the workbook or the database to a new location, the PivotTable won't be able to find the database. By refreshing the PivotTable in a macro, you can add some additional code to tell the PivotTable that the database is in the same folder as the workbook. Then, if you move the workbook to a new location, as long as you move the database with it, the application will continue to work.

A PivotTable stores its information in something called a *pivot cache*. Multiple PivotTables in a workbook can share the same pivot cache. A pivot cache has its own object, a PivotCache object. The PivotCache object has a *Connection* property that stores where to go to get the data. If the database is always in the same folder as the application workbook, you can set the *Connection* property to look at that folder.

1. In the Visual Basic Editor, add this code from the practice file Code12b.txt into Module1 (on the Insert menu, click File):

```
Sub RefreshPivot()
    Dim myConnect As String
    myConnect = "ODBC;"
    myConnect = myConnect & _
        "Driver={Microsoft dBase Driver (*.dbf)};"
    myConnect = myConnect & "DBQ="
    myConnect = myConnect & ActiveWorkbook.Path
    ActiveWorkbook.PivotCaches(1).Connection = myConnect
    ActiveWorkbook.PivotCaches(1).Refresh
End Sub
```

This macro constructs a new connection string. Most of the string is constant. It's simply broken into three statements to make each one easier to read. The last part of the string retrieves the *Path* property of the active workbook, which gives the folder name where the workbook is stored.

Assuming that the active workbook is stored in the C:\ExcelVBA folder, the final connection string would be *ODBC;Driver={Microsoft dBase Driver (*.dbf)};DBQ=C:\ExcelVBA*. This is the minimal connection string necessary to connect to a dBase file database. After you create a database using Microsoft Query, you can look at the *Connection* property of the PivotCache object to see what it created. The string returned by the *Connection* property can be very long. You can try leaving out parts to determine which are required.

2. Save the Chapter12 workbook.

3. Press F5 to run the RefreshPivot macro. You should see the message in the status bar showing that the data is being refreshed.

Note If the macro produces an error, the PivotTable becomes invalid. You must close the workbook without saving changes, open the copy you saved, and then try to resolve any errors.

You've now created the core functionality of the application. The PivotTable retrieves the data from the external database, and the chart presents the data in a visually appealing way. Your next task is to create an effective mechanism for interacting with the application.

Creating a Graphical Interface

A graphical interface, such as a map, can be an effective way of presenting choices. Instead of selecting the name of a state from a list, the user can simply click within the state boundary.

Insert a map

First, you need to create a map on the worksheet. You can import pictures from Excel's clip art gallery or from a file in Windows. For this example, you'll import the picture from a file.

1. Select Sheet2 in the Chapter12 workbook. Rename the sheet as **Main**.

2. Press Ctrl-A to select all the cells, and then change the color that used to be Sky Blue to dark gray.

3. Select cell D3, and from the Insert menu, Picture submenu, click From File.

Be especially sure to save the workbook at this time.

4. Change to the folder containing the practice files for this book, select the Map.wmf file, and click Insert.

5. From the Format menu, click Picture, click the Size tab, set the height to 3.5 inches, and then click OK.

Drawing button

6. If necessary, click the Drawing button to activate the Drawing toolbar. Click the Draw menu on the Drawing toolbar, click the Ungroup command, and click Yes when asked whether to convert the picture to a Microsoft Office drawing.

Fill Color button

7. Click the arrow next to the Fill Color button, and choose Fill Effects.

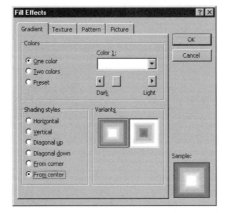

8. In the Fill Effects dialog box, select One Color as the Gradient, and select From Center as the Shading Style. Then click OK.

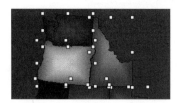

The new format applies to each state.

The shading makes the states look something like jewels. Once you convert an imported picture to a Microsoft Office drawing, you can take advantage of the numerous impressive formatting features available to shapes.

9. Save the Chapter12 workbook.

The map is ready. You could have the user simply click on the state background, but adding the two-letter codes for the states will make things easier for people who get Nevada and Arizona confused.

Add state codes to the map

You could use command buttons to add the state code to the map, but buttons have limited formatting capabilities. Instead, try using WordArt text, so you can make the state codes look attractive.

1. On the Drawing toolbar, click the Insert WordArt button. Select the fifth style on the third row, and click OK.

Insert WordArt button

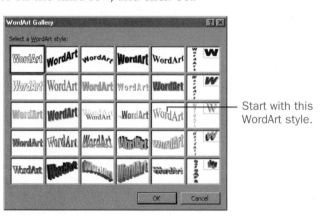

Start with this WordArt style.

If you accidentally drag a state instead of the WordArt object, click the Undo button to move it back.

2. In the Edit WordArt Text dialog box, type **WA** as the text, and click OK.

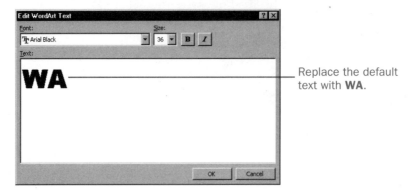

Replace the default text with **WA**.

3. From the Format menu, choose Word Art, specify .35 inch as the Height, .5 inch as the Width, and click OK. Then drag the label for the state to the middle of the map of Washington State.

Drag the label to the middle of the state.

Later, you'll assign a macro to run when you click the state name. If you include the state code as part of the name of the graphical object, you'll be able to use a single macro for all the states.

4. Change the name of the WordArt object to **lblWA**. (Click in the name area to the left of the formula bar.)

5. While pressing the Ctrl key, drag a copy of the WA label to each of the remaining six states.

6. Change the text of each WordArt object to the appropriate state code (OR, ID, CA, NV, UT, and AZ), and change the name of each WordArt object to the appropriate label (lblOR, lblID, lblCA, lblNV, lblUT, and lblAZ).

Tip As long as the WordArt toolbar is visible, you can quickly change the text of a WordArt shape by using the keyboard. Press the Tab key to select the shape you want to change. Press Alt-X to execute the Edit Text command from the WordArt toolbar. Type the new text. Press the Tab key to activate the OK button and then press the Enter key. Repeat for the next shape. Unfortunately, there's no keyboard shortcut for activating the Name box.

---

7. Select the map for Washington State. Give it the name **picWA**. Give an analogous name to the map of each state (picOR, picID, picCA, picNV, picUT, and picAZ).

8. Save the Chapter12 workbook.

By assigning names ending in the two-letter state code to both the WordArt object and the map for each state, you can streamline the process so that the user can click either the letters or the background to run the macro.

Link a macro to the graphical objects

Earlier in the chapter, you created a SetPivot macro. That macro can display any state, provided that you pass it the appropriate state code. Coincidentally, the state code is the last two letters of the name of each object for each state. You therefore need to create a macro that can retrieve the name from the object and extract the code for whichever state the user clicks.

In a macro, Excel's Application object has a property named *Caller*. The *Caller* property gives you the name of the object that the user clicked to run the macro. Visual Basic has a function named *Right* that extracts letters from the right side of a word. You can use the *Right* function to extract the state code from the name that the *Caller* property returns. It's tedious to assign encoded names to each object, but the benefit is that a single macro can handle all the states.

1. On the Drawing toolbar, click the Select Objects button. Then drag a rectangle around the entire map. You should see sizing handles around each of the seven states. Click the Select Objects button again to turn it off.

Select Objects button

2. Right-click on the map, and choose the Assign Macro command. When you select multiple objects before assigning a macro, you assign the same macro to each object, the same as assigning the macros one at a time.

3. In the Assign Macro dialog box, type **ShowMe** as the macro name, and click New.

4. Enter these statements as the body of the ShowMe macro:

```
Dim myName As String
Dim myCode As String

myName = Application.Caller
myCode = Right(myID, 2)
SetPivot myCode
```

5. Activate Excel and, with all states still selected, click the Draw menu and the Group command on the Drawing toolbar. Then press the Esc key to deselect the map. This groups all the states into a single group, which will be convenient when it's time to hide and show the map. Fortunately, even if you group the states, the *Caller* property still returns the name of the specific item that you click.

6. Save the Chapter12 workbook, and click anywhere inside the border of Nevada. The Data sheet should appear and display the orders for Nevada.

The *Application.Caller* property is a convenient tool for making a single macro handle any of several objects.

Note When you use the Control Toolbox to add an object, you create an ActiveX control. Multiple ActiveX controls can't share a single macro, because they use event handler procedures, and an event handler can link to only one object.

Add a background logo

You can also use WordArt to add an attractive logo for the EIS application. Later in the chapter, you'll animate the logo.

Insert WordArt button

1. Activate the Main worksheet, and click the Drawing toolbar's Insert WordArt button.

2. Select the fourth style on the fourth row and click OK. Type **Miller** and press the Enter key, type **EIS** and press the Enter key again, type **Textiles**, and then click OK.

Start with a built-in format.

WordArt Shape button

3. The new WordArt object has the appropriate colors, but it has a strange shape. You can easily adjust the shape. On the WordArt toolbar, click the WordArt Shape button, and select the Button (Pour) shape (the rightmost shape on the second row).

WordArt Same Letter Heights button

WordArt Alignment button

4. On the WordArt toolbar, click the WordArt Same Letter Heights button. Then click the WordArt Alignment button and choose the Stretch Justify option.

5. Drag the top-left sizing handle to the top-left corner of cell C3, and drag the lower-right sizing handle to the middle of the bottom of cell H22.

Many shapes have an adjustment marker that allows you to modify the shape. It appears as a yellow diamond to the left of center in the WordArt object. Later in the chapter, you'll see how a macro can change the adjustment.

6. Drag the adjustment marker to the left until it's about a quarter of an inch from the outside circle.

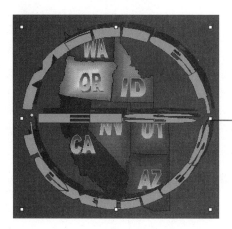

—Drag the Adjustment handle to change the shape.

7. On the Drawing toolbar, click the Draw menu, choose the Order submenu, and click Send To Back.

8. Turn off the row and column headings. (From the Tools menu, click Options, click the View tab, and then clear the Row And Column Headers check box.)

9. Press the Esc key to deselect the logo, and then save the Chapter12 workbook.

The logo looks good, but you can make it even more attractive by animating it.

Animate the logo

Animating a WordArt object is easy. The macro simply makes many small changes to the adjustment values that are available. When you adjust shapes in a macro, however, Windows doesn't refresh the screen until the macro has completed. In many cases, you'll be glad that Windows doesn't refresh the screen, because your macro runs faster that way. When you're animating a shape, however, you want the screen to refresh each time the macro adjusts the shape.

1. Activate the Visual Basic Editor, and click at the bottom of the module. From the Insert menu, click File, change to the folder containing the practice files for this book, and double-click the Code12c file. This StartUpAnimation macro appears in the module:

```
Sub StartUpAnimation()
    Dim myLogo As Shape
    Dim myMap As Shape
    Dim i As Double
    Set myLogo = Worksheets("Main").Shapes(1)
    Set myMap = Worksheets("Main").Shapes(2)

    Application.EnableCancelKey = xlErrorHandler
    On Error GoTo ErrorHandler

    myMap.Visible = msoFalse
    myLogo.Adjustments(1) = 91
    myLogo.Adjustments(2) = 0.5
    myLogo.TextEffect.Tracking = 0.1
    Worksheets("Main").Select
    Application.ScreenUpdating = True

    For i = 91 To 166 Step 5
        myLogo.Adjustments(1) = i
        DoEvents
    Next i
    For i = 0.5 To 0.18 Step -0.02
        myLogo.Adjustments(2) = i
        DoEvents
    Next i
    For i = 0.1 To 1.5 Step 0.1
        myLogo.TextEffect.Tracking = i
        DoEvents
    Next i
    For i = 0.2 To 0.455 Step 0.02
        myLogo.Adjustments(2) = i
        DoEvents
    Next i

ErrorHandler:
    myLogo.Adjustments(1) = 166
    myLogo.Adjustments(2) = 0.455
    myLogo.TextEffect.Tracking = 1.5
    myLogo.Visible = msoTrue
    myMap.Visible = msoTrue
End Sub
```

This macro consists of five parts, separated by blank lines. The first part simply declares some variables and assigns references to the two shapes on the worksheet.

The second part and the fifth part work together to allow you to skip the animation by pressing Ctrl-Break. The *On Error Goto ErrorHandler* statement tells the macro to jump to the ErrorHandler label if there's an error. The *EnableCancelKey* property tells Excel to consider it an error if the user presses Ctrl-Break. The statements in the final part (after the label) simply set the shape adjustments to their final values and display both the shapes.

See Chapter 8 for more information about the On Error statement.

The third part of the macro sets the logo shape adjustments to their initial values, hides the map, and makes sure that screen updating hasn't been turned off by an earlier procedure. It then activates the Main worksheet, ready to show the animation. The *Tracking* property controls how much WordArt letters overlap.

Note The constants *msoTrue* and *msoFalse* are identical to the ordinary Visual Basic constants *True* and *False*. The *mso-* prefix stands for "Microsoft Office"; for some unknown reason, the designer of the Shape objects decided to create *True* and *False* values that are unique to Microsoft Office. You can use the *True* and *False* constants with Shape objects, but when you enter a statement using a Shape object, the Auto List offers only *msoTrue* and *msoFalse*.

The fourth part of the macro does the real animation. It consists of four loops, which change three different settings of the logo shape. You can find appropriate start and end values for an animation by turning on the recorder and making manual changes to the adjustments for a shape. Much of the process is simply trial and error. The *DoEvents* statement is the secret to making an animation work. This statement tells Windows to refresh the screen (refreshing is an "event" that Windows should "do"), without waiting for the macro to end.

2. Save the Chapter12 workbook, click in the StartUpAnimation macro, and press F5 to test the macro. You may want to set breakpoints in the macro and step through parts of the macro.

See Chapter 8 for information about setting breakpoints.

Your application now has both functionality and an effective user interface; however, it's still obviously part of Excel. Now is the time to package the application by removing any distracting toolbars, window features, and menu commands and by making the macros run automatically.

Packaging the Application

Packaging the application consists of bending the appearance and behavior of Excel's workspace to match your wishes. Many of the settings you'll need to change—such as the window size and the appearance of the toolbars—can also be customized by the user. Excel stores changes to those settings. For example, after a user changes which toolbars are visible, Excel saves the settings when the program closes and restores them the next time the program starts.

If your application changes customization settings, it must restore them to the original state when the application closes. For example, if your application hides all the toolbars when it opens, it should redisplay the toolbars when it closes.

Replace and restore the menu bar

A Windows application can have many toolbars, but only one menu bar. The way to remove Excel's menu bar is to replace it with a custom menu bar of your own. When the application closes, removing the custom menu bar automatically restores Excel's standard menu bar. A menu bar is simply a command bar—just like a toolbar—that you designate as a menu bar. You give the menu bar a name when you create it, and you can then use that name to delete it. For this application, name the menu bar EIS.

1. In the Visual Basic Editor, add this procedure to the module:

```
Sub ZapMenu()
    On Error Resume Next
    CommandBars("EIS").Delete
End Sub
```

The *On Error Resume Next* statement allows you to use this macro to ensure that the custom menu is deleted, without worrying about whether it was ever created or not. When the application is working perfectly, the menu bar should never exist when the macro creates it, and it should always exist when the macro deletes it, but while you're developing and testing the application, you might sometimes run the ZapMenu macro when the menu has already been deleted. In that case, having the macro ignore the error makes your life simpler.

The menu bar for this application will have two commands: Exit and Return To Main. Before creating the macro that adds the custom menu bar, you can create the *sub* procedures the commands will need.

2. Add this procedure to the module:

```
Sub ExitEIS()
    ZapMenu
    ActiveWorkbook.Close
End Sub
```

This procedure closes the active workbook. This is the macro that the Exit button will run.

3. Add this procedure to the module:

```
Sub ReturnToMain()
    Worksheets("Main").Select
End Sub
```

This procedure activates the Main worksheet. This is the macro that the Return To Main button will run.

4. Now you're ready to add the macro that adds the custom menu bar. Click at the bottom of the module, and from the Insert menu, click File and double-click the Code12d file to add this procedure to the module:

```
Sub SetMenu()
    Dim myBar As CommandBar
    Dim myButton As CommandBarButton

    ZapMenu
    Set myBar = CommandBars.Add(Name:="EIS", _
        Position:=msoBarBottom, _
        MenuBar:=True)

    Set myButton = myBar.Controls.Add(msoControlButton)
    myButton.Style = msoButtonCaption
    myButton.Caption = "E&xit"
    myButton.OnAction = "ExitEIS"

    Set myButton = myBar.Controls.Add(msoControlButton)
    myButton.Style = msoButtonCaption
    myButton.Caption = "&Return to Main"
    myButton.OnAction = "ReturnToMain"
    myButton.Visible = False

    myBar.Protection = msoBarNoMove   msoBarNoCustomize
    myBar.Visible = True
End Sub
```

This macro consists of five parts separated by blank lines. The first part simply declares a couple of variables.

The second part of the macro runs the ZapMenu macro to make sure the EIS menu bar doesn't already exist, and then it creates a new EIS menu bar. Passing *True* as the value of the *MenuBar* argument is what makes this new command bar into a menu bar. Putting the menu bar at the bottom of the screen makes it look less like a conventional menu bar.

The third and fourth parts of the macro add the two commands to the menu bar. Initially, the Return To Main command is invisible.

The fifth and final part of the macro protects the new menu bar. This property has an enumerated list of values that you can assign to it to control what you will and will not allow users to do to the menu bar. You can add values together to further control what you will allow. This macro doesn't allow the user to move or customize the new menu bar.

5. Save the Chapter12 workbook and run the SetMenu macro and the ZapMenu macro.

In summary, replacing Excel's menu bar is easy: you just create a new one of your own. Restoring Excel's menu bar is even easier: you just delete the one you created.

You still need to make the Return To Menu command visible whenever the Data worksheet becomes active, and to make it invisible whenever the Data worksheet becomes inactive. This looks like a job for event handler procedures—one to hide the command and one to show it. You can create a single procedure with an argument, and then you have the event handlers call that procedure.

1. Insert this procedure into the module:

```
Sub CommandVisible(IsVisible)
    On Error Resume Next
    CommandBars("EIS").Controls(2).Visible = IsVisible
End Sub
```

The *On Error Resume Next* statement again allows you to avoid inconveniences while building and testing the application—in case this procedure runs when the menu hasn't been created. The other statement makes the command visible or invisible, depending on the value of the argument.

Project Explorer button

2. Click the Project Explorer button, and double-click the entry for the Data worksheet.

3. Insert these two event handler procedures:

```
Private Sub Worksheet_Activate()
    CommandVisible True
End Sub

Private Sub Worksheet_Deactivate()
    CommandVisible False
End Sub
```

Whenever the Data worksheet becomes active, the Return To Menu command will become visible. Whenever the worksheet becomes inactive, the command will disappear.

4. Reactivate the module, close the Project window, save the Chapter12 workbook, and run the SetMenu macro.

5. Activate Excel and switch back and forth between the Data and Main worksheets. Watch to see the command appear and disappear.

6. Run the ZapMenu macro.

You can package the application pleasingly by creating a window that's precisely the right size for the table and chart. When the application closes, however, you should restore the window back to the way it was. Restoring the window is harder than restoring Excel's menu bar, because you must make the macro remember the original size of the window.

You can store the size of the window in a variable, but when you use *Dim* to declare a variable inside a procedure, the variable lasts only as long as the procedure is running. You can keep a variable from disappearing by using the word *Static* to declare the variable.

1. Insert this partial procedure into the module:

```
Sub SetWindow(State)
    Const myWidth = 540
    Const myHeight = 320
    Static myOldWidth
    Static myOldHeight
    Static myOldTop
    Static myOldLeft
    Static myOldState


End Sub
```

You'll use this same procedure to change the window and to restore it. The *State* argument will determine which task the procedure will carry out. By using a single procedure for both tasks, you can store the old values right here in the *SetWindow* procedure using the *Static* keyword. The *Const* statements give the new custom values for the height and width. A *Const* is a constant value. You can use it like a read-only variable. Giving the width and height new values at the top like this makes them easy to change if you want to adjust your application later.

2. Click in the blank line before the *End Sub* statement of the SetWindow procedure, and from the Insert menu, click File and then double-click the file Code12e. That inserts the following part of the macro:

```
If State = xlOn Then
    myOldWidth = Application.Width
    myOldHeight = Application.Height
    myOldTop = Application.Top
    myOldLeft = Application.Left
    myOldState = Application.WindowState
    Application.WindowState = xlNormal
    Application.Width = myWidth
    Application.Height = myHeight
    Application.Caption = "Miller Textiles EIS"

    ActiveWorkbook.Unprotect
    ActiveWindow.WindowState = xlMaximized
    ActiveWindow.Caption = ""
    ActiveWorkbook.Protect , True, True

    ProtectSheet xlOn, "Main"
    ProtectSheet xlOn, "Data"
```

(continued)

```
Application.DisplayFormulaBar = False
Application.DisplayStatusBar = False
ActiveWindow.DisplayHorizontalScrollBar = False
ActiveWindow.DisplayVerticalScrollBar = False
ActiveWindow.DisplayWorkbookTabs = False
```

This is the first half of an *If...Else...End If* structure. It runs if the value of the *State* argument is *xlOn*. The value *xlOn* is a built-in Excel constant. Using the constant makes the macro easier to read than using an arbitrary number, and using a built-in constant is easier than creating a custom constant.

Setting the window consists of three parts. The first part stores the old height, width, top, left, and window state of the Excel application window in the static variables. It then assigns new values to those properties. When you resize the application window, you should always set the *WindowState* property to *xlNormal* first, because if the application is maximized, you can't change the width or the height. This part also customizes the Excel application caption.

The second part of the *If...Else...End If* structure makes sure that the workbook window is maximized and protected. You must unprotect it before attempting to maximize it. Setting the caption to an empty text string keeps the workbook name from appearing in the caption bar. The final statement of this part of the structure protects both the structure and the windows of the workbook. ProtectSheet is a procedure you'll create shortly that protects or unprotects a sheet. You give it the sheet name and specify whether protection should be on or off.

The third part of the *If...Else...End If* structure is mostly for your convenience as you develop the application. You could protect the worksheets interactively, but then you'd always have to unprotect them interactively to make any changes. Likewise, you could hide the scroll bars, the sheet tabs, the formula bar, and the status bar interactively, but sometimes they're useful while you're developing the application.

3. Click before the *End Sub* statement of the SetWindow procedure, and insert the file Code12f to add this final part of the macro:

```
Else
    Application.Caption = Empty
    If Not IsEmpty(myOldWidth) Then
        Application.Width = myOldWidth
        Application.Height = myOldHeight
        Application.Top = myOldTop
        Application.Left = myOldLeft
        Application.WindowState = myOldState
    End If
    ProtectSheet xlOff, "Main"
    ProtectSheet xlOff, "Data"
    ActiveWorkbook.Unprotect
    Application.DisplayFormulaBar = False
```

```
      Application.DisplayStatusBar = False
      Application.DisplayFormulaBar = True
      Application.DisplayStatusBar = True
      ActiveWindow.DisplayHorizontalScrollBar = True
      ActiveWindow.DisplayVerticalScrollBar = True
      ActiveWindow.DisplayWorkbookTabs = True
   End If
```

These statements are the second half of the *If...Else...End If* structure.
Basically, they undo everything the statements in the first half did. Again,
checking whether the *myOldWidth* variable is empty is for your convenience
while you're developing the macro. When you make certain changes in
Visual Basic for Applications—such as adding or deleting a procedure—
the value of static variables can be lost, effectively replacing the value
with zero. Checking to see if the *myOldWidth* variable is empty keeps the
macro from shrinking the application window to a tiny block on the
screen if you happen to do something that resets the static variables.

4. Click at the bottom of the module, and insert the file Code12g to add
this macro:

```
Sub ProtectSheet(State, SheetItem)
    If State = xlOn Then
        Worksheets(SheetItem).EnableSelection = xlNoSelection
        Worksheets(SheetItem).Protect , True, True, True, True
    Else
        Worksheets(SheetItem).Unprotect
    End If
End Sub
```

This is the macro that the SetWindow macro calls to protect a worksheet.
Setting the *EnableSelection* property to *xlNoSelection* prevents the user
from selecting any cells when the worksheet is protected.

5. You now need a way to run the SetWindow macro with the appropriate
arguments. Insert these two macros in the module:

```
Sub InitView()
    SetMenu
    SetWindow xlOn
End Sub

Sub ExitView()
    ZapMenu
    SetWindow xlOff
End Sub
```

6. Save the Chapter12 workbook and test the InitView and ExitView
procedures.

Static variables are a valuable tool for remembering values that must be restored later.

Remove and restore toolbars

The procedure for removing and restoring toolbars is very similar to that for changing and restoring windows: store the old values before making changes, and then use the stored values to restore the workspace. Storing toolbars, however, adds a new twist. Storing the size of the window always requires exactly three static variables for three and only three values (height, width, and state), but storing the list of visible toolbars can involve an unknown and varying number of toolbars.

As you know, Excel organizes multiple objects into collections. In fact, the toolbars themselves are in a collection. Visual Basic will actually allow you to create your own custom collection; you can make a collection of only those toolbars that need to be restored. Collections are powerful tools, and this example shows only a very simple (but extremely useful) way to take advantage of them.

1. Click at the bottom of the module and insert the file Code12h to create this procedure:

```
Sub SetBars(State)
    Static myOldBars As New Collection
    Dim myBar

    If State = xlOn Then
        For Each myBar In Application.CommandBars
            If myBar.Type <> 1 And myBar.Visible Then
                myOldBars.Add myBar
                myBar.Visible = False
            End If
        Next myBar
    Else
        For Each myBar In myOldBars
            myBar.Visible = True
        Next
    End If
End Sub
```

Once again, a single procedure handles both the changing and the restoring, so that a static variable can store the old values. This time, however, the static variable is declared as a *New Collection.* Declaring a variable as a New Collection tells Visual Basic that you want to create a collection of your own.

The first half of the *If...Else...End If* structure loops through each of the items in the application's CommandBars collection. If the command bar is a menu bar, its *Type* property is *1* and you should not hide or restore it. Otherwise, if the command bar is visible, you want to add it to your custom collection and then make it invisible. To add an item to a custom collection, you use the *Add* method followed by a reference to the item you want to add. The second half of the *If...Else...End If* structure simply loops through the custom collection, unhiding every toolbar in it.

2. You can launch SetBars from the InitView and ExitView macros, the same as you did with SetWindow. Insert the statement **SetBars xlOn** before the *End Sub* statement of the InitView macro.

3. Insert the statement **SetBars xlOff** before the *End Sub* statement of the ExitView macro.

4. Save the Chapter12 workbook and test the InitView and ExitView procedures.

This section didn't give details about all the ways you can use a custom collection, but even if you use a custom collection only for storing items from a standard collection—essentially copying the code from this chapter—you'll find it a valuable tool.

Complete the package

All the pieces are in place for the finished application. You just need to make it happen automatically when the workbook opens.

1. Activate the Project Explorer window, and double-click ThisWorkbook.

2. Insert this event handler for when the workbook opens:

```
Private Sub Workbook_Open()
    Application.ScreenUpdating = False
    RefreshPivot
    InitView
    StartUpAnimation
End Sub
```

Every time the workbook opens, you want to check for new data in the database, customize the environment, and play the initial animation. Setting *ScreenUpdating* to *False* restricts the amount of flashing you see on the screen.

3. Insert this event handler for when the workbook closes:

```
Private Sub Workbook_BeforeClose(Cancel As Boolean)
    ExitView
    ActiveWorkbook.Saved = True
End Sub
```

Every time the workbook closes, you want to restore the environment. You also want to keep Excel from asking whether to save changes. Setting the *Saved* property of the active workbook to *True* makes Excel believe that it has been saved, so it doesn't ask.

4. In the ExitEIS macro, insert the statement **ExitView** before the *ActiveWorksheet.Close* statement. The *Workbook_BeforeClose* event handler needs to run ExitView in case the user closes the workbook by clicking Excel's Close Window button.

> **Note** Theoretically, the ExitEIS macro shouldn't have to run ExitView. ExitEIS closes the window, and the event handler should run when the window closes regardless of what causes it to close. For some reason, however, the event handler doesn't run the ExitView macro if the ExitEIS macro triggered the event. It's just another reminder that Visual Basic for Applications was created by humans.

5. If you have a digital signature, sign the Visual Basic for Applications project to avoid the warning message when you open it. (See Chapter 1, "Signing Personal Macros.")

6. In Excel, hide the ChartData sheet. (Format menu, Sheet submenu, Hide command.)

7. Rename Sheet3 to **Blank**. Turn off the row and column headers. Select a cell several rows and columns away from cell A1. Save the workbook while the Blank sheet is active so that the user won't see anything when the workbook first opens.

8. Close the workbook, and reopen it. Test the application and close the workbook.

The application is beautiful. It has functionality. It has an effective user interface. It's well packaged. Congratulations!

Chapter Summary

To	Do this
Import data from an external database into a PivotTable	In step 1 of the PivotTable Wizard, select the External Data Source option. In step 2, click Get Data, and create a new data source for the external database.
Keep a PivotTable the same size, even if it has blank items	Double-click the tile of the field whose items you want to show, and select the Show Items With No Data check box.
Change the default format for the cells in a workbook	From the Format menu, click Style. Select the Normal style and change the formatting to the desired default.
Link a text box to the contents of a cell	Create the text box on a worksheet. Press the Esc key to select the container box. In the Formula bar, type an equal sign and the cell address you want to link to the text box.
Use a macro to refresh the data in a PivotTable	Assign a new value to the *Connection* property of a PivotCache object.
Convert an imported picture into Office 97 shape objects	Select the picture, click the Draw menu on the Drawing toolbar, and choose Ungroup.
Determine which object launched a macro when the macro is attached to several objects	Use the *Application.Caller* property to find the identifier of the object.

To	Do this
Force the screen to refresh while animating a shape object	Include a *DoEvents* statement in the macro.
Make Ctrl-Break trigger an error that you can trap	Assign *xlErrorHandler* to the *Application.EnableCancelKey* property.
Replace Excel's standard menu bar	Create a new menu bar using the *CommandBars.Add* method with *True* as the value of the *MenuBar* argument.
Make a variable retain its value from one time you run the macro to the next	Use the keyword *Static* to declare the variable instead of *Dim*.
Prevent the user from selecting any cells on a worksheet	Assign *xlNoSelection* to the *EnableSelection* property of a worksheet, and then protect the worksheet.
Create a custom collection for storing references to objects	Declare a variable as New Collection. Then use the *Add* method on the collection variable to add new items to the collection.

For online information about	Ask the Assistant for help using the words
Retrieving data from an external data source	"External data" (in Excel's Assistant)
Automating shape objects	"Shape object" (in the Visual Basic Editor's Assistant)
Using custom collections	"Collection object" (in the Visual Basic Editor's Assistant)
Using static variables	"Variable lifetimes" (in the Visual Basic Editor's Assistant)

Preview of the Future

You've now completed all the chapters in this book. You've created simple macros using the macro recorder. You've explored the wealth of objects available in Excel. You've learned how to use Visual Basic for Applications commands and statements to control an application. You've made macros easy to run using forms, toolbars, menu commands, and ActiveX controls. And you've built a packaged application.

Excel and Visual Basic for Applications are both very powerful and complex tools. You can use the Review and Practice section to solidify what you've learned, and then continue learning new skills with both Excel and Visual Basic for Applications for a long time. The concepts and skills you've learned in this book will enable you to write useful and powerful applications now, and they'll also serve as a good foundation as you learn more about Excel and Visual Basic for Applications.

Review and Practice

Review and Practice Objectives   Estimated time: 30 minutes

You'll will review and practice how to:

- Create a form that interacts with a worksheet.

- Use Microsoft ActiveX controls.

- Create event-handler procedures.

- Use optional arguments with a subroutine.

- Use conditional statements.

- Handle errors.

In Part 4, you learned how to create an efficient user interface using Microsoft Visual Basic for Applications forms, controls, and events. In this review and practice section, you'll create a form to make a worksheet easy to use.

You're working with the controller at Miller Textiles to evaluate some possible uses for capital. Sometimes you want to consider the short-term possibilities, and sometimes you want to consider the long-term possibilities. You've already created the worksheet found in the Savings workbook.

	A	B	C	D	E	F	G
1					StartDate	1/1/2000	
2					Years	0	
3					Months	1	
4					Days	0	
5	Period	Date	Value		Invest	$1,000	
6	0	1/1/2000	$1,000		Rate	8%	
7	1	2/1/2000	$1,007				
8	2	3/1/2000	$1,013				
9	3	4/1/2000	$1,020				
10	4	5/1/2000	$1,027				
11	5	6/1/2000	$1,034				
12	6	7/1/2000	$1,041				
13	7	8/1/2000	$1,048				
14	8	9/1/2000	$1,055				
15	9	10/1/2000	$1,062				
16	10	11/1/2000	$1,069				
17	11	12/1/2000	$1,076				
18	12	1/1/2001	$1,083				
19							

— These values...

...control these dates.

The worksheet shows how much an investment will grow over 12 periods. Column A contains the period number, column B contains the date at the end of each period, and column C shows the amount the investment is worth at the end of each period. Cells F5 and F6 allow you to enter the desired initial investment amount and the expected monthly rate of return. The value in cell F1 determines the starting date of the investment. The values in cells F2, F3, and F4 allow you to define the length of each time period. The number in cell F2 (the Years cell) tells how many years are in each period. The number in cell F3 (the Months cell) tells how many months are in each period. The number in cell F4 (the Days cell) tells how many days are in each period. Typically, two of the three cells contain zeros.

The formulas in the worksheet are in the Date column (B6:B18) and the Value column (C6:C18). You don't need to understand the formulas in the worksheet in order to create the form, but you might find them interesting. The Date column cells contain a formula that calculates the ending date of the period, using the StartDate, Years, Months, and Days values. Here's the formula, divided into rows to make it more readable:

```
=DATE(YEAR(StartDate)+Years*Period,
 MONTH(StartDate)+Months*Period,
 DAY(StartDate)+Days*Period)
```

The DATE function creates a date given year, month, and day values. The first argument consists of the YEAR function, which extracts the year of the start date, incremented by the number of years per period times the period number. The second argument does the same for the month portion of the date, and the third argument does the same for the day portion of the date. Changing the *StartDate, Years, Months,* or *Days* values automatically changes the dates—easily switching between a two-week investment and one lasting several decades.

The Value column cells contain a formula that calculates the value the investment will have at the date in the future. Here's the formula:

```
=FV(Rate/12,Period*Years*12+Period*Months+Period*Days/30,0,-Invest)
```

A completed Part4 workbook is in the Finished folder. Your macros don't need to match the sample exactly.

Microsoft Excel's FV function calculates the Future Value of an investment, given the interest rate, the number of periods, the amount invested each month, and the initial investment amount. The first argument (*Rate*) divides the rate by 12 to convert it to a monthly interest rate. The second argument (*Periods*) sums the number of months represented by the *Years, Months,* and *Days* values. To get months, the *Years* value is multiplied by 12, and the *Days* value is divided by 30. The third argument (*Payment*) is zero, because the only payment you will make will be the initial investment. The fourth argument (*Present Value*) is the original investment, converted to a negative number to show that you are paying the money.

Create a Form

You want to create a form that makes it easy to change the values in the StartDate, Years, Months, and Days cells. You'll create the form's user interface, add the functionality, and then implement the form, integrating it into Excel.

Step 1: Create the form

The first step is to create the form's user interface. Create a new form that contains all the controls you'll need to control the worksheet.

1. Save a copy of the Savings workbook as **Part4.**

2. In the Visual Basic Editor, create a form and add to it the ActiveX controls to create this dialog box.

The dialog box should have the following 10 controls. The frame should contain the three option buttons listed in the table.

Type	Name	Caption/Text	Accelerator
Label	lblStartDate	Start Date:	S
TextBox	txtStartDate	1/1/2000	-
Frame (group box)	grpType	Increment Type	-
OptionButton	optYears	Years	Y
OptionButton	optMonths	Months	M
OptionButton	optDays	Days	D
Label	txtIncrement	1	-
Label	lblIncrement	Increment Amount:	A
SpinButton	spnIncrement	-	-
CommandButton	BtnClose	Close	C

3. Make sure the tab order of the controls in the dialog box matches the order in the table. The txtIncrement control has a *txt-* prefix even though it is a label, because the form treats it as a read-only text box. The lblIncrement control comes after the txtIncrement control so that its accelerator key will activate the spnIncrement SpinButton.

4. Set both the *Min* property and the *Value* property of the spnIncrement control to 1.

5. Run the dialog box. Try out the tab order and the accelerator keys.

For more information about	See
Creating a form	Chapter 11, "Creating a Form's User Interface"
Adding controls to a form	Chapter 11, "Creating a Form's User Interface"
Setting control properties	Chapter 10, "Using a Loan Payment Calculator"
Setting the tab order	Chapter 11, "Set the tab order for controls"

Step 2: Add Simple Event Handlers to the Form

As part of the form's user interface, you should add some simple event handlers to make the controls behave properly. You can make the Close button close the form, and the spnIncrement control change the caption on the txtIncrement control.

1. Add an event handler to the btnClose control's *Click* event to unload the form.

2. Add an event handler to the spnIncrement control's *Change* event to assign the value of the control to the txtIncrement control's caption.

3. Run and test the form.

For more information about	See
Adding event handlers to a control	Chapter 11, "Add command buttons"
Unloading a form	Chapter 11, "Add command buttons"

Step 3: Make the Option Buttons Change the Worksheet

You're now ready to add the macros that create the form's functionality. The form has three option buttons that correspond to the three period-type cells on the worksheet. Each option button should set its own period-type cell to the value of spnIncrement, while changing the values of the other two period-type cells to zero. Since the code for the three option buttons is similar, you can create one common subroutine that does the work for all three. If you pass the name of the range to the subroutine, the subroutine can change the value of all three cells to zero and then assign the proper value to the one cell.

1. Create a subroutine named *DoChange* with a single argument named *NewType*.

2. Inside the subroutine, assign zero to the ranges named Years, Months, and Days.

3. Assign the value from spnIncrement to the range whose name was passed as the *NewType* argument.

4. Create event handlers for the *Click* event of each of the three option buttons. Inside the event handler, call the *DoChange* subroutine, passing the name of the appropriate range (Years for optYears, Months for optMonths, and Days for optDays).

5. Test the form.

   You should see the Year, Month, and Day cells change when you select each option. If you change the spin button, the next time you change an option, you should see the new increment number in the cell.

For more information about	See
Creating a subroutine	Chapter 2, "Simplify the subroutine statements"
Adding an argument	Lesson 8, "Add arguments to a custom function"
Changing the value of a range	Lesson 4, "Exploring Ranges"

Step 4: Make the Spin Button Change the Worksheet

The option buttons change the worksheet as soon as you click them, but the spin button doesn't change the worksheet directly. You can make the spin button call the *DoChange* subroutine, but you don't want it to change which cell gets changed. If you store the value of the changing cell in a *Static* variable, and make the *NewType* argument optional, you can have the option buttons change the name of the range, while the spin button changes only the value.

1. In the DoChange macro, make the *NewType* argument optional, and give it the default value of "" (an empty string).

2. Add a new Static variable named *OldType*.

3. Test to see whether the *NewType* value is equal to "". If so, assign its value to *OldType*. If not, assign its value to *OldType*.

> **Tip** Rather than assign an empty string as a default, you can use IsMissing to test for a missing optional argument. For example, use **IsMissing(NewType)** to test for whether a value was passed for the *NewType* argument. If you assign a default value to an optional argument, the argument's value will never be missing.

4. Add a statement to the spin button's event handler that runs DoChange without an argument.

5. Test the form. Try it once changing an option button first, and then try changing the spin button without changing an option button first.

6. Add an event handler to the Form's *Initialize* event that runs the DoChange subroutine with *Months* as the argument. (You'll need to save the workbook with the initial increment set to one month.)

7. Test the form again.

For more information about	See
Default arguments	Chapter 8, "Make arguments optional"
Conditional statements	Chapter 7, "Using Conditionals"
Static variables	Chapter 12, "Change and restore windows"
Initializing a form	Chapter 11, "Initialize the text box"

Step 5: Make the Text Box Change the Worksheet

The option buttons and the spin button all change the worksheet immediately. The text box allows you to type a date. You'd like the text box to change the worksheet immediately as well, but only if it contains a valid date. If you declare a variable as a Date, Visual Basic will refuse to assign anything other than a date to it. You can then assign the result of that date to the StartDate cell on the worksheet.

1. Create an event handler for the text box's *Change* event.

2. At the top of the macro, declare a variable *myDate* with Date as its type.

3. Add a statement that will go to the label *ErrorHandler* if an error occurs.

4. Assign the value of the text box to the *myDate* variable.

5. Assign the value of the *myDate* variable to the StartDate range.

6. Insert the label **ErrorHandler:** immediately before the End Sub statement.

7. Test the form, typing various values into the Start Date box.

For more information about	See
Using dates with variables	Chapter 3, "Store values in variables"
Handling errors	Chapter 8, "Handling Errors"

Step 6: Implement the Form

Your form now has all the functionality it will need. You're ready to integrate the form into Excel. You can make the workbook automatically open the form, and make closing the form automatically close the workbook.

1. Change the name of the form to frmDates.

2. Create an event handler for the *Open* event of the Part4 workbook.

3. In the event handler, add a single statement to show the frmDates form. Use *False* as the argument to the *Show* method to open the form as non-modal. This will allow you to change the investment amount or the interest rate without closing the form.

4. Create an event handler for the form's *QueryClose* event. (Put the code in the *QueryClose* event rather than in the *btnClose_Click* event, in case the user closes the form by clicking the Close icon in the top-right corner of the form.)

5. In the event handler, add a single statement that closes the workbook without saving changes. (Use *ThisWorkbook* to refer to the workbook that contains the macro. Watch for arguments to the *Close* method to avoid saving changes.)

6. If you have a digital signature, sign the project.

7. Make sure the initial values on the worksheet match the initial values on the form before you save it. (StartDate is 1/1/2000; Months is 1; Years and Days are 0.)

8. Test the form by closing the workbook and reopening it. (If you need to open the workbook without running the macro, press and hold the Shift key as you open it.)

For more information about	See
Naming a form	Chapter 11, "Creating a Form's User Interface"
Creating an event handler for opening a workbook	Chapter 12, "Complete the package"
Displaying a form	Chapter 11, "Creating a Form's User Interface"
Closing a workbook without saving changes	Chapter 3. "Using Auto Lists to Learn About Objects"
Digitally signing a project	Chapter 1, "Signing Personal Macros"

Part 5

Appendixes

Alternative Techniques

Microsoft Excel typically provides several methods for accomplishing the same task. Some methods use menu commands, some use keyboard shortcuts, and some use toolbar buttons. This appendix contains one or more alternative methods for carrying out many of the tasks described in this book.

Chapter 1

Task	Alternatives
Show a toolbar	Right-click any toolbar and click the desired toolbar.
	From the View menu, the Toolbars submenu, click the toolbar name.
Record a macro	Click the Record Macro button.
	From the Tools menu, the Macro submenu, click Record New Macro.
Stop recorder	On the Microsoft Visual Basic toolbar, click the Stop Recording button.
	From the Tools menu, the Macro submenu, click Stop Recording.
Display the Macro dialog box to run a macro	On the Visual Basic toolbar, click the Run Macro button.
	From the Tools menu, the Macro submenu, click Macros.
	Press Alt-F8.
Show the Visual Basic Editor	Display the Macro dialog box, select a macro, and click Edit.
	On the Visual Basic toolbar, click the Visual Basic Editor button.
	From the Tools menu, the Macro submenu, click Visual Basic Editor.
	Press Alt-F11.

Task	Alternatives
Run a macro from Visual Basic for Applications	Press F5.
	On the standard toolbar, click the Run Sub/UserForm button.
	From the Run menu in the Visual Basic Editor, click Run Sub/UserForm (or Run Macro).
	From the Tools menu, click Macros, select the macro, and click Run.

Chapter 2

Task	Alternatives
Delete the rows containing the selected cells	From the Edit menu, click Delete, and choose the Entire Row option.
	Press Ctrl– (minus sign).
	Press Shift-Spacebar to extend the selection to the entire row, and choose the Delete command from the Edit menu.
Step through a macro	Press F8.
	Show the Debug toolbar, and click the Step Into button.
	On the Debug menu, click the Step Into command.
Display the Goto dialog box in Excel	On the Edit menu, choose the Go To command.
	Press Ctrl-G.
	Press F5.
Select the current region	Press Ctrl-Shift-*.
	Press Ctrl-* (on the numeric keypad).
	Click the Select Current Region toolbar button. (To add the Select Current Region button to a toolbar, right-click any toolbar and choose Customize. On the Commands tab, select Edit. Drag the Select Current Region button to a toolbar.)
Close a workbook file	From the File menu, click Close.
	Press Ctrl-W.
	Press Ctrl-F4.
Delete a worksheet	From the Edit menu, click Delete Sheet.
	Right-click the worksheet tab, and click Delete.

Chapter 3

Task	Alternatives
Delete a line in a macro	Select the entire line, and press the Delete key.
	Press Ctrl-Y.
Show the Locals window	On the View menu in the Visual Basic Editor, click Locals Window.
	On the Debug toolbar, click the Locals Window button.
Change which statement will execute next	Drag the yellow arrow in the left margin of the code window.
	From the Debug menu, click Set Next Statement.
	Press Ctrl-F9.
Show the Immediate window	From the View menu, click Immediate Window.
	Press Ctrl-G.
	On the Debug toolbar, click the Immediate Window button.
Get help on a keyword	Click the keyword, and press F1.
	On the Help menu, select Microsoft Excel Help. In Help, select the Index tab, type the keyword, and press the Enter key.
Show the global list of methods and properties	With the cursor on a blank line, press Ctrl-Spacebar.
	Press Ctrl-J.
	From the Edit menu, click List Properties/Methods. On the Edit toolbar, click the List Properties/Methods button.
Show a list of constants	Use Auto List.
	Press Ctrl-Shift-J.
	From the Edit menu, click List Constants.
	On the Edit toolbar, click the List Constants button.
Show the Object Browser	On the Standard toolbar, click the Object Browser button.
	Press F2.
	From the View menu, click Object Browser.

Chapter 4

Task	Alternatives
Change a cell to bold	Click the Bold toolbar button.
	Press Ctrl-B.
	Press Ctrl-1, and select the Font tab.
Change selected cell font to italic	Click the Italic toolbar button.
	Press Ctrl-I, and select the Font tab.

Chapter 5

Task	Alternatives
Activate a sheet in a workbook	Click the Sheet tab.
	Press Ctrl-Page Up or Ctrl-Page Down to move to the next or the previous sheet.
Select an item in a chart	Click the item.
	Select the item in the Chart Objects list on the Chart toolbar.
	Press the Up Arrow key and Down Arrow key to move between groups of objects. Press the Left Arrow key and Right Arrow key to move from object to object.
Select a graphical shape on a worksheet	Click the shape.
	To select all shapes and other objects, press Ctrl-G, click the Special button, select the Objects option, and click OK.
	To move from shape to shape, select one shape and then press the Tab key.

Chapter 7

Task	Alternatives
Set or remove a breakpoint	Click in the margin.
	Press F9.
	From the Debug menu, click Toggle Breakpoint.
	On either the Debug toolbar or the Edit toolbar, click the Toggle Breakpoint button.

Task	Alternatives
Run to the statement containing the cursor	From the Debug menu, click Run To Cursor.
	Press Ctrl-F8.

Chapter 8

Task	Alternatives
Edit a formula in a worksheet	Click the Edit Formula button in the Formula bar.
	Press F2.

Chapter 9

Task	Alternatives
Move a control on the worksheet	Drag the control with the mouse.
	Press any of the arrow keys to "nudge" the control.
Select a property in the Properties window	Click the property name.
	Simultaneously press Ctrl-Shift and the first letter of the property name.
Move between areas of the Properties window	Click in the area.
	Press the Tab key
Exit Design Mode	On the Visual Basic toolbar, click the Exit Design Mode button.
	From the Run menu in the Visual Basic Editor, click Exit Design Mode.
Show the Project window	On the Standard toolbar, click the Project Explorer button.
	Press Ctrl-R.
	From the View menu, click Project Explorer.

Chapter 11

Task	Alternatives
Insert a user form	Click the Insert UserForm button.
	From the Insert menu, click UserForm.
	In the Project window, right-click to show the shortcut menu, and then from the Insert submenu, click UserForm.
Show the Properties window in the Visual Basic Editor	Click the Properties Window button.
	Press F4.
	From the View menu, click Properties Window.
Run a form	Press F5.
	From the Run menu, click Run Sub/UserForm.
	On the Standard or Debug toolbars, click the Run Sub/UserForm button.
Display the Find dialog box in Excel	From the Edit menu, click Find.
	Press Ctrl-F.
Hide a row	From the Format menu, the Row submenu, click Hide.
	Press Ctrl-9.
Show a row	From the Format menu, the Row submenu, click Unhide.
	Press Ctrl-Shift-9.
Hide a column	From the Format menu, the Column submenu, click Hide.
	Press Ctrl-0.
Show a column	From the Format menu, the Column submenu, click Unhide.
	Press Ctrl-Shift-0.

Chapter 12

Task	Alternatives
Show the Style dialog box	From the Format menu, click Style.
	Press Alt-' (apostrophe).
Move a field in the PivotTable Wizard to the page, column, row, or data area	Drag the field tile.
	Press Alt-P, Alt-C, Alt-R, or Alt-D, respectively.
Show the PivotTable field dialog box	Double-click the PivotTable field tile.
	Select the field tile, and press Alt-L.
Scroll to the next procedure in a module	Use the scroll bars.
	To scroll down, press Ctrl-Down Arrow. To scroll up, press Ctrl-Up Arrow.
Go to a specific procedure in a module	Scroll to the procedure.
	Click on the name of the procedure, and press Shift-F2.
	Select the procedure name from the Procedure list at the top of the code window.
	Click outside any procedure, press F5, select the procedure, and then click Edit.

Checking Your Configuration

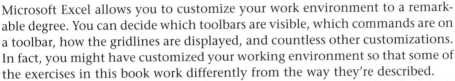

Microsoft Excel allows you to customize your work environment to a remarkable degree. You can decide which toolbars are visible, which commands are on a toolbar, how the gridlines are displayed, and countless other customizations. In fact, you might have customized your working environment so that some of the exercises in this book work differently from the way they're described.

In general, this book assumes that your environment matches Excel's default settings. This appendix describes the settings that affect the way exercises work in this book. If you find that your copy of Excel or the Microsoft Visual Basic Editor doesn't behave the way the book describes, compare your custom settings with those described here.

Excel Environment

The settings for Excel are separate from the settings in the Visual Basic Editor.

Windows

- The workbook window is maximized.

- The Excel window can be either maximized or resizable.

Toolbars

- The Standard and Formatting toolbars are visible.

- After Chapter 1, the Visual Basic toolbar is visible.

- The menus and all toolbars contain the default commands.

To control which toolbars are visible, click Customize from the Tools menu, click the Toolbars tab, and then put a check mark next to only those toolbars that you want to see.

To reset the toolbars, click Customize from the Tools menu and then click the Toolbars tab. Select a toolbar or menu name, and then click the Reset button.

Add-Ins

This book doesn't require that any add-ins be installed. For the most part, installing or removing the add-ins that come with Excel shouldn't affect any of the exercises in this book (except that if you've installed the AutoSave add-in, you might occasionally be prompted to save the open workbooks). If you're uncertain whether an add-in might be affecting the way the exercises in this book are working, you can safely disable all the add-ins you've installed.

To disable an add-in, click Add-Ins from the Tools menu, select the add-in name, and remove the check box next to the name.

View Options

This book assumes that the following View options are set. View options that aren't mentioned don't matter.

- Show Formula Bar.
- Show Status Bar.
- Show All Objects.
- Don't Show Formulas.
- Show Gridlines.
- Gridline color is Automatic.
- Show Row and Column Headers.
- Show Horizontal Scroll Bar.
- Show Vertical Scroll Bar.
- Show Sheet Tabs.

To set the View options, click Options from the Tools menu, click the View tab in the dialog box, and select the desired options.

Calculation Options

This book assumes that the following Calculation options are set. Calculation options that aren't mentioned don't matter.

- Calculation is Automatic.
- In the Workbook options group, Accept Labels In Formulas is selected.

To set the Calculation options, click Options from the Tools menu, click the Calculation tab in the dialog box, and select the desired options.

General Options

This book assumes that the following General options are set. General options that aren't mentioned don't matter.

- R1C1 Reference Style is turned off.
- Sheets In New Workbook is 3.
- User Name is set to your name.

To set the General options, click Options from the Tools menu, click the General tab in the dialog box, and then select the desired options.

Visual Basic Editor Environment

The Visual Basic Editor environment has customization settings that are independent of Excel. To display the Visual Basic Editor, click the Visual Basic Editor button on the Visual Basic toolbar in Excel.

Windows

- All windows are closed except the code window.

- The code window is maximized.

Toolbars

- The Standard toolbar is visible.

- The menu and toolbars contain the default commands.

To control which toolbars are visible, click Customize from the Toolbars submenu of the View menu, click the Toolbars tab, and then put a check mark next to only the Standard toolbar.

To reset the toolbars, click Customize from the Toolbars submenu of the View menu, and then click the Toolbars tab. Select a toolbar or menu name, and click the Reset button.

Editor Options

This book assumes that the following Editor options are set. Editor options that aren't mentioned don't matter.

- Auto Syntax Check is turned on.

- Require Variable Declaration is turned off (until possibly after Chapter 8).

- Auto List Members is turned on.

- Auto Quick Info is turned on.

- Auto Data Tips is turned on.

- Auto Indent is turned on.

- Default to Full Module View is turned on.

- Procedure Separator is turned on.

To set the Editor options, click Options from the Tools menu, click the Editor tab in the dialog box, and select the desired options.

Editor Format Options

This book assumes that the following Editor Format options are set. Editor Format options that aren't mentioned don't matter.

- Normal Text has Auto for Foreground, Background, and Indicator.

- Execution Point Text has Auto for Foreground and is Yellow for Background and Indicator.

- Breakpoint Text is White for Foreground, and Dark Red for Background and Indicator.

- Comment Text is green for Foreground, and Auto for Background and Indicator.

- Keyword Text is dark blue for Foreground, and Auto for Background and Indicator.

- The Margin Indicator Bar is turned on.

To set the Editor Format options, click Options from the Tools menu, and click the Editor Format tab in the dialog box. Select the desired type of text, and choose the options you want.

General Options

This book assumes that the following General options are set. General options that aren't mentioned don't matter.

- Notify Before State Loss is turned off.

- Error Trapping is set to Break In Class Module.

- Compile On Demand is turned on.

- Background Compile is turned on.

To set the General options, click Options from the Tools menu, click the General tab in the dialog box, and select the desired options.

Docking Options

This book assumes that the following Docking options are set. Docking options that aren't mentioned don't matter. (These window settings don't affect the way anything in the book works, but they might make your screens appear different from the captured screens in the text.)

- All windows are Dockable. (The Object Browser is Dockable after Chapter 3.)

To set the Docking options, click Options from the Tools menu, click the Docking tab in the dialog box, and select the desired options.

Index

A

absolute references, 103–4
Accelerator property, 219
access key (accelerator key), 215
Activate method, 127
   with ChartObject objects, 126
ActiveCell property, 40, 73, 86, 87
ActiveCell statement, 92
ActiveChart property, 123, 124
ActiveX controls, 217–18, 221, 236
AddDates macro, 39–41
AddFields method, 137, 138
Add method, 80, 83
Address property, 110–11
AddShape method, 116
AddTotals macro, 149–51
AdjustChart macro, 295–96
ampersand (&), 212, 214–15
animating a logo, 303–5
A1 notation, 95, 105, 108
AppendDatabase macro, 41–47
   stepping through, 43–45
appending
   to the database, 41–47
   a row with formulas, 55–56
AppendRow macro, 55–56
Application object, 34, 73
argument(s)
   adding to custom functions, 183
   multiple, 21
   named, 21
   optional, 186
   properties distinguished from, 20–21
Arrange method, 82
ArrangeStyle argument, 82
Array function, 118, 137
Auto List feature
   declaring variables to enable, 83–84
   learning about objects in, 79–84
   learning constant values with, 81–83
Auto List Members feature, 34
Automation, 6
Auto Quick Info feature, 34

B

BackColor property, 117
background logo, 302–3
Before keyword, 231
blank cells, selecting only, 35–36
Boolean data type, 64

breakpoints, 173–77
   temporary, 176–77
Button argument, MouseMove event, 223
Buttons argument, *MsgBox* statement, 165–66

C

C++, 7
calculated ranges, 99–102
Calculate method, 169
Caller property, 301
Cancel argument, 231
Cancel button, 41
   If structures and, 162, 163, 164
cancelling events, 231–32
Caption property, of command buttons,
   218–19
Category pivot field, 135, 137
Cells property, 97–99
Change Button Image command, 212
ChangeChart macro, 127
Channel pivot field, 135, 137
chart objects (ChartObject objects), 121–31,
   127. *See also* PivotCharts
   formatting, 130–31
   locations of, 124
   modifying a macro that creates, 122–24
   recording a macro that creates, 121–22
   recording a macro that modifies
     attributes of, 127–29
   referring to existing embedded, 124–27
   writing a macro that modifies, 129–30
Chart property, 126, 127, 128, 130
ChartType property, 122
check box, with a related text box, 256–58
CheckFiles macro, 195, 196, 198
CheckRun macro, 165
child windows, 88, 89
Classes list, in Object Browser, 85
Click event, 222
Close method, 47, 81
closing a file, saving changes while, 44, 47
collections
   custom, 312
   looping through, with *For Each* loops,
     167–68
   navigating down by using, 71–72
   ranges as, 96–99
ColorFormat objects, 117
ColorIndex property, 68–69, 120

OFFSET function, 101
Offset property, 99, 100, 101
On Error GoTo ErrorHandler statement, 197, 305
On Error Resume Next statement, 190–91, 193, 195, 198, 296, 306
Open event, 228
OpenText macro, 31–34
OpenText method, 33
option buttons, 254–55, 320–21
    implementing, 270–71
Option Explicit statement, 18, 34, 188
Orientation property
    of data fields, 142
    of PivotFields, 136, 138

P

page field, 136
PageFields collection, 138
parent objects, navigating up by using, 69–71
Parent property, 69
Paste Special command, 19
PasteSpecial method, 20
personal signatures (digital signatures), 22–25
PivotCharts
    creating, 290–92
    formatting, 293–94
    macro to adjust, 295–96
PivotField objects (PivotFields collection), 133–46, 135–38
    building, 133–38
        creating a default PivotTable, 134–35
        manipulating pivot fields, 135–36
    charting a row from, 152–54
    macro to change states, 294–95
    macro to refresh, 296–97
    making multiple changes to, 137
    manipulating individual items within, 138–40
    refining, 138–46
        finding PivotTable ranges, 143–44
        manipulating data fields, 140–42
        manipulating pivot items, 138–40
    retrieving external data into, 283–85
        creating a PivotChart, 290–92
        defining the PivotTable, 285–88
        definition of the data, 283–85
        formatting a PivotChart, 293–94
        formatting the PivotTable, 288–90
    synchronizing two, 151–52
pivot items, manipulating, 138–40
points, specifying the location and size of an object using, 116
Position property, 138
    of PivotFields, 137, 138
printing a report, 273–74
PrintOrders macro, 173–77

Private keyword, 220
projects, 224–26
Project window, 224
    showing, 331
prompting the user
    for a date, 40–41
        If structures, 162–64
    for new values, 56
Properties window, 331
property(-ies)
    arguments distinguished from, 20–21
    changing multiple, 12–16
    changing the value of, in the Locals window, 66–68
    methods distinguished from, 21–22
    in Object Browser, 85
    showing the global list of, 329
    toggling the value of a, with a macro, 17
protecting worksheets, 246–48
Protect method, 248
ProtectSheets macro, 167, 170–71
Public keyword, 230
Public variables, 230–31

Q

Query Wizard, 284–85

R

RAND function, 182
Random function, 182–83, 186, 187
Range class, 98
Range objects, 91–102
    calculated, 99–102
    as collections, 96–99
    formulas built with address of, 108–11
    in Object Browser, 86
    putting values and formulas into, 106
    Range property of, 94–96
    simplifying *Select* groups, 93
    simplifying *Select...Selection* pairs of statements, 92–93
Range property
    with *Array* function, 118
    uses of, 94–96
R1C1 notation, 38, 104–11
read-only properties, 66
recording macros (recorded macros)
    actions, 18–25
    alternative technique for, 327
    converting a formula to a value with a macro, 19–21
    with menu commands, 18–19
    to create a chart, 121–22
    to create a rectangle, 114
    editing, 16–18
    to fill missing values in selected cells, 37–38
    to format currency, 9–12

to merge cells vertically, 12, 14–15
to modify chart attributes, 127–29
in modules, 15
to open a report file, 29
relative movements, 45–46
that run other macros, 49–50
rectangle
  recording a macro to create a, 114
  writing a macro to create a, 115–17
Refresh On Open option, PivotTable, 296
relative movements, recording, 45–46
Relative Reference button, 45
relative references, 103
RemoveGrid macro, 16–17
renaming, shapes, 119–21
report, printing a, 273–74
Require Variable Declarations check box, 188
Resize property, 99, 101
Return To Menu command, 308
RGB property, 120, 131
Right function, 301
Rnd function, 182, 183, 184
RowFields collection, 138
Rows property, 97, 99
Run Macro button, 10
run mode, 221
run-time errors, 188

S

SaveChanges argument, *Close* method, 47
saving, changes while closing a file, 44, 47
SchemeColor property, 120
ScreenUpdating property, 313
selecting
  an irregular range of blank cells, 35–36
  the current region, 36
SelectionChange event, 227–30
Selection object, 12
Selection property, 40
selection (selecting; selected cells), filling
  with values, 37
Selection statement, 92
Select...Selection pairs of statements, 92
SelectShapes macro, 117–19
Select statement, 92
SelLength property, 273
SelStart property, 273
SetBars macro, 312–13
SetFocus method, 273
Set keyword, 64
SetMenu macro, 307, 308
SetObject macro, 69–70
SetPivot macro, 294–95, 301
SetSourceData method, 122
SetWindow macro, 309–11
Shape class, 115
ShapeRange objects (ShapeRange collection), 118, 119

Shapes collection, 116, 118, 119
  methods and properties for, 115–16
Shapes property, 115, 118
shapes (Shape objects), 117–20, 124, 126, 127, 131
  Activate method not available to, 126
  modifying existing, 117–19
  renaming, 119–21
  types of, 116
Shift argument, MouseMove event, 223
shifting a column, 53–54
shortcut keys, assigning, to macros, 10, 14
ShowMe macro, 301
Show method, 274
signatures, personal (digital), 22–25
snapping drawing objects, 218
spin buttons, 238–42, 247, 321–22
StartOfMonth function, 259–60
StartRow argument, 32
StartUpAnimation macro, 304–5
state codes, adding to maps, 299–301
statements
  how to read, 12
  splitting into several lines, 21, 32, 33
State pivot field, 135, 136, 137
static variables, 311
StatusBar property, 178
stepped area chart, 290
stepping through macros
  AddDates macro, 40
  alternative technique for, 328
  AppendDatabase macro, 43–45
  FillLabels macro, 38–39
  ImportFile macro, 31–33
  StoreValue macro, 63
StoreObject procedure, 64
StoreValue macro, 62–64
String data type, 63–64
subroutines, 50
subroutine statements, simplifying, 50
Sub statement, 12
Sum of NET column, in PivotTables, 141
Sum of UNITS column, in PivotTables, 141–42
SynchronizeCharts macro, 129–30
SynchTables macro, 152
syntax errors, 188

T

tables. *See also* PivotTable objects
  adding totals to, 149–51
tab order for controls, 262–63
TakeFocusOnClick property, 219, 221
TestInput macro, 162–64
TestRandom macro, 186
text box, 322
  check box with a related, 256–58

Reed Jacobson

is Vice President, Consulting, for LEX Software, a company that specializes in custom development services using Microsoft Excel, Visual Basic, SQL Server, and other products. LEX Software is one of the original companies invited to participate in what later became the Microsoft Solution Provider program.

Reed received a B.A. in Japanese and Linguistics, an M.B.A. from Brigham Young University, and a graduate fellowship in Linguistics from Cornell University. He worked as a Software Application Specialist for Hewlett-Packard for 10 years and ran his own consulting firm for 5 years.

Reed is the author of *Excel Trade Secrets for Windows*, *Microsoft Excel Advanced Topics Step by Step*, and *Office 2000 Expert Companion*. He has given presentations on Excel at Tech•Ed and other Microsoft conferences and seminars; he has also created training video tapes for Excel and contributed articles to *Inside Visual Basic*.

Reed Jacobson
LEX Software
P. O. Box 3632
Arlington, WA 98223
rjacobson@lexsoft.com

The manuscript for this book was prepared and galleyed using Microsoft Word 97. Pages were composed by Helios Productions using Adobe PageMaker 6.52 for Windows, with text in Stone Serif and display type in ITC Franklin Gothic. Composed pages were delivered to the printer as electronic prepress files.

Cover Designer: The Leonhardt Group
Cover Illustrator: Todd Daman
Interior Graphic Designer: James D. Kramer
Interior Graphic Artist: Helios Productions
Principal Compositors: Sybil Ihrig, Helios Productions / Ann Shaver
Technical Editor   Douglas Giles
Copy Editor   Fran Aitkens
Principal Proofreader: Deborah O. Stockton
Indexer: Maro Riofrancos

MICROSOFT LICENSE AGREEMENT

Book Companion CD

IMPORTANT—READ CAREFULLY: This Microsoft End-User License Agreement ("EULA") is a legal agreement between you (either an individual or an entity) and Microsoft Corporation for the Microsoft product identified above, which includes computer software and may include associated media, printed materials, and "online" or electronic documentation ("SOFTWARE PRODUCT"). Any component included within the SOFTWARE PRODUCT that is accompanied by a separate End-User License Agreement shall be governed by such agreement and not the terms set forth below. By installing, copying, or otherwise using the SOFTWARE PRODUCT, you agree to be bound by the terms of this EULA. If you do not agree to the terms of this EULA, you are not authorized to install, copy, or otherwise use the SOFTWARE PRODUCT; you may, however, return the SOFTWARE PRODUCT, along with all printed materials and other items that form a part of the Microsoft product that includes the SOFTWARE PRODUCT, to the place you obtained them for a full refund.

SOFTWARE PRODUCT LICENSE

The SOFTWARE PRODUCT is protected by United States copyright laws and international copyright treaties, as well as other intellectual property laws and treaties. The SOFTWARE PRODUCT is licensed, not sold.

1. **GRANT OF LICENSE.** This EULA grants you the following rights:

   a. **Software Product.** You may install and use one copy of the SOFTWARE PRODUCT on a single computer. The primary user of the computer on which the SOFTWARE PRODUCT is installed may make a second copy for his or her exclusive use on a portable computer.

   b. **Storage/Network Use.** You may also store or install a copy of the SOFTWARE PRODUCT on a storage device, such as a network server, used only to install or run the SOFTWARE PRODUCT on your other computers over an internal network; however, you must acquire and dedicate a license for each separate computer on which the SOFTWARE PRODUCT is installed or run from the storage device. A license for the SOFTWARE PRODUCT may not be shared or used concurrently on different computers.

   c. **License Pak.** If you have acquired this EULA in a Microsoft License Pak, you may make the number of additional copies of the computer software portion of the SOFTWARE PRODUCT authorized on the printed copy of this EULA, and you may use each copy in the manner specified above. You are also entitled to make a corresponding number of secondary copies for portable computer use as specified above.

   d. **Sample Code.** Solely with respect to portions, if any, of the SOFTWARE PRODUCT that are identified within the SOFTWARE PRODUCT as sample code (the "SAMPLE CODE"):

      i. **Use and Modification.** Microsoft grants you the right to use and modify the source code version of the SAMPLE CODE, *provided* you comply with subsection (d)(iii) below. You may not distribute the SAMPLE CODE, or any modified version of the SAMPLE CODE, in source code form.

      ii. **Redistributable Files.** Provided you comply with subsection (d)(iii) below, Microsoft grants you a nonexclusive, royalty-free right to reproduce and distribute the object code version of the SAMPLE CODE and of any modified SAMPLE CODE, other than SAMPLE CODE, or any modified version thereof, designated as not redistributable in the Readme file that forms a part of the SOFTWARE PRODUCT (the "Non-Redistributable Sample Code"). All SAMPLE CODE other than the Non-Redistributable Sample Code is collectively referred to as the "REDISTRIBUTABLES."

      iii. **Redistribution Requirements.** If you redistribute the REDISTRIBUTABLES, you agree to: (i) distribute the REDISTRIBUTABLES in object code form only in conjunction with and as a part of your software application product; (ii) not use Microsoft's name, logo, or trademarks to market your software application product; (iii) include a valid copyright notice on your software application product; (iv) indemnify, hold harmless, and defend Microsoft from and against any claims or lawsuits, including attorney's fees, that arise or result from the use or distribution of your software application product; and (v) not permit further distribution of the REDISTRIBUTABLES by your end user. Contact Microsoft for the applicable royalties due and other licensing terms for all other uses and/or distribution of the REDISTRIBUTABLES.

2. **DESCRIPTION OF OTHER RIGHTS AND LIMITATIONS.**

   - **Limitations on Reverse Engineering, Decompilation, and Disassembly.** You may not reverse engineer, decompile, or disassemble the SOFTWARE PRODUCT, except and only to the extent that such activity is expressly permitted by applicable law notwithstanding this limitation.

   - **Separation of Components.** The SOFTWARE PRODUCT is licensed as a single product. Its component parts may not be separated for use on more than one computer.

   - **Rental.** You may not rent, lease, or lend the SOFTWARE PRODUCT.

   - **Support Services.** Microsoft may, but is not obligated to, provide you with support services related to the SOFTWARE PRODUCT ("Support Services"). Use of Support Services is governed by the Microsoft policies and programs described in the user manual, in "online" documentation, and/or other Microsoft-provided materials. Any supplemental software code provided to you as part of the Support Services shall be considered part of the SOFTWARE PRODUCT and subject to the terms and conditions of this EULA. With respect to technical information you provide to Microsoft as part of the Support Services, Microsoft may use such information for its business purposes, including for product support and development. Microsoft will not utilize such technical information in a form that personally identifies you.

- **Software Transfer.** You may permanently transfer all of your rights under this EULA, provided you retain no copies, you transfer all of the SOFTWARE PRODUCT (including all component parts, the media and printed materials, any upgrades, this EULA, and, if applicable, the Certificate of Authenticity), **and** the recipient agrees to the terms of this EULA.

- **Termination.** Without prejudice to any other rights, Microsoft may terminate this EULA if you fail to comply with the terms and conditions of this EULA. In such event, you must destroy all copies of the SOFTWARE PRODUCT and all of its component parts.

3. **COPYRIGHT.** All title and copyrights in and to the SOFTWARE PRODUCT (including but not limited to any images, photographs, animations, video, audio, music, text, SAMPLE CODE, REDISTRIBUTABLES, and "applets" incorporated into the SOFTWARE PRODUCT) and any copies of the SOFTWARE PRODUCT are owned by Microsoft or its suppliers. The SOFTWARE PRODUCT is protected by copyright laws and international treaty provisions. Therefore, you must treat the SOFTWARE PRODUCT like any other copyrighted material **except** that you may install the SOFTWARE PRODUCT on a single computer provided you keep the original solely for backup or archival purposes. You may not copy the printed materials accompanying the SOFTWARE PRODUCT.

4. **U.S. GOVERNMENT RESTRICTED RIGHTS.** The SOFTWARE PRODUCT and documentation are provided with RESTRICTED RIGHTS. Use, duplication, or disclosure by the Government is subject to restrictions as set forth in subparagraph (c)(1)(ii) of the Rights in Technical Data and Computer Software clause at DFARS 252.227-7013 or subparagraphs (c)(1) and (2) of the Commercial Computer Software—Restricted Rights at 48 CFR 52.227-19, as applicable. Manufacturer is Microsoft Corporation/One Microsoft Way/Redmond, WA 98052-6399.

5. **EXPORT RESTRICTIONS.** You agree that you will not export or re-export the SOFTWARE PRODUCT, any part thereof, or any process or service that is the direct product of the SOFTWARE PRODUCT (the foregoing collectively referred to as the "Restricted Components"), to any country, person, entity, or end user subject to U.S. export restrictions. You specifically agree not to export or re-export any of the Restricted Components (i) to any country to which the U.S. has embargoed or restricted the export of goods or services, which currently include, but are not necessarily limited to, Cuba, Iran, Iraq, Libya, North Korea, Sudan, and Syria, or to any national of any such country, wherever located, who intends to transmit or transport the Restricted Components back to such country; (ii) to any end user who you know or have reason to know will utilize the Restricted Components in the design, development, or production of nuclear, chemical, or biological weapons; or (iii) to any end user who has been prohibited from participating in U.S. export transactions by any federal agency of the U.S. government. You warrant and represent that neither the BXA nor any other U.S. federal agency has suspended, revoked, or denied your export privileges.

DISCLAIMER OF WARRANTY

NO WARRANTIES OR CONDITIONS. MICROSOFT EXPRESSLY DISCLAIMS ANY WARRANTY OR CONDITION FOR THE SOFTWARE PRODUCT. THE SOFTWARE PRODUCT AND ANY RELATED DOCUMENTATION IS PROVIDED "AS IS" WITHOUT WARRANTY OR CONDITION OF ANY KIND, EITHER EXPRESS OR IMPLIED, INCLUDING, WITHOUT LIMITATION, THE IMPLIED WARRANTIES OF MERCHANTABILITY, FITNESS FOR A PARTICULAR PURPOSE, OR NONINFRINGEMENT. THE ENTIRE RISK ARISING OUT OF USE OR PERFORMANCE OF THE SOFTWARE PRODUCT REMAINS WITH YOU.

LIMITATION OF LIABILITY. TO THE MAXIMUM EXTENT PERMITTED BY APPLICABLE LAW, IN NO EVENT SHALL MICROSOFT OR ITS SUPPLIERS BE LIABLE FOR ANY SPECIAL, INCIDENTAL, INDIRECT, OR CONSEQUENTIAL DAMAGES WHATSOEVER (INCLUDING, WITHOUT LIMITATION, DAMAGES FOR LOSS OF BUSINESS PROFITS, BUSINESS INTERRUPTION, LOSS OF BUSINESS INFORMATION, OR ANY OTHER PECUNIARY LOSS) ARISING OUT OF THE USE OF OR INABILITY TO USE THE SOFTWARE PRODUCT OR THE PROVISION OF OR FAILURE TO PROVIDE SUPPORT SERVICES, EVEN IF MICROSOFT HAS BEEN ADVISED OF THE POSSIBILITY OF SUCH DAMAGES. IN ANY CASE, MICROSOFT'S ENTIRE LIABILITY UNDER ANY PROVISION OF THIS EULA SHALL BE LIMITED TO THE GREATER OF THE AMOUNT ACTUALLY PAID BY YOU FOR THE SOFTWARE PRODUCT OR US$5.00; PROVIDED, HOWEVER, IF YOU HAVE ENTERED INTO A MICROSOFT SUPPORT SERVICES AGREEMENT, MICROSOFT'S ENTIRE LIABILITY REGARDING SUPPORT SERVICES SHALL BE GOVERNED BY THE TERMS OF THAT AGREEMENT. BECAUSE SOME STATES AND JURISDICTIONS DO NOT ALLOW THE EXCLUSION OR LIMITATION OF LIABILITY, THE ABOVE LIMITATION MAY NOT APPLY TO YOU.

MISCELLANEOUS

This EULA is governed by the laws of the State of Washington USA, except and only to the extent that applicable law mandates governing law of a different jurisdiction.

Should you have any questions concerning this EULA, or if you desire to contact Microsoft for any reason, please contact the Microsoft subsidiary serving your country, or write: Microsoft Sales Information Center/One Microsoft Way/Redmond, WA 98052-6399.